UNFINISHED BUSINESS

Michelangelo Antonioni

Unfinished Business

SCREENPLAYS
SCENARIOS
AND
IDEAS

Edited by
Carlo di Carlo and Giorgio Tinazzi
Translated by Andrew Taylor

Marsilio Publishers
New York

Library of Congress Cataloging-in-Publication Data

Antonioni, Michelangelo.
    [Film nel cassetto. English]
    Unfinished business : screenplays, scenerios, and ideas / edited
 by Carlo di Carlo and Giorgio Tinazzi ; translated by Andrew Taylor.
        p.   cm.
    Ten treatments and scripts for unproduced films.
    Includes two essays by the editors.
    ISBN 1-56886-051-X
    I. Di Carlo, Carlo, 1938-   . II. Tinazzi, Giorgio. III. Title.
 PN1997.3.A5813   1998
 791.43'0233'092--dc21   98-29373
                                                             CIP

Original Italian edition:
I film nel cassetto
Copyright © 1995 Marsilio Editori®

Translation copyright © 1998 Marsilio Publishers

Of the present edition © 1998
Marsilio Publishers
853 Broadway
New York, New York 10003

ISBN 1-56886-051-X

Marsilio Publishers' books are available from:
Consortium Book Sales & Distribution
800-283-3572

CONTENTS

UNFINISHED BUSINESS

INTRODUCTION

Thinking in the Absence of Image

Most film directors do not come up with their own subjects, or even write their own screenplays. They are contracted
by a producer to give dramatic shape to this or that story. In
this sense they are somewhat like the conductor of an orchestra. A more select group of directors are more like the composer—conceptualizing the piece, scoring it, distributing its
musical lines among a wide range of registers, chords, and
instruments. Michelangelo Antonioni is one of those directors.
In fifty-five years of filmmaking, he has thought up almost all
the subjects for his films, scripted and cast them, meticulously
overseeing each shot and cut. Before becoming a director
Antonioni was in fact a writer—more specifically, a film critic,
but also a screenwriter (of Roberto Rossellini's *A Pilot Returns*,
1942, as well as other works up to and beyond Federico Fellini's
The White Sheik, 1951). After making his first documentary in
the 1940s and his first feature film in 1950, this "composer,"
or writer/director, then invented some of the most original
idioms in the budding new language of cinema. When attempt-
ing to understand these idioms, one finds it helpful to consider
them a part (the most important part, without question, but
still only a part) of Antonioni's larger written oeuvre. To begin
with, there are the many reviews and more than thirty articles
on film in which he, a voice in the neorealist chorus affiliated

with the journal *Cinema*, tested his ideas as early as the second half of the 1930s. Then there are the rich fictional writings—the dozens upon dozens of stories, sketches, and reminiscences that are partially collected in *Quel bowling sul Tevere* (*That Bowling Alley on the Tiber*) (Einaudi, 1983). Then there are Antonioni's reflections on cinema and art in general, and the accounts of his poetics and filmmaking practices recorded in *The Architecture of Vision* (Marsilio, 1997). Finally there are the scenarios and screenplays—both for completed films eventually viewed by thousands as well as for films never shot. In addition to these practices of Antonioni the writer, one would also want to consider Antonioni the musician, the young violinist who performed his first public concert at nine years of age, and the painter, whose select works are reproduced in *Montagne incantate*. Fictional, poetic, pictorial, essayistic, and cinematic, the parameters of Antonioni's art are not easy to fix. The eighty-six-year-old artist, who suffered a stroke in the 1980s, who received a Lifetime Achievement Oscar in 1995, and who has another film currently in the making, seems the very embodiment of unfinished artistic business. The temporal expanse of his work is equally broad, bearing witness to cultural developments spanning two-thirds of a century—from the era of Mussolinian Fascism to the explosion of neorealism, from the throes of postwar Italy to the terroristic scene of the 1970s, from the urgencies of philosophical existentialism to the quizzical postmodern dérive of the century's end. Antonioni is virtually the sole survivor of that grand generation of Italian filmmakers that once boasted Rossellini, Visconti, De Sica, Fellini, and Pasolini. In terms of sheer longevity, he is an extraordinary touchstone of 20th century Italian culture. Even if he had never made a single film, the testimony of his writings alone would warrant the attention of historians.

Unfinished Business is just one element in that written record. A translation of *I film nel cassetto*, it collects ten scenarios, sketches, and screenplays that Antonioni never found the chance to film, even though some of them (particularly *The Crew*) were dearer to his heart than those cinematic projects he did complete. For the story of how and why some scripts got made and others did not, one should turn to the essay by Carlo di Carlo that concludes this volume. It is essentially the old tale of the director proposing, the producer disposing, and the market, of course, determining outcome and inevitably being wary of Antonioni's highly cerebral art. In forty-eight years, Antonioni made close to the same number of films (less than two dozen) as Pasolini did in fourteen, Fellini in twenty-three, and Visconti in thirty-four. For a true sense of the density of his work, however, as di Carlo reminds us, one must note that Antonioni wrote another twelve completed screenplays that were not produced, six co-written screenplays, fifteen original treatments, and approximately forty documentary treatments. *Unfinished Business* provides an important piece of this collateral work, including two screenplays.

Considering these writings alongside Antonioni's films is somewhat like studying a poet's drafts of his poems, or a novelist's outlines for a novel. Reading these pieces, the films we are familiar with slowly reveal elements of their inspiration and genesis, the theoretical horizon against which they stand, and the imaginative options from which they emerge. We find the same predominance of female protagonists, the triangular structures of love, the disappearances, homicides, or suicides, the intangibility and evanescence of all signs and identities. Gradually, what changes as we see Antonioni supplementing his images with words and his dramas with exposition is his artistic profile. We develop a deeper sense of the intellectual ambitions that accompanied his stylistic innovations. We witness the social-philosophical ramifications of his taciturn art. Above all, we better understand that crucial claim that he made when he said, in *The Architecture of Vision*, that his films were "documents, not of a completed thought, but of a thought in the making" (58). The reason behind Antonioni's idea of film as a "thought in the making" seems mainly to be his wish to emphasize that a huge dimension of filmic significance is determined in the actual process of production: in the scouting of locations, in the decisions about frame and shot, in the spatial disposition of characters, in the expressive implications of color, in the extemporaneous nature of performance, and, finally, in the copious adjustments to the script that all this thought-in-the-making entails. Antonioni is more determined than most other directors to stress that the "meaning" of a film can only be located in these actual constructions of the visual drama. It does not exist independently of, or prior to, the labor occasioned by each detail of composition. At the same time, one must reckon with the other side of this vision of film as an enactment of thought, the dimension captured by the original Italian title of *The Architecture of Vision*, *Fare un film per me è vivere* or *Filmmaking is Living to Me*. Only in the aesthetic process, as Schiller famously announced, is a person truly human. If filmmaking is a species of thinking, then that thinking in turn is the deep unfolding of life, an essentialization of existence. Nothing is what it is except through the form that it assumes. Hence certain lines in the script take on a different meaning depending on whether they're spoken against the background of a wall or a street; and "a line spoken by an actor in profile doesn't have the same meaning as one given full-face" (*Architecture*, 28).

The same can be said about the film as a whole. As a verbal, dramatic, and visual document of a "thought in the making," the film does not necessarily unravel a single, coherent story. In Antonioni's case, it is more often built out of "flashes, ideas that come forth every other moment." That is why Antonioni speaks of his "old conviction"—already back in 1940—that "to make good cinema you need virtually nothing but an image [i.e., the meteorological change upon which the first scenario, *Green Land*, is based] from which other more precise images can germinate in a way that can only be realized on film" (page 2 of this volume). A mere sensation can generate a film even though the story remains far from clear. One day, "I invented a film while looking at the sun," asserts Antonioni, "the meanness of the sun," just as he thought up *The Cry* by staring at a wall (*Architecture*, 61, 91).

The resulting work might be considered an elaboration of a

mood, feeling, or conflict—the "thought" by which these are eventually expressed. After all, as Antonioni puts it in *Quel bowling sul Tevere*, "My thoughts are almost always films" (199). When critics then ask him what he "intended to say" with a particular film, the question seems to beg the notion of film as thought, making Antonioni feel that the best he can do is "respond along these lines: 'In that period, certain events happened in the world, I saw certain people, I was reading certain books, I was looking at certain paintings, I loved X, I hated Y, I didn't have any money, I wasn't sleeping much.' " The thinking-that-is-a-film remains fused to the experience from which it arose. That is why Antonioni did not take exception to that early assessment of his cinema as "internal neorealism," for it recognized that his films were interested in the "innermost thoughts" of a character, in the subjective effects of a dramatic scene, in the forces that move us to act in one way instead of another. This type of cinema does not necessarily record either a meaningful story or a completed understanding, but rather a hermetic process of interpretation. If the work is successful it will occasion a similar experience in the spectator. "A film does not need to be understood," Antonioni believes. "It is enough if the viewer feels it" (*Architecture*, 8, 25-26, 57, 168). If much of the thought-in-the-making takes place during the process of production, other portions of it occur before, around, and outside the shooting—to begin with, in the life and mind of the person making the decisions. In the largest sense, however, the thought-in-the-making is embodied in the collective, national, historical experience, not to mention in the ontological relationships between humans and their natural or artificial habitats (which Antonioni analyzes in the screenplay *Tecnicamente dolce* [*Technically Sweet*], published in 1976 but not included in this volume). However much a film may aspire to convey a sense of the entirety of this thought-in-the-making, it can only articulate a part. The rest, no doubt, will be better expressed by writing, painting, or singing; by playing, working, or loving; by musing, sitting, or simply gazing. In fact, for Antonioni, this gazing is probably the most fundamental of all cognitive activities, leading Biarese and Tassone to quote him as saying that essentially "painting and writing are developments of a gaze" (*I film di Antonioni*, 169). The intellectual experience that develops from a gaze—with the instruments of art—is potentially vaster than that provided by any single film. Many, in fact, question how successfully Antonioni's films actually communicate this developing intellect that arises from merely dwelling in the world. So many parts of these films draw attention to quite the opposite phenomenon—the failure of human understanding, the obstacles to intuition and emotional clarity, the impenetrability of signs and things—that by the end of the films the thought-in-the-making is all but undone. Antonioni himself confesses, his films present "abortions of observation" much more frequently than full-fledged visions. And that brings us back to his writings, seeking explanation. So much is unsaid in Antonioni's films that the impulse to uncover his intentions is greater than it is in the case of, say, Fellini, Pasolini, or Bertolucci. His films pose more difficulties of comprehension than theirs do, often revolving around unsolvable conundrums (What happened to Anna in *The Adventure*? Why does the boy lose the use of his legs in *Red Desert*? Why does Jack Nicholson's character in *The Passenger* risk his life to assume the identity of a stranger?). Not that the screenplays or writings answer these questions; but they do help us proceed beyond the expectation of an answer, making us recognize how many other, much simpler occurrences are just as questionable. The most abstract of Italian filmmakers, Antonioni has little regard for conventional methods of displaying character and unfolding action in cinema. He uses methods of illumination that have more in common with poetry, painting, and music. The irony that emerges from his prose—even after erudite references to philosophers such as Wittgenstein, Heidegger, and Max Scheler—is that only the image is eloquent. What is seen makes sense. As it is "aborted," that flash of significance leads to a thought. That thought develops into—and by means of—a film. And that film reaffirms and recuperates the power of the image. Tinazzi and di

Carlo, like others before them, thus properly stress: important as writing is to Antonioni, it would be a mistake to lend it more authority than the film toward which it looks. The screenplay is only a preliminary articulation of a thought that properly takes shape in film. "These are the limits of the script," says the director, "to give words to events that refuse words." Writing a screenplay is just "describing images with provisional words, words which will no longer do" (*Architecture*, 70). For Antonioni images are empirically and epistemologically prior to all else. The images are what, in the absence of a film, the words of a script try to clarify. And even when a film, at least a film by Antonioni, is present, the spoken words are frequently the least convincing part. The images seem to have more autonomy and power. Could it be that Antonioni himself is prone to the criticism he directs at Visconti's *Ossessione* of 1943? The dialogues of that film appear dated after many decades, he observes, "not because they are wrong, but because they no longer fit the images" (*Architecture*, 208). Time wears out words faster than anything. Moods, situations, and moments resist their explanatory power. The ten treatments/projects/screenplays that make up *Unfinished Business* span the forty years between 1940 and 1980. The essays by Giorgio Tinazzi and Carlo di Carlo thoroughly contextualize these scripted projects, relating them not only to the other work Antonioni was engaged in at the same time, but also to their historical moments, and to Antonioni's films and their recurring themes. Tinazzi analyzes the intrinsic merit of these writings one by one, while di Carlo recounts the trajectory of Antonioni's cinematic career throughout the decades in question, detailing the fortunes of these scripts never converted to images. After reading them and measuring them against the films with which we are familiar, it becomes clear how that conversion from word to image occurs. What is more fascinating and challenging to the reader, however, is the opposite and apparently prior conversion—from image/experience to word, or to thinking in the absence of image.

Thomas Harrison

UNFINISHED BUSINESS

GREEN LAND[1]

On November 1st 1937, the *Corriere della Sera* published a guest column that was somewhat out of the ordinary. It wasn't the theme that was odd (as far as that goes, we're accustomed to seeing editorials in almost any style); rather, it was the fact that the article concerned filmmakers. The author of the piece was Guido Piovene; the title was "Notes for a Novel." At first, it might seem strange that cinema was invoked in the context of an explicitly literary project. And yet, right from the beginning, before the author himself had spoken of the possibility of his idea being developed into a film, I had begun to think about cinema. The subject matter itself had led me to think that film might be the idiom in which the piece could find its most faithful and effective representation.

I remember discussing the column at length with friends at the time, and some maintained that the novel would be better suited than any other medium to express the subtle transition of countries and peoples from one state of being to another of which Piovene speaks. A novel can take pages and pages to analyze this transition, dwelling at length on details that have an immediate poetic value. Cinema instead, with its need for spectacle, is denied the luxury of such pauses. While others

[1] 1940. In *Bianco e nero* 10 (October 1940): 959-972.

might favor the novel form here, I saw it as a film. And still today, as I take up the column again, I cannot re-read it without substituting for its words a scenario from my own imagination. It is natural that for Piovene, a writer, an idea should flow in all its freshness directly to his pen; how else can it be made into art? But there is also something for the eye in his writing, something which makes one strongly and instinctively desire a concrete and colored vision of that world he describes, a world which is extinguished in a chilly puff of wind and behind which lingers suggestive songs that are truly sung and echo in our ears.

You will not find a plot in these "Notes": they only offer enough hints to give an idea of what might be, and so I will try to sketch it out here in my own way. But there is a drama there, and what a drama! Besides, on this point I remain faithful to an old conviction: namely, that to make good cinema you need virtually nothing but an image (like that provided by Piovene's "Notes") from which other more precise images can germinate in a way that can only be realized on film. It will be a great day when filmmakers customarily jot down in three lines those films they will make at their leisure, as Chekhov did with his tales.

Thus there is a use in demonstrating how possibilities to give life to beautiful things can be found anywhere, even where one would least expect it: in editorials, for example. Often I have happened to discover in this type of prose motifs that are perfectly suited to filmmaking: it was merely a matter of having the talent and experience to make the difficult translation. I remember another piece by Piovene called "The Flower of Gems," which in other times would have delighted those directors accustomed to more intimate scenarios, offering them a chance to emulate Pabst in *Crisis*.

But in this case it was a declared fact; there was no doubt about it, wonder of wonders, the writer himself had recognized the potential of making the "Notes" into a film: this was a rare and wonderful show of support from an artist working in one medium for another.

We may therefore calmly examine the "Notes" on the basis

of purely filmic criteria. Before doing so, however, it might be advisable to acquaint the reader with the "Notes" themselves, with the proviso that their hypothetical realization should be imagined—and I wish to emphasize this—in technicolor:

How many years ago was it? I don't remember: but certainly I have read about and heard people say that the coasts of Greenland, or parts of them, once blossomed in the warm air of the Gulf Stream which used to pass nearby. And that those coastal areas were graced by civilized towns. But the Gulf Stream changed course and the ice slowly came down from the hinterland to the sea, and the people of the towns migrated toward the snow-covered, now barren fields.

I don't know the names of those towns, the date of this migration, or the geography of the coast; I'm not even sure that what I'm telling you is true. This image is just a notion of mine floating atop a sea of ignorance. Even now I don't want, as people normally would do, to look up the entry for "Greenland" in the encyclopedia in order to educate myself. I'm perfectly happy with this image, an image of a field of wheat in the sun, a meadow of little blue flowers that are gradually blown away by a cold blast of wind.

But what a subject for a novel or a film, for the writer or director who had the imagination and the courage to create it.

If I had to make a novel out of it, I would begin with a family of farmers living near the coast but not too far from a town. Between their carefully plowed fields and the shoreline, there would be a line of sand dunes, almost a cliff. The beach would seem like the edge of hell.

It would be a pebble beach, now covered, now exposed by the sea. Forever damp, the small, round, white stones scattered in abundance over the beach would glisten in a sinister fashion, veined with red like the bones of a baby lamb. For a long distance one could walk along the sea skipping from rock to rock, among deep pools of water full of many-branched strands of seaweed, made life-like by a fluid movement like the abdominal muscles of an oriental dancer. The open sea would have the most beautiful colors, like minerals collected in a museum: reds, greens, sulfur yellows, white bleached to silver by the sun. In the distance one would see bigger rocks of the same colors, and, according to the time of day and the weather, they would sometimes be lit from above by brilliant white rays of sun and sometimes glow red as if lit from within.

My farmers would live above the sand dunes. They would live with their backs to the sea, looking inland, with their minds fixed on their small world, the horses, the cows, the fields of grain, the garden planted with potatoes. They would hate the sea and would never look at it, even though it is just a few steps away, on the other side of the dunes. Their offspring would be fishermen and sailors, but they would still hate the sea. For them, sailing would be like challenging the devil, like a gambler trying to beat the house. Even if they were fishermen, they would be unable to swim (which is typical for those from the North), and they would wear heavy clothes at sea, so that if they were shipwrecked, they would avoid a prolonged struggle with the waters.

They would look inland towards a green plain, swept by raging winds in which the light would create a trembling aura of apricot and rose. Showers would pass unnoticed, and so would the rainbows and the crows. On fine days, the light would be unchanging, without reverberation, suggesting an image of peaceful eternity.

Now one day, someone from this homestead, grazing his horses, stops with a jerk. The meadow grass for a moment becomes almost silver and then returns to what it was before. The man notices that the silhouette of his house becomes sharper, as if it were the focus of some evil intent. The horses whinny as they look inland, from where a freezing wind cuts through the air like a living thing. In places, the waters of the sea take on that paradise-blue color, like the iris of an eye, as only happens to the sea when it has white sand on the bottom or is framed by icebergs.

This only happens for a moment, as if the stretch of coastline were passing through the steady beam of a spotlight. But gradually one moment blends into the next, and the farmer *thoughtfully weighs the grains of whitish, unripened wheat.*

I imagine that the mood of the people in the condemned town becomes more refined and more artificial, as if an exquisite, dying civilization were being formed in that moment.

Refugees bring news of plains that one day are blossoming and the next are deserted before the advancing iceflows. Almost as a defensive gesture, the gentle crafts of needlework and miniature painting begin to flourish, along with the jewelry trade, and more humane laws are passed. Young people behave in a softer manner and adopt more extravagant hairstyles. But some are attracted by the triumphant brutality of Nature and almost try to enact it in their own lives and play at being brutal themselves. Bands of them run away to the deserted slopes and become hunters or bandits. The town declares them public enemies and closes its doors to them.

The days of past wealth, as they fade from the memories of the living, pass into a heroic mythology which the populace morbidly savors. In the beer cellars, people dance beside wall paintings of larger-than-life heroes who carry bushels of wheat as big as pine trees and bunches of grapes with berries the size of fists. The stories take on an air of the surreal.

The traditional festivals that accompany the natural cycle of the seasons are still celebrated, but they take on something of a pathetic tone. Girls still gather outside the gates of the town to celebrate the arrival of May, though the hills are now covered with a more wiry grass and the flowers in their hair seem more vivid among the bare trees than they once were. I cannot forget their bright, shining eyes, their pale, soft cheeks flushed pink, and their graceful, eighteenth-century movements or their sparkling charm in the last cold light of day.

I can even imagine the day when the townsfolk have to take to their ships and leave that ice-bound coast. It would be a fine, clear day, and the motionless ships in the little harbor with their banners and pennants and flags would be like splashes of sunlight or streaks of blood on the sparkling silver sea. I like to think of those people, so hostile to the sea, who lived without ever looking at it, with their eyes fixed instead on the meadows and the church steeple, suddenly venturing out upon the ocean as if in mortal combat with the devil, forced to abandon their town to the enemy.

Of course, as soon as the ships weigh anchor, the abandoned city would be invaded by bandits and wayfarers who would crowd the docks, shouting and begging those leaving to take them on board. And the fleeing townspeople, gathering at the stern, certainly would weep for them and give them their blessing, telling them where to find the necessities of life in their empty houses. But they wouldn't go back for them, and their conversation with those on shore would be carried on until they were out of earshot.

But the most exciting thing of all for the imagination to contemplate is a family who decides to stay behind, who doesn't forsake the laws of civilization. A young married couple with two children. The parents, gentle and polite, slightly simple as the culture of the place requires, look out of their window at an expanse of snow which seems to glow in the night, even though there is no moonlight. Then they look at their children, at their rumpled hair and their faces that don't understand what's going on. I think that those two people, still young, at that moment feel themselves slipping physically into a cruder existence, feel their bodies aging. Little by little their minds are emptied and they are left with no memories. They know they were not the ones responsible for creating the children who now face them, but a natural phenomenon that has made them different, and they know that they will grow up as two barbarians. In the cold wind that blows down from the Pole, these two are a foretaste of the end of the world.

If it is true—as it most certainly is—that, when all is said and done, the only pieces of cinema that count are those of absolute novelty or absolute beauty, then it is no less true that these absolutes are obtainable only insofar as all other elements are subordinated.[2] There can be no doubt about this, but I would

---

[2] On this see: P. M. Pasinetti, "Predica natalizia," *Cinema* 84.

nevertheless like to play the role of producer for a moment.

I know full well what a shrewd producer seeks in a screenplay. Considering above all else the needs of the industry, he looks for several external features that can give the film glamour, something novel that immediately captures the imagination of the public. So, for example, the setting might be the decisive element, or the period: some historical periods are more photogenic—as regards costumes and settings—than others. In our case, the period is not defined, and it is the producer's task to choose the one he thinks best. As for the setting, it would seem to me that you couldn't ask for anything more suggestive or unusual than that in Piovene's article. The times in which we live are rather barren of originality, and such novelty as this must be held very precious.

But there is more. The audience, like a little child, possesses an interest in natural wonders that can never be satisfied, reserving for those events a sort of ecstatic amazement: Nature is always a formidable and unknown power, which man (at least the average man) feels but does not know, and Nature's spectacles are grandiose, fearsome, tragic. But most often the audience is simply fascinated by them. If these spectacular events impact on part of the human race, then fear is added to fascination, as well as a little hatred towards Nature mingled with pity for the unfortunate human beings caught up in it all. But whatever the case, interest in Nature always exists. That is why I see an excellent opportunity to engage the attention of the audience in that freezing-over of the coast of Greenland; in that inexorable descent of the glaciers towards the sea, reducing the land to a narrow strip and bringing with it the destruction of towns and countryside; in that emigration of entire peoples to warmer lands; in that end-of-the-world atmosphere. In this lies the eternal myth of man engaged in a struggle with the elements.[3]

[3] As for the historical background – to which it would be as well not to attribute too much importance – the following quote should provide enough information. In E. Ruggero's book *Il Mare* we read: "In the history of inhabited countries, they say that the east coast of Greenland was once dotted with towns, villages, and vegetation. They also say that a 'sudden change' in the Gulf Stream which gives life to these northern lands was responsible for its death."

But this is still not enough to satisfy our shrewd producer. He knows his audience through and through, and he is well aware how they like to see people like them, who love and hate each other in the grip of situations which, seen with a bit of an imagination, are similar to their own; he knows how they like to see characters with whom they can become involved, or even better, in whom they can recognize themselves. Thus, having settled upon a genre (sentimental, dramatic, satirical, etc.), the producer will look for a knot of feelings, a clash of ideas or ideals, the terms of a struggle; in short, a tightly defined and psychologically dynamic focus which will captivate the viewer and draw him in, amaze him and entertain him. This is all, of course, found in Piovene's article; the subject itself suggests several dramatic possibilities. For the story of these people, so simple and egalitarian, so dominated by Nature, is the very story of their environment.

However, if I am not mistaken, I am digressing from how a producer thinks and that is only to be expected. For at a certain point, once the shrewd producer has recognized that his general requirements have been satisfied, he should withdraw with good grace and leave the field open to imagination, inspiration, and creativity; in other words, he should allow the director and his collaborators a free hand in the creation of that absolute novelty and beauty which we mentioned before that is the *raison d'être* of any work of art.

So, when Piovene wanted to make a novel out of his idea, he began with a family of farmers living near the coast but not too far from the town. If I were to make a film of it, I don't see why things should be substantially different; I would just prefer our family to live in a house just outside the town gates so there would be no need to forego the pleasure of close participation in town life. And it would be a peaceful little town, with that delightful air of a *Kermesse* (*mutatis mutandis*, obviously), festive and at the same time slightly rustic.

Imagine it: this little wooden town with houses that are demure and clean like dolls' houses, with flowers on their balconies and pitched roofs, with streets not too wide nor too straight, offering harmonious views, with lots of little bridges spanning the river that divides the town in two and serves to transport timber down from the mountains to the estuary. But we already know that our town has no interest in the sea, even though it is so close. Every now and then it would be good to remember this deep-seated hatred of the sea—partly motivated by fear, I would emphasize. Every once in a while, there are fishermen walking along, but they are not as numerous as the farmers with their scythes or picks or whatever else they carried on their shoulders in those days. And more than boats on the river, you see farm carts with their wheels—two wooden discs, squeaking—as they go down the streets. Young children run around them pulling out handfuls of hay and scattering them on the ground. In this way, even the town has the strong flavor of the countryside. Besides, it doesn't take long to get from the main square to the open countryside: ten minutes, a quarter of an hour at most. From that point, golden fields and emerald pastures stretch away, broken here and there by dark smudges, darkest along the banks of the river, on whose frozen surface the children go skating in the winter. Then the fields begin to climb the slopes of the hills, up, up to the forests and the sparkling glaciers, almost always crowned by clouds. Just looking at them you can imagine the roar of the noisy torrents and the steep waterfalls in which they dissolve. "On fine days, the light would be unchanging, without reverberation, suggesting an image of peaceful eternity." (I think a cameraman could have fun with that.) In the other direction, almost a bulwark against the ocean, lies the bank of sand dunes: high dunes, wiry clumps of grass sprouting from their tops, a hellish vision.

Against this background, life flows happily along, with songs and dancing, with beautiful, generous women, with love that is natural and easy, and with girls who, as Piovene says, celebrate the arrival of May on the hills outside the town. I would add, though, that this probably isn't the only thing they celebrate there; in fact, I would insist on this. But since there was Christianity in those days, we'll have a multicolored procession wind its way through the streets every so often: and every-one kneels down as it passes and makes the sign of the cross, because they are devout folk, even though in the evening, they run out again into the hills to do you-know-what; for love is a pure gift of God when it is healthy and not morbid, when it is simple and natural.

Our farmers' home is a normal farmhouse, rather dark in color, its windows outlined in white, framed by climbing plants, and near the fields. The family, hailing from Norway originally, has owned those fields for centuries and they have always lived there, that is, ever since the first colonists landed at that place. They have always plowed that land, and their ancestors are buried under the shadows of the trees in the town grave-yard. And none of them has ever looked back at the sea (I'd make it almost a tradition among them, at this point, a super-stition); the storms from the North drive the seagulls to flap around the furrows in the fields, but the farmers keep their gaze turned inland, "their minds fixed on their small world, the horses, the cows, the fields of grain, the garden planted with potatoes." And when the seagulls come on certain days to flutter over the farm, they are considered birds of ill omen.

Inside the house can be found, among others, the old father, rough, vulgar, and with tousled hair; then there is the son, as strong as an ox, shy but not averse to a good joke and noisy laughter with his friends. Like all in his family, he is faithful to the land and has given himself to it body and soul, even though in his moments of relaxation he does not disdain the pleasures and companionship of the town.

And here is the point when a girl becomes indispensable to the plot, at least as far as I am concerned. There are lots of them in the town, pretty ones too; but among them all, one stands out for her grace and femininity and verve. Just so we understand what we are talking about, I imagine her looking like the girl in *Giovanotto, godi la tua giovinezza* (*Young Man, Enjoy Your Youth*). A photograph of that girl was printed in newspapers and magazines, amid fields of grain, with a scarf on her head and her lips parted in a radiant smile as she bent to glean the wheat. That's how I imagine our girl. Strong in the power of her youth and with a free, lively attitude toward life, she's the typical—albeit rather exaggerated—model of femininity in our town. I repeat that I do not know the North, even less how it was in those days, and I cannot guess what limits that culture's morality imposed on her, but there is a modern expression that fits what I want to say about her: she is "a bit of a flirt" when it comes to young men. For some time she has known how our young farmer loves her, but she isn't interested in him, or perhaps she enjoys seeing him suffer (but perhaps that is not very Nordic). In any case, her head is certainly very full of beautiful stories: out beyond the houses, the green fields on the slopes of the hills are the places to find love and all its wonders, the love so necessary to a young, healthy body, and it would be stupid to give it up by creating obstacles and ties. In short, let's be honest: according to our Italian morality she would be an "easy" girl, really promiscuous.

However, it is probable that at a certain point, the young man, conquering his own shyness, gets up the courage to speak to her and then gets the brush off or perhaps an ironic "yes" on condition that she herself is not tied down, and as a result of this he completely loses his head. And it is probable that all sorts of trouble erupts because of this love, which even makes him neglect the fields, and we can imagine the fury of his rough old father, his mother's crying, and the anxious surprise of his young sisters.

At this point the big event begins. Listen to Piovene: "Now one day, someone from this homestead, grazing his horses, stops with a jerk. The meadow grass for a moment becomes almost silver and then returns to what it was before." Just for a moment. Then: "[G]radually one moment blends into the next, and the farmer thoughtfully weighs the grains of whitish, unripened wheat." The writer doesn't say how much time elapses between the first symptoms of the freeze and the departure of the population. A lot, one presumes, if "the days of past wealth" are able to emerge "from the memories of the living" and become a "heroic mythology": reality doesn't

11

become myth that quickly. At least, that would be the most realistic hypothesis. In actual fact, if you wanted to trace the evolution of Greenland as far as it is known, you would have to spread it out over three or four centuries. But I think that in a film you would have to speed things up, in order to make it more dramatic. And nothing stops us from imagining in a single film a disaster that happens in the space of three or four years, a half-decade at most. We are in the realm of legends here and everything is possible; we can even contradict the science of geomorphology if we want to.[4] Unless, that is, we want to make one of those films in which whole generations live out their destinies and the young actors from the beginning become great-great-grandfathers at the end. These films have the passage of time embedded in their very structure; it's their guiding premise, and this brings with it a rather suspicious melancholy. It is true that here, where Nature has the protagonist's role, the story would take on another, more robust meaning. But anyway, there are many possible ways of filming it, and of these I have undertaken to explore only one and I'll stick to that.

I said that everything—or nearly everything—that Piovene imagined would take place over the course of a half-decade at the most. In that exquisite, dying civilization, feelings become more refined and more artificial. The noble crafts of needlework and miniature painting flourish, along with the art of the jeweler. More humane laws are passed, while certain young men, enacting the brutality of Nature in their own lives, become hunters and bandits, and the city declares them outlaws. Our family instead continues to fix its attention on the land. Plowing, sowing, and harvesting are now done with greater care, lovingly, and the old man and his son and the whole family fight desperately to reverse the dwindling returns from the soil. The winters are endless, the white of the

---

[4] But there is no need. It is well known that ocean currents are subject to variations in direction and flow which can occur with remarkable suddenness. If there is any contradiction it is with the history of the Gulf Stream but this is a conscious departure that is very familiar to most filmmakers.

mountains has gradually spread along the horizon, the grass
has lost its greenness, and the hardened earth has become less
fruitful. But our farmers redouble their efforts, they work
with angry obstinacy, still incredulous about their situation
and deluding themselves that a miracle will happen; they will
be the last to give in and it will take the tears of the women
and the constant urging of friends to persuade the old man
and his son to go, united as they are with all the people on
the farm in their struggle. Their departure will be more sor-
rowful than you can imagine.

In the meantime, the son's relationship with the girl has
also undergone a change. She has not been insensitive to what
is going on around her; like all Nordic people she is deeply
attached to Nature and her mood has followed its destiny and
taken on a "tragic, pathetic" quality. We can now see in her
too those "bright, shining eyes, those pale, soft cheeks flushed
pink and those graceful, eighteenth-century movements." Life
in the town has already become less cheerful. As it has become
more refined, it has lost its former exuberance and the feeling
of recklessness that had previously characterized it. Little boys
no longer scatter handfuls of hay from the wagons onto the
road, having a vague sense of how precious it is; from behind
closed doors laughter is now more subdued; in the taverns the
singing of the occasional drunk is no longer so noisy; and out
on the fields the birch trees are stunted and shriveled. Women
have become more thoughtful, more chaste (if in fact they were
in the past truly promiscuous and not merely open and sincere), and they are less flirtatious; or rather, they have a greater
awareness of sin and a deeper desire for redemption. The men
are likewise more taciturn.

The foreboding mood of a nightmare hangs in the atmosphere, imperceptible but undeniable, and the girl feels it. She
becomes more serious, perhaps more virtuous, as she feels the
need for someone or something to protect her from that thin
air, that meager light, that subtle fear which is spreading all
around. She is no longer so whimsical; now we see her more
often sitting at the window sewing, and perhaps it might be

nice to think that she is sewing her own trousseau (or something similar, according to local custom). Little by little, not out of cold calculation but instinctively, her behavior towards the farmer changes, and she now feels a need for warmth which drives her towards him. And the two are happily united. At this point, an outlaw who is in love with her might offer an opportunity to portray that brutality so different from the refinement of the dying town, though there is no need to develop that idea here. We can of course concentrate on the scene of the departing ships, the "main scene," as the producer would call it.

And there, in fact, are the ships at anchor in the little bay, or fjord it would be better to say, with their rectangular, Norman-style sails unfurled. Piovene would like to see pennants and flags like splashes of sunlight or streaks of blood, but actually I don't see it that way; I think such a festive air is not really appropriate. Rather, I see a subdued sadness, a heartfelt resignation to their fates on the faces of the fleeing townspeople as they slowly and calmly bid farewell to their native land. Row boats full of people and household goods leave the quay and head out to the ships, the last being the one that carries our family. "Of course, as soon as the ships weigh anchor, the abandoned city would be invaded by bandits and wayfarers who would crowd the docks, shouting and begging those leaving to take them on board. And the fleeing townspeople, gathering at the stern, certainly would weep for them and give them their blessing, telling them where to find the necessities of life in their empty houses. But they wouldn't go back for them, and their conversation with those on shore would be carried on until they were out of earshot." And I imagine a furious fight breaking out among those who are left behind, desperate and unreasonable, a fight that immediately dies down of its own accord; and the outlaws watch the ships sail away into the distance and perhaps feel a shiver of cold run down their spines.

And now we see the coast from on board one of the ships, as it slips away. It is still green but has no vitality. The refugees stare at it, standing at the stern. Among them we see the two young people holding hands like teenagers. They don't seem as interesting now. As is appropriate, he seems to be deeply moved; each new glance towards the land is like a caress, and he cannot pluck up the courage to make it his last. But this emotion doesn't last for long. In fact, it is not long before his gaze wanders from the land and comes to rest on the young girl. He is thinking that his country did not die for nothing since it has given him her hand to hold.[5] And the girl, for her part, leans towards him with a feeling of helplessness, but this doesn't last long either; after she has had one last look at the narrow strip of land on the horizon, her eyes come to rest hopefully on the open sea, and her eyes are the same color as the water.

It is now the old father who appears most interesting, standing at a slight distance from them. He surely must have a lump in his throat as he stands there with his windswept white hair, gazing steadily at the land and gritting his teeth. His eyes are moist so that they almost seem covered by a veil: he looks at the shore, the houses, the hillside and the woods, the white mountains . . . Through the veil of his tears he can see the white of the mountains coming down, down the slopes toward the fields, the grain, the farm; they will soon all be covered over with white, with a layer of ice. Then, as if a spring inside him had been released, he seems to explode into action. Drawing himself up to his full height, he begins to hurl a stream of abuse at the land, shouting, ranting, swearing. His fury only adds to the emotions of those around him. It is beautiful to see those other men, each as strong as an ox, and those calm women sobbing, and the old man towering over them all, cursing and waving his fists and swearing as the ship heads out to sea and the water becomes a cold, metallic, blue-green color, as if it already felt the coming freeze—whilst the seagulls fly under

---

[5] It may seem extremely difficult, if not impossible, to express such a state of mind on film, and yet I am convinced that a sensitive director working with a good actor would manage it just fine.

the sinking sun, whirling in a sinister fashion under the sky of that Green Land.[6]

This is a sketch of the plot as I would do it if I was commissioned to write the screenplay. But I cannot omit a few last words about the color.

It will not have escaped anyone's attention that color must play a big part in our film: not to be flamboyant or as mere decoration but as an integral part of the story. Here color will suggest not only the climate, it will represent psychological developments, the drama itself—visually. The colors will develop and gradually fade away. Listen to how Piovene lets his imagination run riot with these colors: "little white stones veined with red"; "the open sea [with] the most beautiful colors, like minerals collected in a museum: reds, greens, sulfur yellows, white bleached to silver by the sun"; and "those far-off cliffs which also have their different colors according to the time of day and the weather . . ." "Green plains in which the trembling light is tinted rose or apricot, fields of grain scattered with little blue flowers and the sky cleft by rainbows"— this is the sort of thing that if you saw it on screen you would say, "That's fake," but it's precisely in those false-looking tints that you will find the true colors of the Far North, where the landscape sometimes takes on the hues of a seemingly unimaginable palette. Then there's that exquisitely sad fading away of everything, the rarefied atmosphere, the last blossoming of flowers, the fringe that borders the advancing white as it caresses

---

[6] In his article, Piovene also talks about a young couple left behind with their two children, etc. The idea is very interesting, but I don't think I would give it much attention. A hint, a suggestion, would serve very well to indicate that feeling of the end of the world that the writer alludes to; however, I would end the film with the departure of the ships. Especially, the figure of the old man (as I have done) for at this moment he is certainly more important than the young people. For them there is the prospect of a new life, and the girl's gaze as she scans the horizon seems anxious but at the same time confident that there will be another land where she can put down roots and which will become her children's home. The old man can feel nothing of that. His life is over; there are no new horizons to comfort him and he will live out his remaining years on foreign soil. That's why he is angry; yes, it is an explosion of impotent rage but it's above all else the last farewell, the last show of his love for that land. Dudley Nichols, the screenwriter for *The Informer*, once wrote that symbols have the highest importance in cinema, as long as they don't seem to be symbols. I think that is precisely the case here.

everything with its deathly cold touch. It is cheerfulness, life itself that fades with the colors. And that's not to mention the aurora borealis or the famous "midnight sun," the description of which is generally the *pièce de résistance* of any writer visiting the Arctic Circle. The twenty-four hour daylight, dusk at eleven o'clock at night, the sun which sinks into the sea but never fully sets, instead hiding in ambush just beneath it, inflaming it and tinging the clouds above with red while the sea takes on the color of burnished steel and makes your eyes hurt to look at it: these are truly apocalyptic sights—or so they say. There are those who would say that these images are impossible to realize on screen with the current state of color technology. But it is clear that if technical difficulties were to frighten us away from trying things in art, then no masterpieces would ever see the light of day. We already have the ability to achieve some surprising effects with color and that should be enough.

Having said that, I don't think there is much more to be said. I believe that everybody would agree on one thing, that the film would undoubtedly come under the heading "colossal," and that should not displease our shrewd producer. As for the title, all films must have one and I think that *Green Land* is most apt to capture the main thrust of the story. Once upon a time, there was a green land . . .

LAST NIGHT, SHOTS RANG OUT[1]

A summer's night in Rome. It's hot. In a bedroom some-where is a girl who can't sleep. She is called Giulia and she's twenty-one. She's the daughter of an unscrupulous businessman who got rich during the war. She studies foreign languages at the university. The window of her bedroom opens onto the de-serted street below. Suddenly, some voices are raised, there's a scuffle, and two gunshots ring out, very close by. Giulia had been reading a book, and she rushes to the window. From there all that can be seen is a part of the street; the rest is hidden by the house next door. But the shots rang out directly below, and a man can be seen dressed in a light colored suit, kneeling wounded in the middle of the road. There's a third shot, and the man falls down dead.

Giulia draws back into the room, terrified. But curiosity gets the better of her. She looks out again. The man isn't there any more. Something has been left behind that looks like a handkerchief. Giulia runs into her father's bedroom, but he hasn't come home yet. She runs to the maid's room, but she's snoring loudly. As she's about to wake her up, Giulia changes her mind and goes back to her room, back to the window. Just

[1] 1949. In *Cinema Nuoyo* 9 (April 1953): 246-248.

at that moment, another man comes round the corner of the house next door, picks up the handkerchief, looks at it carefully, and puts it in his jacket pocket. Then he apparently senses Giulia's lighted window and looks up. Giulia shivers; the man hesitates for a moment. He is tall and thin. Giulia is terrified; she lets down the blind and slips into bed.

The first thing she remembers when she wakes up the next morning is the ugly event that she witnessed. She flips through the newspaper, but there's no mention of it. She goes out to buy others: nothing. Nobody has reported the crime. Did she dream it? Sometimes one remembers things one has dreamt as if they were real. She goes to see a friend who lives nearby. Her friend had indeed heard the shots but was careful not to get out of bed: one often hears shooting at night. The shots always seem to be right outside your window, but usually they are echoes from far away, or just someone letting off firecrackers. Giulia tells her friend what she saw, but Elena is skeptical. How come the newspapers don't talk about it then? A man has died and everything is like normal.

Elena has an idea. Go to the police station nearby and inquire about it. The press probably has its reasons for keeping quiet. Giulia is a witness, the only witness, and her statement could be important. For certain, the police will be racking their brains for a lead and they will welcome her with open arms. But at the police station they say they don't know anything about it.

Evening comes and Giulia has calmed down. She goes round to some friends who are showing a 16mm home movie. She tries to tell her story about what happened the previous night, but nobody seems interested. In fact, they start joking about it. One of them, Luigi, tries to frighten her: "If the guy saw you, then he'll kill you too. You'll see, he'll be back. Killers always come back to the scene of the crime." Everybody laughs, even Giulia. But as she's getting into bed a few hours later, she's still a little bit tense. She wakes up with a start in the middle of the night. The window is open and there is a deep silence all around. Giulia puts on the light and gets up. She feels an irresistible urge to go over to the window. She takes a peek out into the street and can't believe her eyes. In the exact spot where the crime was committed, there is a man's shadow, standing still behind the corner of the house next door. After a moment, the shadow moves, the man appears and stops again: he's lighting a cigarette. He is tall and thin. Giulia could swear that he's the same man from the night before, especially when he blows out the match and looks up at her. And that's not all: he starts motioning to her. Giulia is seriously frightened now. She draws back hurriedly and switches off the light. When she looks out again, the man has gone.

Giulia gets back into bed. But this second episode has almost disturbed her more than the first. Especially because the next morning, as she leaves the house to go to the university, the first person she sees is the man from the previous night. Giulia hurries away as quickly as she can; the man gets into an old Topolino[2] and follows her. Giulia gets onto a streetcar with the man following behind in his car. Is it a joke? This is getting worrisome. At last, she gets to the university. She meets some friends and, while she's with them, feels more comfortable. The little car has disappeared. But suddenly, this time very close by, the same man appears. Giulia notices that he's younger than she thought, twenty-seven or twenty-eight most likely. But what does he want with her? Is it really about this murder business?

To her enormous surprise, she sees that he greets one of her friends. She immediately asks her friend who he is. "He's a student,[3] I can't even remember his name." So, he's a student. This reassures her a bit. But at the same time it confuses her. Before, she had thought of him as a criminal; now she doesn't know what to think. Could he be a killer or an accomplice when he's so well-dressed and so distinguished? Over the next few days, the young man doesn't miss an opportunity to try and get near her. He manages to get himself introduced and walks with her down the streets of the campus. In short, he's

---

[2] One of the early cars produced by the Fiat company. [Translator]

[3] The term *fuori corso* suggests a student who has exceeded the time to graduate and rarely takes classes but is still technically registered. [Translator]

trying to flirt with her. And Giulia goes along with it, partly from curiosity, and partly because this boy, with his air of elegance and good manners, attracts her in spite of everything. They see each other again. The girl can't get over her original reluctance; sometimes she's even afraid of him and swears to herself that she won't see him again. But neither can she ignore her growing affection for him, and it's that affection that gradually diffuses her original diffidence. For her part, Elena enjoys her friend's little flirtation and tries to convince her that her fears are groundless, absurd.

The young man's name is Michele. He's in the School of Architecture, he says, and only has a few courses left to take; he'll graduate in October. One evening, they go out together to a jam session at Mario's bar on the Via Pinciana. There are two bands: New Orleans jazz and be-bop. A hell of a noise. They meet a friend of Michele's who comes over and introduces himself loudly to Giulia. His name is Beppe Z. He seems amazed to see Michele, though it's not clear why. "What about her?" he says, nodding at Giulia. "Where did you pick her up?" He laughs with amusement but it's a strange laugh. Equally strange, Michele quickly leads Giulia away. Outside, for the first time, he tells her he loves her, and they have their first kiss. Everything is very sweet. The shadow that hangs between them and the memory of that night have almost completely disappeared. Giulia has never talked to Michele about it; she would like to, but she hasn't got the nerve. Elena also advises her not to: her suspicions might offend him. But several things now happen to cast new shadows over Giulia's peace of mind and give her fresh doubts. The first is a robbery. A valuable ring was missing from a school friend's house, and it came out that it was their mutual friend Luigi who took it (there was a lot of talk about this). Someone turned him in to the police and he was arrested. When she hears about it, Giulia can't believe her ears. If Luigi is a thief, then anything's possible: maybe people who seem to be on the level actually aren't. Maybe Michele is a murderer. In short, who is this Michele anyway?

The next day, Giulia goes to her father's office to ask a

member of his staff to find out about the young man. As she gets there, she has a disturbing experience. There is a man coming out of the office just at the same moment that she is trying to get in. In fact, she has to step back to let him pass; he's leaning in the doorway and seems to be on the verge of tears, his lips are trembling, almost with rage. He's muttering to himself: "Thief . . . thief." Then he notices Giulia and he gets a grip on himself. And before the girl passes him, he says: "Keep well away from here, miss. They're all a bunch of ruffians." Giulia's mother is dead. Her father is very fond of her but he doesn't pay as much attention to her as he should. Still, she loves him and to hear bad things about him from this stranger seems incredible to her. Her father, a crook! His secretary, his accountant, his clerk and employees—all ruffians! The world seems to have turned upside down.

Anyway, she goes inside. And there she finds everyone in a happy mood. Her father is laughing, and when he sees her, he comes towards her and hugs her. He puts his staff and office at her disposal. She wants information? That's his strong suit. He lives and breathes it. And in fact, after two days she gets her information. It seems that Michele's family is of modest means. His father is dead and his mother has remarried. He has a sister. He has no permanent job, yet his lifestyle seems to be beyond his means. As he gives her the news, her father asks who was interested in Michele. "A girlfriend of mine," Giulia lies. "Tell your friend to drop him," is the reply. And he will not say any more than that. Giulia is very upset by all this. When she sees Michele again she tries to spot the signs of a good-for-nothing in him. But she can't: he's so calm, smiling and affable. In his arms she forgets everything. But this time she plucks up courage and tells him what is on her mind.

She tells him about that tragic night, when she first saw him, and about the following night and what she suspected. She had thought that Michele would protest and be offended but instead a shadow comes over him. He becomes sad. Then he explains to her that on that night he had gone to a party on Via Such-and-Such. Giulia wants to know whose party. Michele hesitates, then gives her a name: it's the family of a doctor who she knows well, since she is friends with their daughter, who is also a student at the university. As he was leaving, Michele saw the face of a girl in the window and thought she was pretty. The following night he went back, secretly hoping to see her again; it was a bit of an adventure and he made signs for her to come down. Then he was curious to see what she looked like by daylight, and he went back the morning after. Then he fell in love with her. It was all very normal.

But there's another question that Michele has to answer. How does he get the money which he obviously spends on his clothes, his car, and so on? Again, Michele seems troubled. But it's only for a moment. He has some friends in business, he says, and every so often they cut him in on a deal. Who are these friends? Another hesitation, and he throws out another name: B. Loris. And immediately, as if he can't help himself, he admits that in the past he's been involved in some shady business, but the very fact that he now admits it openly to her, the person whom he loves most in the world, means that he's sorry for it. One thing is for sure though; he's never killed anyone. "Do I look like the type who would kill someone?" No, Giulia doesn't think he does. But then, many things don't seem to be what they are and vice versa. She doesn't understand anything anymore. She would have liked his words to calm her, but unfortunately they don't. When they part, the little shadow that was between them, rather than being blown away, has become darker.

Giulia talks about it repeatedly with her friend Elena, who tells her not to make a drama out of it. "A flirtation is just a flirtation. It should be taken lightly." But Giulia's not the type to do that, and besides, her feelings for Michele are too strong *not* to be taken seriously. Giulia is fighting a battle with herself. When the day and time of her next meeting with Michele come around, she decides to test him and doesn't show up. It is evening. Michele waits a long time, more than an hour. Then, disappointed, he leaves. He goes by the Glow-Worm, a night club in Villa Borghese, and he stops to listen to the band and a black woman singing. He gets more and more anxious. He goes to the phone in the bar next door. He speaks into the receiver and says: "It's me . . . I wanted to tell you that I can't come tomorrow . . . Nor the day after. I don't think we should see each other any more. I just wanted to tell you . . . It's been going on two years now; it had to come to an end sooner or later . . . Yes, it's better over the phone: there won't be a scene that way . . . Bye."

Then he goes into the nightclub and starts dancing with one of the hostesses. He holds her tightly, resting his cheek against hers. The girl looks at him surprised, but she doesn't seem to mind. When the dance is over, Michele suggests they go out. The girl can't leave work. So they sit at a little table apart from the others and Michele orders some champagne. It's still early and there aren't many people about. At the other tables, the other hostesses are by themselves. Out of the blue, Michele fires a question at his companion: "Will you go to bed with me?" The girl pretends to be offended, but Michele insists in a way that she has never heard before. "Why me?" she asks. "There are lots of girls in here." Michele still insists. "I want to know if you would be willing to do it with me. Please, be honest." "Of course, you're a good-looking boy." So they agree to see each other again later, at three o'clock, when she gets off work. He'll wait for her at the Hotel Como. They part, almost tenderly.

At a quarter past three, the girl goes into the Hotel Como. She asks for Michele, but Michele is not there; he hasn't come. The girl is very annoyed; she leaves the hotel feeling humiliated and walks away unsteadily on her high heels. Michele is under Giulia's window. He whistles softly, then again more loudly. Two, three, four times. At last, Giulia appears at the window. They make signs to each other. After a bit, the main door of the apartment building swings open and the two young people fall into each other's arms. She is in her dressing gown and Michele caresses her, hugs her, and kisses her madly, which frightens and at the same time delights Giulia. The girl resists as long as she can but finally gives in. The next day Giulia goes out with a group of her friends. She seems happy, laughing and joking with everybody.

Just at that moment, Giulia's attention is caught by the name on a shop sign: B. Loris. It's the man Michele had mentioned when talking about his business associates. Giulia goes towards the shop. It's a men's clothing store, a very elegant store. Overcome by curiosity, the girl goes inside and asks to talk to the shop owner, ready with an excuse that she wants to buy something. But when she finds herself face to face with Mr. B. Loris, her courage deserts her. He's a harmless looking guy, a bit slick though he seems quite refined. Giulia gets her story muddled and ends up telling the truth: she'd like to know about Michele. The man is intrigued, but he can tell her little. Michele bought a secondhand car from him and paid for it in cash, that's all. He knows Michele only slightly. They are not business partners. Giulia apologizes and leaves. She's confused. So why did Michele give her this guy's name? Now the shadows and doubts start to return. And it's precisely those shadows, those doubts, that persuade her to do something she would never normally dare.

This happens two days later, at the university. Giulia meets Laura, the doctor's daughter in whose house Michele claims to have spent that infamous evening. The two girls aren't close but they greet each other like friends. Laura even teases her saying: "We're neighbors and we never even see each other." Giulia takes advantage of the remark immediately: "Well of course not, you don't invite me to your parties." Her friend is surprised. What parties? It's six months since she organized a party at her house. In fact, she was just thinking about having another one next Sunday; she hopes Giulia will be able to come. Giulia says yes and walks away. An icy hand seems to grip her heart: there's another of Michele's lies, more serious than the previous ones. Guided by a strange kind of instinct, she goes to the university registrar's office. She knows one of the girls who works there quite well, and she asks about Michele. Her friend flips through the files and can't find Michele's name. She goes to some old files: there he is. He was indeed enrolled in the

School of Architecture for two years. He took an exam. But he hasn't paid any fees in three years; in other words, he's no longer a student there.

Giulia feels the tears welling up inside her: another lie and it seems to confirm all the other ones. She runs home: she has no doubts now, it's all true. She has to deal with two feelings, each as strong as the other: cut off all ties with Michele, or help him back onto the straight and narrow and sacrifice herself for him. But that evening the newspapers arouse new emotions in her. They've found the body of an unknown man in the Tiber; he'd died a few days previously from gunshot wounds and apparently had been thrown into the river. It could be the same body from that night. The newspaper says which mortuary the body is being held in for identification by the public, and Giulia phones Michele to invite him to go with her to see the man. If he's innocent, the girl thinks she will be able to tell from his reaction. She needs to test him. No need to say that she's hoping Michele will pass the test. Giulia has never been in a mortuary. As soon as she goes inside she feels a vague sense of unease, and at the sight of the body, she feels she could literally faint. How can anyone recognize him, disfigured like that? She makes them show her the light clothes that she remembers so well: they are the ones of the man who was shot underneath her window. Michele is not unaffected by it all. Giulia seems to read in his face a kind of turmoil, like amazement and rage mixed together. But he recovers quickly and is there for the brief interview Giulia has with the policeman at the mortuary who wants to know what reason she had for viewing the body. Giulia hadn't foreseen this and is caught off guard. She tells everything she knows. The policeman asks her to go with him to the police station, where they subject her to a battery of questions. Questions about the man she claims to have seen picking up his handkerchief. Giulia hesitates, glances at Michele, and then says that she can't remember. When they finally let her out, she is exhausted. Instinctively, she had told them as little as possible, but she has surely hurt Michele. If they arrest him, it would be as if she had personally turned him in. She's desperate and bursts into tears, hugging the young man and begging for his forgiveness. Michele reassures her: nothing will happen to him because he's got nothing to do with the whole thing. Understand? Nothing to do with it.

However, Giulia can't quite manage to believe him. She continues to see him because she doesn't really have any proof that he's guilty. And she hopes, she still hopes. She is in a state of continual anxiety. The newspapers aren't talking about the crime anymore now; obviously, the police are conducting their investigation in the strictest of confidence. Each time they see each other, Giulia is scared Michele won't come because he's been arrested. When they are alone together, a wall seems to separate them. Both of them feel it, especially Michele who is well aware of the need to convince her of his innocence if he is to really make Giulia his. The young man gets more and more nervous, as if he is struggling with some private trouble of his own. Moreover, he's beginning to run out of money and he has no job. He confides in his sister, but even with her he keeps something back, that secret of his that won't allow him any peace. And one day, confronted with Giulia's unwavering distrust, he tells her in exasperation of his decision not to see her again until he can give her proof of his innocence.

Three days go by. On the morning of the fourth day, Elena runs to Giulia's house with a newspaper in her hand. They've arrested the murderers. There are two of them. Giulia feels faint, so her friend reads her the names: fortunately, Michele is not one of them. The first name means nothing to them, but Giulia has heard the second mentioned several times. She racks her brains and finally comes up with the answer. The name was Beppe Z. and it was Michele's friend from the jam session. The victim, the newspaper informs them, was an American who was in Rome on business: an antiques dealer. It seems he was carrying a large sum of money on the night of the crime, which naturally is now missing. The arrest of the murderers came about through an anonymous tip to the police.

For Giulia, discovering that one of the killers was a friend of Michele's is the final blow. She goes to her next date with the young man to tell him exactly what she thinks of him and to break up with him for good, but Michele doesn't turn up. She waits for him for three quarters of an hour and then goes home. It's as if her world had collapsed around her. It's impossible to deceive herself any more. That evening, she tosses and turns in her bed, unable to sleep. It's almost midnight when Michele calls. Giulia rushes to the phone but her father beats her to it. "Giulia's in bed," he says. So the girl goes back to her room; all things considered, maybe it is better this way. It's a warm night, the window is wide open, and memories flood in with the humid night air.

After a while, the silence is broken by a low whistle. Giulia jumps. There it is again . . . and again. Giulia runs to the window—she's right, it's Michele. This is how she saw him on that first night, with his face turned up to look at her, smiling. For a moment she is tempted to lean out, or go downstairs, but she gets a grip on herself. What good would it do? It would only make things more difficult for him. Michele whistles again a couple of times and then goes away. There, Giulia thinks to herself, it's over. The next day is Sunday and at the home of Laura, the doctor's daughter, the party is taking place. Elena drags Giulia along with her, secretly telling their friends to keep an eye on her: "She needs distracting, she has a big crush on someone." Elena even asks Roberto, Laura's brother, to flirt with her a bit. And Roberto doesn't need to be asked twice; he's always liked Giulia. But he has to work hard to get over the girl's silence, and even then, after a couple of hours, she claims she's tired and wants to go home. Roberto offers to escort her.

As they are going downstairs, the noise of the front door opening and closing makes Giulia lean over the banister to see who it is. It is just a casual glance, but she gets a shock. It's Michele. He stops on the floor beneath them, rings the bell, and, after a moment, the door is opened for him. He must live there if he has a key to the front door. "Who lives in that apartment?" Giulia asks. Roberto smiles enigmatically: "A lady," he answers. Giulia goes home very worried. A lady? So

Michele has a lover. And he was at her house that night, and because he's a gentleman, he didn't want to say so. The bitterness of this discovery is outweighed by her joy in having found an explanation for everything. And she had doubted him, she had believed he was guilty.

The next morning she wakes up in a kind of frenzy. She must see Michele immediately, apologize to him for standing him up on the previous night, and for everything else too. She calls him, but Michele isn't in; he didn't come home last night and nobody knows where he might be. He often does this. Defeated, Giulia hangs up the receiver. Where can she find him? Why is he always out? She's too preoccupied to do nothing, and she goes out and starts to walk the streets in the vain hope of running into him. But it's useless, and around midday, exhausted and downcast, she goes home.

Michele is there, leaning on the wall of the building opposite. They step into the hallway of Giulia's building and hug each other, as if they hadn't seen each other for months. Then they go out again. Giulia has a ton of things to tell him. "I know everything," she begins. Michele looks at her, worried. But Giulia chatters on almost happily: "There's a woman in your life and you were with her that night and you didn't want to tell me. Don't deny it because I saw you." Michele is quiet for a moment, thinking. Then he admits it; it's true, he has a lover. He was there that evening, and there were also other people too, including the dead man, Beppe Z., and the other man who was arrested. Those three went off together and a little later he left too. He found the handkerchief in the street and recognized it. It's a pocket handkerchief, silk, and it belonged to Beppe Z. He picked it up and the rest she knows.

Giulia seems satisfied with the explanation. She's happy, and Michele seems to be too, though perhaps a bit less so. Suddenly a strange excitement seems to come over him and he swears to the girl that he won't see that woman any more. He'd already broken everything off, but the evening that Giulia had seen him go into the apartment, he'd been so humiliated when she hadn't turned up to their date that he had given in to temptation. He's a skunk, a good-for-nothing, and he asks her to forgive him. He reproaches himself bitterly, almost in tears. But now it's over, he'll get work, they'll marry and be happy.

In the afternoon, Giulia gets a phone call. It's Roberto again and he would like to see her. She goes out and they set off together. Roberto begins by reassuring her: he has not asked to meet her because he wants a date. In fact, he's certain that after their talk he'll be even less likely to get one. But he does respect her and he feels it is his duty to warn her about certain people. Giulia is immediately uneasy. She doesn't need anybody's advice, she says brusquely. She knows perfectly well who and what Michele is; he doesn't have secrets from her any more. "But one secret," Roberto insists, "just one, I am sure he hasn't told you yet." Since Giulia doesn't believe him, Roberto goes on: "You know the lady who lives in the apartment below mine?" Giulia has never seen her. "Come with me then," says Roberto, and he leads her to a bar, to the telephone at the back. He dials a number and hands the receiver to Giulia, telling her to ask for Mrs. Bardelli (that was the name that Giulia had read on the brass plate on the door). At the other end of the line, a man answers her. "May I speak with the lady of the house, please?" Giulia asks. "I'm sorry, there isn't one." "But isn't this the Bardelli house?" "Yes, this is Mr. Bardelli."

Giulia hangs up. What does it all mean? Roberto makes her sit down at a table in a corner. "Don't be naive, Giulia. People like that do exist, you know." But Giulia obstinately refuses to understand. "Maybe he and Michele had business together," she says, her voice trembling. "Call it business if you like," Roberto continues, "after all, he does do it for the money." Giulia can't hold back her tears. She cries out that it's a trick Roberto has made up to get her away from Michele but he won't succeed because she loves him. Then she stops. This is so big it almost seems to her she doesn't love him any more. Roberto lets her get it all out of her system and then walks her home. "I hope that one day you'll thank me for this little talk. You can't imagine what it has cost me," he tells her as they part. Giulia doesn't even answer. She walks off without even

31

saying good-bye, wrapped up in her own thoughts, feeling as if she hates Michele, Roberto, and all the men on earth. At home, her father is waiting for her, very worried. The police have called to see her, she must go down to the station at once. Giulia would like to go alone, but her father insists on going with her. As they walk, she tells him what it's probably about. At the police station they show her the handkerchief that Michele had picked up that night. Does she recognize it? Yes, she does. But how come they have it? They tell her not to worry and show her the two men they arrested to see if she recognizes one of them as the one who picked it up. Giulia hesitates—can she lie to the police? "No, it wasn't either of them," she says. "Then it must have been somebody else who knew what they'd done and turned them in to us," the policeman concludes. A question immediately springs to Giulia's mind: "Do you think that that person was an accomplice?" The reply is very confident: "Absolutely not. Whoever sent this letter [and he waves the anonymous tip] with this handkerchief as evidence cannot be their accomplice. It would have been too dangerous. These two would have given us his name instantly." Giulia's father grins: "Nice friends they have!" "Well, who knows what the story behind it all is," the policeman says. "The dead man was one of *those* if you know what I mean . . . Things like that are always messy."

Giulia walks out of the police station like a robot. She doesn't even hear her father giving her a lecture: "I told you not to get involved. Idiots! If they managed these things well . . . But no, they go and get him fished out of the river and they all spy on each other!" Giulia's not listening. What does it matter to her anymore if Michele is innocent? It is strange though, that was the one thing he was truthful about. At home she shuts herself in her room and won't see anyone, not even Elena, who comes round to see her soon afterwards. She must decide what she's going to do about Michele. How can she see him again, with what she now knows? Suddenly the phone rings and of course it's Michele. The young man is still in the same mood as when they last saw each other: calm, happy, and full of enthusiasm because that day he has just had a job offer. He wants to see her right away, but Giulia says that she can't right now, her father is suspicious and is watching her too closely. It would be better to meet at midnight, under her window, like so many other nights. Giulia has a plan.

She looks up a number in the telephone directory and dials: "Bardelli speaking," the man's voice from before answers. Giulia tells him that Michele will be waiting at exactly midnight on Via Such-and-Such, in front of number . . . It's urgent. "Tell him that Giulia sent you." At midnight Giulia hides behind the blinds of her bedroom window. After a few moments, Michele appears. The young man stops and looks up at the window. As usual, he whistles several times, but Giulia doesn't move an inch. A few seconds go by, then another man crosses the road and approaches Michele. It's Bardelli—Michele turns away, obviously annoyed. They exchange a few hurried words and Michele looks up towards Giulia's room. At that precise moment, Giulia shows herself at the window; she's trembling and her face is streaked with tears, though the two men below cannot see it. For a moment they watch her, then Bardelli goes off around the corner of the building next door.

Michele stands still, looking up at the window. He looks shaken and he calls out her name, softly so that it's hardly audible: "Giulia . . . Giulia." The girl goes back into her room; she can hardly control her sobs, she stands rooted to the floor, listening to the tense silence that is broken only by the sound of her name. A gunshot rings out on the street below. Giulia cries out and rushes over to the window: Michele is stretched out face down on the street, lifeless. His hand still clutches the revolver. It is just after a quarter past midnight in the summertime. It's warm and people are still awake. Windows open, some passersby run to help. Someone asks why this boy should have killed himself, at his age, right there.

STAIRS[1]

1. *The deserted steps of the Valle Giulia,[2] surrounded by greenery. The camera pans slowly over the steps while two calm voices are heard speaking clearly:*

HIM: . . . it's just the way things are. You must see that I can't do without you any more. That's all. Try and understand me, Giovanna, I can't live without you.

HER: Since when have you had all these ideas in your head?

The camera continues to pan over the deserted steps, finally coming to rest on two young people in the distance who are climbing up them, stopping every now and then to rest.

HIM: Since this morning. I need to live with you . . . let's get married!

HER: But don't you know what your sister said to me? Don't you know that she came round deliberately to stop it?

HIM: Who cares? I love you.

2. *Two young people (not the ones from the previous scene) are coming down the steps of a church. It is obvious they have just been married. They are dressed in everyday clothes. No*

---

[1] 1950. Treatment for a documentary film. In C. di Carlo, *Michelangelo Antonioni* (Rome: Bianca e Nero, 1964), 131–133.

[2] An area of parkland in Rome. [Editor]

one is with them except for their witnesses. The couple say good-bye to them without much fuss and get into a taxi. The bride's bouquet is left lying on the ground.

3. Several people are going up the steps to an airplane. The steps are immediately removed, the plane leaves. Someone waves a handkerchief.

4. A little woman emerges onto the landing of a middle-class apartment complex; she leans out over the stairwell and calls:
WOMAN: Giorgio! Giorgio!
From down below a little boy calls back.
BOY: Yeah?
WOMAN: Come upstairs!
BOY: I'm playing with my meccano[3]! . . .
WOMAN: I'll give you meccano, I'll . . .
A second woman in her nightgown, with her hair all messed up, emerges from another door to put out the trash. A man goes by with a shopping bag.

5. The courtyard of a public housing project. There are landings everywhere, connected to each other by outdoor staircases. The postman arrives; people look out into the courtyard, some run downstairs to fetch their mail. Lots of chatter among the neighbors. Someone is washing clothes in the central well.

6. A maid comes down a sweeping, mammoth staircase and opens the front door. A glimpse of a car and an elegant lady getting out of it who comes inside.
LADY: Is their any mail for me?
MAID: Yes, ma'am. A telegram.
They start to go up the stairs.

---

[3] A popular Italian children's toy, similar to an erector set. [Editor]

LADY: Where did you put it?

MAID: Upstairs.

LADY: Stupid girl. What do you want to go and leave it lying around like that for?

MAID: But the master is out . . . If you had been back late I would have hidden it.

7. *A very poor house. Outside, two sets of stairs lead to the upstairs floors. There are women and children: great poverty. But there's a girl singing a love song as she washes the dishes outside.*

8. *Ballerinas coming down the little stairs at the side of a stage. At the bottom there are others, singing and dancing to piano music. The music stops, and the dancers sit down and stretch out, exhausted. The man at the piano beats time with his finger to a very sad rhythm.*

9. *People getting onto the escalator in a department store; the camera goes up with them. As they go up, one voice emerges over the noise of the others in conversation with someone:*

SHOP ASSISTANT: It's poplin, madam, very good quality . . . pure brushed cotton.

CUSTOMER: How much is it?

SHOP ASSISTANT: 950.

CUSTOMER: Ah . . . Well, perhaps not . . . that's expensive . . . too expensive . . . really . . .

The customer's voice keeps repeating, "It's too expensive . . . much too expensive."

10. *A thin man, visibly ill and tired, going up a staircase. At the top, there's the door to an office. The man looks as if he's about to enter when he sees a notice and stops. The sign says: "No Openings." Disappointed, the man turns back down the stairs.*

11. *A beautiful house (in Pratica di Mare[4]), two buildings made into one with a central staircase covered by a glass roof. A man runs down a corridor and through a door, leaving it ajar so that he can peek through it. A little later, a woman comes up the staircase and stands furtively by the door, which the man immediately opens and takes her in his arms.*

12. *A staircase lined with rows and rows of mirrors. We see women's legs among veils of material.*
In a Milanese accent, a woman's voice: Well, then . . . come on guys . . .
A man's legs walk into the picture; they stand still for a moment in front of the women. Then one of the women starts to go up the stairs and the man follows her.

13. *A building under construction, the scaffolding sticking up into the sky. A bricklayer climbs up a step ladder with a large bucket of cement. You can see the exhaustion on his face.*

14. *A factory chimney with metal rungs on the outside to climb to the top. And in fact, there is a worker climbing up to the top, carrying his tools with him. The drop below him is terrifying.*

15. *Clear sky again, the top of a ladder sticking up into it. It's a fireman's ladder. From the bottom of the picture, smoke comes into view. The ground seems to move, though in fact it's the ladder that's swaying. At the bottom you can just glimpse a squad of soldiers marching.*

16. *We go into a barracks. It's very dark and a skinny soldier is busy washing the dirty steps. Other soldiers tramp down them and get it all dirty again with their muddy boots, just after he had gotten it clean. An officer comes by and shouts at*

---

[4] A seaside resort near Naples. [Editor]

the soldier washing the steps who stands to attention and nods his head: yes sir, yes sir . . .

17. *A hospital with several nurses pushing a stretcher with a patient on it. This patient stretches his arm out over the edge of his stretcher, and a man walking beside him holds his hand. Then the stretcher is taken into an elevator and disappears. At the side, you can see some stairs. The other man's eyes are red.*

18. *On a little landing, there's a woman crying, almost hugging a man. Behind them, there is the precipitous drop of a stairwell. The two of them are talking in desperate voices.*
HIM: . . . nothing, nothing. There's nothing we can do.
HER: But didn't you tell him you've got children . . . a family?
HIM: He says so has he.
HER: Oh, my dear . . . What are we going to do? We haven't got a dime!

19. *The second floor of a smart hotel, near the staircase. At the bottom you can see the lobby. A group of well-fed businessmen are chatting. They've got briefcases and leather wallets, fancy pens and rings. They're writing lots and lots of numbers, doing the accounts. Next to them, a very young, very beautiful girl, elegantly—almost flashily—dressed, is leafing through a foreign fashion magazine.*

20. *A crowd surges forward up a wide staircase brandishing placards with political slogans.*

21. *On the steps of the Courthouse there are several lawyers, recognizable by their somewhat theatrical mannerisms. Other people are passing by too. There are clerks and little old ladies who are lost and asking which way they should go, but no one tells them; they just shrug their shoulders. You can hear snatches of conversation.*

VOICES: . . . The hearing is fixed for the twenty-eighth . . . Don't think I'm going to let you screw me over this time . . . My dear attorney . . . Four hundred thousand lire, you understand? Do you understand? . . . Etc.
Two policemen walk by, completely indifferent to it all.

22. *The interior of a jail. Two guards are walking a prisoner towards a little iron ladder that leads up to the next floor. He's an old man, with white hair.*

23. *The staircase in an old age home. Several old men are making their way up the stairs with difficulty, using their walking sticks to help them. At the bottom you can see a garden with other old men sitting on benches.*

24. *Four men are coming down the staircase of a modest house . . . with a coffin. On the street you can see people waiting with their hats off, and there are flowers.*

25. *The staircase in an asylum; several nurses are trying to control a furious patient who is waving his arms and screaming. The screaming blends into the music, which is itself a scream.*

ONE OF OUR CHILDREN[1]

For many Italian children, mostly from the lower middle classes, added to the burden of living through the Second World War are some strange memories. During the war, they had put on uniforms and marched to the sound of fanfares. And they were real fanfares, not the sound of angelic trumpets from the gramophone on Christmas day while their grandparents helped buckle them into toy suits of armor they had received as a present. No, these were real trumpets and real uniforms and even real guns. There they were, marching along to the beat of drums—they were Mussolini's youth movement. These too were real experiences.

Then everything changes. There is a lot of confusion and everyone tells these children that it's the guns and drums that are to blame. No one has the time or inclination to explain it to them any better than that. The children from Mussolini's youth movement go back to school and find they are democrats. Life isn't easy, and children from the middle classes come from families that were hit pretty hard by the war and who haven't sorted out their own ideas yet. While the war was on,

---

[1] 1950-51. Treament co-written with Giorgio Bassani and Suso Cecchi D'Amico. In *Cinema* 138 (1954): 417-420.

the children got used to having no exams and to quick, easy lessons, and so they got out of the habit of studying, and the habit wasn't replaced by a willing attitude. Besides, their honest parents certainly don't seem to have enviable lives which might be something to emulate. Some of the children rebel and start to use the weapons they learned to handle during the war in order to get money, as they see gangsters doing in American films. The ones who go back to school, and that's most of them, get back into the daily routines of childhood as if they were tired old men. Every now and then, the newspapers talk about "traumatized youth"; the label is a popular one, and the children do their best to live up to the portrait of disenchantment that people paint of them. Some of them even start to think nostalgically about the days of uniforms and guns and hand grenades. They find people and images that are able to reawaken not only their nostalgia but even their belief that it is possible to take over the reins of a nation that is still afraid of them, since their past behavior had been so unpredictable. They will be the new storm troopers or triumvirs or mercenary captains. These children say to themselves that they are young and strong.

Arturo Bolla is young, but he has rather delicate health and he certainly shouldn't go outside as he does with no coat in this spring weather. He is eighteen years old and he's studying book-keeping at the technical high school, or at least that's what he is supposed to be studying. Arturo Bolla has two girl-friends and few friends. His father was in the militia under the Fascist Party,[2] though he denied having had any political duties when it was expedient for him to deny it. But then he proclaimed it loud and clear when it was convenient to getting his back pension paid. Then he found a job and didn't talk about politics any more; it doesn't even interest him now. He knows very little about his son. At first, the boy's nostalgia for the old days was flattering, almost like a tribute to his father. For

---

[2] *Vice federale* was a local political official in the Fascist Party as opposed to state bureaucrats or army officers. [Translator]

example, he was happy with Arturo's contempt for his mother when she suggested economizing by using his father's gray woolen jacket from the militia as a housecoat. And it was out of self-regard that Mr. Bolla didn't protest or stop his son from taking part in political demonstrations, even though he would be happier knowing that his son was busy studying. Mr. Bolla thinks that his son will grow up in his own way. The important thing is that in the meantime he should stand on his own two feet, and it seems Arturo is perfectly capable of that. He's always out, always busy: a sign that he must be doing something.

Arturo Bolla is fond of his parents out of habit, but deep down he is profoundly contemptuous of his father, who he thinks has never been decisive enough. Because when you get right down to it, that's the quality he most admires. Underneath the solemn supports of patriotism, ideology, and so on, what governs Arturo Bolla's actions is always the desire to escape from mediocrity, to do something dangerous and heroic, to boss around all the people (and there are lots of them) whom he considers inferior to himself.

Arturo Bolla is a member of an extreme right wing party, but he is also a member of another political group that shares the same beliefs but goes a bit further and is in the vanguard of the movement. Of course, the official party is very keen to make use of this group, though it denies any contact with it when it's expedient to do so. And of course, the extremists are keen to lend a hand to the moderates in the hope that they can drag them along behind them and set an example to those who are more fainthearted.

The story we have to tell takes place over two days and begins in the morning during a very noisy political demonstration at the university. Arturo Bolla has received the call to action together with several of his comrades, for they come from outside the campus and are therefore immune to any sanctions by the university authorities (reprisals, he calls them). The demonstration is the usual sort of hubbub which is occasionally directed against some anti-Fascist professor; two or three hundred students take part in it, deliberately to make trouble. They throw water bombs and stink bombs until the police are finally called in to urge the students to call it off, at first with gentle persuasion and then with more assertive tactics. A certain number of youths who seem to come from outside the university—that is, the troublemakers—get carried off to the police station. Among them is Arturo Bolla. A brief interrogation, a stern lecture: about an hour in total and it's all done. It is the first time that Arturo has been taken into custody by the police, and the peaceful resolution to the matter is rather disappointing for him. He hangs around the streets where calm reigns undisturbed, and then he makes his way to party headquarters. It's the basement of an old warehouse which never gets any sunlight. There's a girl who spends half her day there sticking address labels onto propaganda sheets which get sent out, postage unpaid. Arturo Bolla looks at the fliers in disgust and then tells the girl exactly what he thinks of them. How can the party leaders not see that this is the time for action? It's not propaganda that they need . . . it's deeds. This morning, it took just a little spark and the whole university was ablaze. The young man gets worked up as he describes the scene: "It looked like the revolution was happening!" he exclaims. Their conversation is interrupted by the arrival of one of the local bosses who tells Bolla in great secrecy that there is marvelous news. Arturo would like to know more, but the other guy is vague. Be patient, you'll receive your orders later today. And you'll be in action again tomorrow.

Arturo is beside himself with joy. Back home, he eats in silence, then he brings his chair into the hallway and begins phoning around in a loud voice so that his father can hear him. The first call is to a girl, Mimma, whom he's mildly interested in. He tells her all about the great deeds of the morning, dramatizing his interview with the police, telling her he's been released to lead them to the others. They're following him everywhere, though he spotted them easily. "Well then, you should stay home," the girl warns him. But Arturo won't have it. He can't stay home, there are big things afoot and he is going to be in the thick of it. So before he's called into action, he'd like to see her. You never know . . . and he arranges to meet her that afternoon. At that moment, his mother appears at the kitchen door. "Didn't you go to school this morning?" she asks. Arturo looks at his mother pityingly, then he looks at his father who is crossing the hall to get his hat on his way out. Arturo's mother is a simple woman, used to her husband treating her as if she didn't have a mind of her own. Arturo tells her that with Italians like her, it is no wonder that the country's history is what it is. "History or no history," his mother replies, "if your father was any sort of man he would give you a clip round the ear that would make sure you don't miss school again. God knows the sacrifices we make. . ." Father and son exchange a knowing look, and Arturo goes back to his telephone calls.

In the late afternoon, Arturo is at the house of one of his comrades. The guy lives in Campo Parioli, and he's "undercover," which is to say that he's on the run from the police. Actually, the police are well aware of where he lives, but they turn a blind eye to it. Bolla has gone to him to get a gun; he thinks that since action is imminent, a revolver will be indispensable, and in fact the comrade straight away finds a way to help him out. So with a gun in his pocket, Bolla goes back to headquarters to get his orders. But the office is deserted and there are no orders yet. A bit annoyed, Arturo goes to where he had arranged to meet Mimma.

In moments of great danger, Arturo Bolla's great hideaway—as he has told his most trusted companions—is a bathing hut on the Tiber owned by Mimma's uncle. That's where he goes now, taking elaborate precautions before going in because there's a man waiting on the sidewalk outside. "He's after me," Arturo tells Mimma, "follow me at a distance." After a few minutes, both of them are inside the cabana. He tells the girl that the other comrades are going to meet him there to discuss some very important matters with him. He takes out the revolver and puts it on the table, within reach. Then he takes a look out onto the street; he's worried because the man is still there, walking up and down. Mimma tries to distract him. She just wants to be hugged; moreover, she's beginning to feel cold, and in any case, she can't be back late or she'll catch it from her mom. She's listening patiently to Arturo's talk, trying to cut him short. And eventually, the boy does forget everything, and he turns his attention fully to his girlfriend. One kiss leads to a second, and then a third . . . Arturo's anxiety is transformed into a torrid, violent urge. They both end up on the ground, deep in each other's arms.

By now, it's evening. Arturo phones home to see if anyone came looking for him there: nothing. He phones headquarters to get his "orders." And in fact he gets them: he must be at a certain café at ten o'clock. There's going to be an important meeting. When Arturo leaves the bar from where he had placed the call (in a sleazy, inconspicuous restaurant), he notices that there is a middle-aged man, leaning against a wall reading his newspaper. "I'm still being followed," Arturo thinks, and slowly, trying to fake indifference, he reaches the corner. Once he's down the next street, he starts running as fast as he can until he makes it around the next corner. Of course, the man hasn't actually moved; he's still there reading his newspaper, waiting for God knows who. But this little episode is crucial for Arturo Bolla. When we next see him at ten o'clock in the café, he has been completely transformed. He has cut off his sideburns and has bleached his hair: he's a completely different man. But he's still nervous. Especially because time goes by and no one turns up. After an hour, Arturo goes to the phone and calls Mimma. He asks her to come and meet him at the café. But Mimma isn't allowed out at that time of night, so Arturo has to call on his other girlfriend who is given more freedom. Her name is Adele and she too is a rabid Fascist. Luckily she lives not very far away, so that after a few minutes she is sitting in front of Arturo who is rapidly losing the air of a political agitator. In fact, he's profoundly disgusted by the behavior of his comrades, who not only don't show up but don't even bother to call him. He is so furious in fact that, throwing his normal caution aside, he drags the girl off to dance in the part of the bar reserved for it. Sambas, slow dances, the boogie-woogie, and more. At midnight he decides to phone the comrade who gave him the news of the next raid. The guy is in bed, sleeping peacefully; he replies that everything has been postponed and says he's sorry he forgot to tell him. Perhaps they'll have some details tomorrow morning. Furious, Arturo slams down the phone in mid-sentence. He drags the girl out with him, and they disappear together into a rather dubious little hotel on the Via del Gambero.

Arturo Bolla doesn't go to school the next day either. He leaves the house after a row over his bleached hair and goes straight to party headquarters. He is full of aggression. But the only person at headquarters is the usual girl sending out her packets of fliers and propaganda. After he has again told her what he thinks of the organization, Arturo grabs some of the packets and goes out. At this point, he's decided he is going to act alone. If the others are all incompetents or cowards, he'll do it all himself. "The first duty that Nature has given to each man and each race is not just to live but to conquer or die," reads an inscription on a wall at headquarters. And he is ready to die for the Fatherland. For he's convinced that all that is needed for the Nation to rise up from its torpor is a gesture, a decisive action and he will do it. With his packets of propaganda he goes toward the mall in Piazza Colonna. It is rush hour and the mall is crammed with the usual "low-lifes," variety show artistes, hostesses, prostitutes, black-marketeers, etc. Arturo Bolla goes into a doorway, and in the outer office of a business he introduces himself and asks to speak with the manager. He is told that the manager isn't in. So with his voice trembling a little, he says that he will wait for him. And he goes into the waiting room with his little packets held tightly under his arm. When he sees that he's alone, he nervously goes over to the window and opens it. The window overlooks the mall and a confused murmur of voices comes up to him from below. Arturo Bolla looks over his shoulder: no one. Then quickly he unties the packets and rains down the fliers; he takes out his revolver and fires two shots into the air. Then he races down the stairs before the security guard can catch him.

The people sitting at tables outside cafés jump but then don't move. Some little children run to pick up the fliers. "So what's it all about?" asks an old man, irritably. Then cynical eyes look over the fliers. "Someone is going to get themselves killed . . . messing about with all this stuff again," someone says. At the entrance to the mall, pale and trembling, Arturo Bolla looks around him. Then he runs straight into a girl who is calmly walking along, trying to swing her hips about as she's seen the movie stars do: it's Mimma. "Hi," she says, without noticing Arturo's excitement. But he drags her away violently. "We must get out of here," he tells her. But Mimma's uncle has reopened the cabana for the summer season that very same day, so it's impossible to hide out there. "And you tell me just like that?" shouts Arturo. "Don't you know that right now every policeman in Rome is looking for me?" He is out of his mind, and he lets off steam at Mimma, who looks at him amazed and tries to calm him down. But that's an impossible task. After a while, Arturo dumps Mimma in the middle of the street and plunges into the traffic.

The first thing he does is to call home to say he won't be there for lunch. Then he goes to take refuge with the doorman of an apartment building in Viale del Re, who is also one of his comrades and gives Arturo something to eat. Arturo tells him he's taken part in a shoot-out with seven other comrades, one of whom was seriously wounded. And he even makes the doorman go and buy some bandages and supplies at the pharmacy which he then takes away with him, supposedly to go and look after the injured comrade. His nerves are stretched to the breaking point. He calls Mimma again but she's still out. Her mother tells him that he can find her at a party given by a mutual friend of theirs. So Arturo goes there. Before he goes up to the apartment, he realizes he has his pockets full of bandages and stuff and he throws them away in the courtyard, in the garbage.

The house is quite crowded; couples are dancing lazily, holding each other tightly. Mimma is there, and you just have to look at her to know that she is having a great time. Arturo sits in a corner, looking detached, not speaking. Mimma questions him in vain. They go out onto the terrace. Arturo says gravely that they are trying to kill him, and it's not easy to resign yourself to dying, even if it is for the good of the Fatherland. Mimma looks at him incredulously. "You know what I think? I think you're a bit obsessed," she says sweetly. Arturo pretends not to hear her. He says she'll see if he isn't right. Everybody is afraid of him: the government, the communists, even his own comrades, who would prefer to continue fighting in the shadows because they don't understand that the moment for action has arrived. "They'll understand when I get killed. Then they'll wake up . . ." he exclaims excitedly.

They go back inside. Someone has come along with the evening newspaper. There's hardly a mention of the episode in the mall. Something about a fanatic who . . . etc. Arturo tears up the newspaper. He's sweating, he's so upset. "Let's dance," Mimma says to calm him down, but the young man shakes his head. They are back inside the room. Arturo touches her arm without saying a word. Maybe he's trying to say something, and for a moment Mimma is unsure what to do. Suddenly, Arturo turns and walks away. In the next room he finds a piece of paper on a table and writes a few lines on it: "My wounds are bloody but I am not betraying the cause. Perhaps it was destiny that it should be me who sacrifices myself. Farewell." He gives the paper to the maid to take to Mimma. Then he goes out, with tears welling up in eyes.

They find him at the first light of dawn, gagged with a small Italian flag, near death, in a boat floating in the middle of the Tiber. A single shot from a revolver through the back of his neck. While the police are trying to reconstruct the last moments of this strange suicide, Mimma stands alone on the river bank looking out, and she too has tears in her eyes.

THOSE FUN-LOVING GIRLS OF 1924[1]

The year 1922 is about to come to an end, the year of "Tango delle capinere."[2]

Carla is getting married. The church is all decked out. Everyone has new clothes. Carla is in white. Lots of flowers, a few tears. She's marrying Giorgio. But she's gazing not at him, but at his brother Ercole, full of sadness because she is so in love with him that she can hardly breathe. Unfortunately, Ercole has never been in the least interested, and so Carla, after suffering incredibly, has resigned herself to marrying his brother. It almost seems like a way of linking herself to him, of starting a family with him, of having him near.

Carla's closest friends are also present at the wedding: Annamaria, Linda, Luisa, Lola. And also her male friends, among them Alberto.

With young people, love is like a breeze among the flowers; it carries pollen from one flower to another according to its whim. For example, everyone knows that for some time Alberto has been courting Annamaria, and they also know that she is bored with it by now. When the wedding ceremony

---

[1] 1956. In *Cinema Nuovo* 85 (June 1956): 362-64.
[2] Literally, "Tango of the Swallows," an extremely popular Italian song of that year; appropriately for this treatment, swallows is also Italian slang for "chicks" or girls. [Translator]

is over and the bride and groom have been sent off amid a forest of fluttering handkerchiefs, Alberto takes Annamaria aside to ask her for some explanation of her conduct. Without beating around the bush, she tells him she intends to break off their relationship, "this marvelous love," as he calls it. She's not enjoying it any more. And besides, she wants to begin a new life.

In their circle, the news of their breakup spreads like wildfire. The person who is happiest about it is Luisa. No one even knows about Luisa's feelings for Alberto, her secret pain at his indifference. But now that he's free, who knows what might happen . . .

Luisa needs to confide in someone, to get some advice. And one of her friends seems perfect for the job: Lola. Everyone confides in Lola. She vicariously lives other people's experiences. She's the oldest of their circle and the least pretty—none of the boys is interested in her but she doesn't complain. She's comfortable with the other girls and doesn't ask for anything except the chance to console them and give them advice.

And she does give Luisa some advice, and pulls out all the stops to get her to meet Alberto. It turns out that Alberto, just to annoy Annamaria and get her back for dumping him, starts to pay a bit of attention to Luisa.

This is a small provincial city, and as we noted earlier, these little events among their circle of acquaintances immediately become public knowledge, though it's not clear how. All that's needed is a glance while they are out dancing, a whispered word . . . and so hardly any time goes by before Annamaria finds out about Alberto and Luisa. Her pride is wounded, and being as fickle as she is, she has a severe attack of jealousy and reacts like a caged tigress. For Annamaria is trapped in her house; her parents won't let her go outside. She is the daughter of a rich industrialist with a beautiful, art-nouveau house full of modern furniture, lots of servants, a car, and several younger brothers. And at that time, the city is in an uproar with armed men camping out in the streets and gardens. It seems all those men are planning to walk to Rome. They must be mad![3]

But Luisa's parents do let her go out at night. Her father tells her that finally a new age will be born and there will be order. So she lets herself be escorted out by Alberto; she loves courting in the middle of all that civic unrest; she feels as if she's living more intensely.

Then the storm passes; life apparently gets back to its normal routine. In the big houses, people drink tea to the sound of the gramophone. "Abat-jour," "Ferriera," "Rose rosse," "Valencia": the girls know all the words by heart and sing them all day long.

But we've left Alberto in the middle of his flirtation with Luisa, and Annamaria more jealous than ever. During one of these afternoon dances at a friend's house, Annamaria and Luisa confront each other. Tears on both sides, and Alberto in the middle, hardly able to contain his joy—he's got two girls crying over him! This will make his friends jealous and allow him to put on a bit of a swagger. In fact, he begins to hang out at the dance halls, where all the jaded skeptics issue their bitter pronouncements while the chorus girls sing in the New Year.

Yes, 1922 is over and we are already in 1923.

Do you remember Carla? Her wedding, with the church all decked out? Her inconsolable glances at Ercole? Well, now she's come back from her honeymoon, sadder than ever. A hideous life is beginning for her. She still feels like a young girl, but she isn't any more; she still feels in love with Ercole, but now she's got Giorgio, her husband, in the house. Her husband! Sometimes, she's so frightened by the idea of it that she would like to run away. Especially because when she married Giorgio, she was kidding herself that she would always have Ercole nearby and he could bring her some vicarious happiness. But when Ercole comes round to see them, Carla doesn't feel happy as she had thought she would; instead,

---

[3] A reference to the march on Rome of 1922 and the rally that brought Mussolini to power. [Editor]

she gets a lump in her throat and feels like she wants to cry.

And so of course, she too goes to confide in Lola. But what advice can Lola give her? All she can do is wait. Time heals all wounds, even unrequited love.

Besides, love isn't the only thing in the world. Luisa knows this, for her romance with Alberto has been rudely interrupted by her family moving to the countryside. Apparently, her father wasn't one of those who walked to Rome; he's a commercial traveler and he was away on business. Now they've organized a sort of trial, and they've expelled him from the Fascist Party. She doesn't really understand what happened because she doesn't know anything about politics, but in their social circle everyone is talking about it. Strange, hot-headed young men are hanging around outside the house, threateningly. Anyway, it's better for the whole family to move to the countryside and stay with Luisa's uncle and aunt.

Luisa is desperate. Life in the countryside is monotonous, they don't even have electricity there. And Alberto will be far away. It's true that he regularly makes the trip to see her, but these visits are becoming rarer and rarer as the weeks go by. Luisa is in despair: perhaps he got back together with Annamaria?

No, that's not how things are. It's also a bolt out of the blue for Annamaria when she learns that Alberto has another girlfriend, a mutual friend to boot: Linda. The troublesome thing is that Linda is pretty and can sing Irving Berlin's "Always" marvelously in the American style. And they also say that her mother has a lot of lovers and this is guaranteed to excite the boys. Emergency measures are needed. And since Luisa is the person most concerned with this whole business, besides herself, Annamaria manages to overcome her former jealousy and go out to meet her in the countryside, bringing her up to date on the news and offering her a provisional alliance against their common enemy. If only they could both go back to the city together, right away . . . Run away to the city even without her parent's permission. Perhaps such a bold move would win Alberto's attention back to them. So they decide to run away that same night in her uncle's horse and buggy.

But during the night, something strange happens. Some men come and get Luisa's father up in the middle of the night and make him go downstairs to the street with them; they can hear Luisa's mother's voice shouting at them to stay where they are, hear her choking sobs. And then the sound of physical blows, like something striking a sandbag. The two girls hug each other tightly in their bed. They're crying too. Why? Their unrequited love for Alberto? Probably, yes. But also because they feel a tremendous, inexplicable fear about the beating that those men are giving another man in the dead of night.

The next day, everyone goes back to the city.

It's a special day for the local "society" people. There's a parade by the cavalry regiment that's stationed in the city, a lovely tournament with an Arab theme. Elegant ladies and gallant officers. Provincial civilities. And it's there that Annamaria and Luisa meet Alberto. He pretends not to notice them, but the two girls corner him. He can't carry on as he is, cheating on them both at the same time. The young man frankly admits that he doesn't care a bit about his new girlfriend, Linda. And very little about Luisa. In short, he's still in love with Annamaria.

Then Annamaria has one of her moods. It's enough for her that she's won. She says that she considers herself to be an emancipated girl, that she wants to keep her independence, and who knows? Flirt with who she likes. And just to add emphasis to her words, she starts flirting with a nearby officer. But Alberto is not prepared to put up with this sort of affront and gets mad at the officer. They have to hold him back from starting a fight. Other people intervene and there's a minor scene. The party has been spoiled, everyone is scandalized: really, these young people have no respect for anything . . .

But the story doesn't end there; it leaves a trail even in the local newspaper. And since the paper is run by Alberto's father, a strong pacifist, he seizes the opportunity to make a stinging attack on the little incident and on the whole cavalry. The high command is outraged. One officer challenges him to a duel. Another scandal. An affront to his honor. Old political scores have to be settled, and the affair gets out of hand. At the end of the day, Alberto's father has to resign from running the paper and thinks seriously about moving to Rome where his family can join him as soon as possible.

All of this directly affects the girls' lives. Luisa, in fact, who was rejected by Alberto during the tournament, pretends to be disillusioned with love, and to cheer herself up she agrees to be courted by Ercole. For a while now Ercole has been pressing his suit rather strongly. She doesn't mind. Ercole is not a bad catch. He's studying literature and writes poems: he even dedicated one to her.

This new love affair between Luisa and Ercole is the most serious thing so far because it throws Carla into a deep depression. She's humiliated; her life is boring. Her marriage to Giorgio seems like a big mistake. Until now, she's been buoyed up by the hope that some day, somehow, she and Ercole will be together; one fine day, Ercole will wake up madly in love with her and carry her off and they'll escape to Paris together and plunge themselves into a whirlwind of pleasure . . . But it's all just a dream. And now that Luisa has come between them, even this dream doesn't have much point.

Moreover, Giorgio has lately been in the grip of some very strange ideas: he has some fanatical friends who talk about Germany, Munich, about some man named Hitler. She thinks it's an excuse to stay out until late. She feels alone and lost.

On the other hand, the love between Ercole and Luisa, which began as a joke, is becoming ever more serious. And then one day the bubble bursts: Luisa's mother finds that she has a key in her possession and refuses to say where it came from. Eventually, they find out that it's the key to a bachelor pad that Alberto sometimes lends to Ercole. Another scandal. The two families won't even greet each other on the street anymore. So the lovers have to resort to underhanded plans, lies, and other tactics so they can keep seeing each other.

But there is one person who unexpectedly comes to their

aid: Carla. She can hardly believe she has an opportunity to involve herself with Ercole. Having no other hope, she resigns herself to living out her love for him through Luisa. And she almost treats it like her own love affair, just so she can feel as if she matters in his life. It's her way of loving him.

But the scandal about the apartment has other repercussions, for Annamaria for one. Annamaria, who can't bear anything or anyone, is really living out the role of the emancipated woman. She smokes cigarettes in public and dances modern dances, including the Charleston; she adores American jazz and plays tennis and even drives a car. But then she is outdone by the scandal of the little love-nest and feels as if she could die of envy. She can't believe how stupid she was that day at the cavalry tournament, when she didn't want to have anything to do with Alberto. She could have had secret, steamy trysts with him in his hideaway, plunging herself into the atmosphere of the clandestine, savoring the taste of sin, but no! Suddenly she finds that one feeling is stronger than all of her little whims: her feeling for Alberto. She's managed to resist seeing him up until now, but not any more. And then one night . . .

It's the end of the year; 1923 is over and 1924 is now here. How time flies!

The little city is in a festive mood; it's a beautiful, cold, crisp, moonlit night, with all-night parties, paper streamers, and fireworks everywhere you look. Annamaria is alone with Alberto, and he takes her into his arms. Everything begins again, only more passionately, with more sighs and more oaths of eternal fidelity, up there in Alberto's hideaway.

But Alberto is more mature now. His father's dismissal from the newspaper, his departure for Rome, have not left the family in a very good financial position, and Alberto himself is in a bit of a delicate position in the city. So he too starts to write articles in order to earn some money. Annamaria doesn't read them; she doesn't even know what they are about. Once, she did glance at one of them; it was about the elections in England, the Labor Party, strange things. She only knows that Alberto, like Giorgio, has changed. When the two friends start discussing politics, they can't stop and end up fighting. In short, they are much less concerned with their girlfriends than before. And she feels jealous, and, at the same time, more in love than ever. She does what she can to take her mind off it all, going frequently to the cinema: Clara Bow, Douglas Fairbanks, Rudolf Valentino are the idols of the moment. Valentino is marvelous with his slicked-back hair.

One day, the newspaper announces that Rudolf Valentino, who is currently visiting Italy, will pass through the city by train. It's amazing. Annamaria goes to the station with her friends. The women go mad; they literally assault the train in order to get a look at the star, cheer for him, touch him. Carla is the only one who is quiet. Her friends have brought her along with them to keep her mind off things, for she's leading a solitary, rather empty life. Since Ercole and Luisa have decided to get married, they don't need her help in order to meet, and so there is no purpose to fill her days. And also because she has realized something terrible, that her love for Ercole is not as strong as it was. She was disappointed by the fact that he took a rather low-paying job and gave up his literary ambitions in order to get married. So now she doesn't have anything to interest her anymore, nothing to believe in, nothing to get excited about. That day at the station, among all those women in ecstasy because Valentino waved and smiled at them from the train, Carla has a sudden crisis and throws herself under a train as it pulls into the station. She is killed instantly.

These are terrible times for the girls. This misfortune, rather than uniting them, drives them apart. They hardly ever see each other now. Linda and Lola live by themselves; they've become close. Some people trade malicious gossip about their lonely friendship. As for Annamaria, she also leads a quiet life. In reality, she's suffering because Alberto has had to join his father in Rome and no one knows when he'll be back. In short, these days, they all feel less like enjoying themselves.

Annamaria is seriously contemplating running away to join Alberto. She doesn't much like his letters to her: they are preoccupied and hasty. She must see him soon, and she has a plan.

But one day her maid informs her that she's met Alberto in the street. How can it be possible? He's come back and hasn't come to see her . . . Where did she meet him? On such-and-such a street. Annamaria rushes over there. It's not a nice day to go outside. There's a general strike on. Apparently, a really important man in Rome has been killed, Matteotti or somebody, and there are riots in the streets. Annamaria is wandering round the half-empty city where the only people are demonstrators and National Guardsmen. She absolutely must get Alberto out of all this.

But Alberto will never get out of it now. Annamaria finds him lying in an empty square, killed by a rifle's bullet.

She's alone now too. She doesn't feel like an emancipated woman any more. She doesn't feel anything. She's just a woman who has lost her lover. How silly that little organ-grinder sounds, playing that song in some far away street: "Quel ciondolo d'or"[4] . . . [5]

---

[4] Literally, "The Golden Pendant," but the Italian has suggestive overtones. [Translator]

[5] In *Cinema Nuovo* 85 (1956), the publication of this treatment was prefaced with the following: *The main characters of the film are: Annamaria, Luisa, Carla, Linda, Lola, Alberto, Ercole, and Giorgio. All the young people are between seventeen and twenty-five and belong to the middle classes in a rich and prosperous northern provincial city.*

In the present treatment there are only suggestions about their respective families, the minor characters, and the locations. The intention here is simply to outline a plot according to the spirit of the times. This has to be a fresh and captivating film, a little romantic and with that same touch of irony and melancholy that songs from that time had. It has the feeling of lost innocence, giving way to what has been called the 'anxiety of modern times.'

Perhaps in reality this change of mood was not as noticeable as it is in the film; perhaps our historical perspective has imposed some changes on it. Obviously, as in all art, there has been a process of transfiguration at work here. But it is not an arbitrary process, for it is a fact that the world has changed since then in both its fashions and its morals. That's why there are some allusions to historical events in the background, in order to give the film greater solidity and set these tenuous love affairs against a background of reality.

But everything is seen through the eyes of the girls as something unimaginable, bigger than they are.

It is also worth noting that I imagined this story in color: subtle colors but warm ones too, scattered here and there with violent splashes because even in the sweetest and calmest love stories there is always a background of pain.

MAKARONI[1]

Spring, 1945. In Germany, the Americans are advancing towards Cologne. The sky is overcast and the roads are crowded with retreating German military vehicles that make their way through a fusillade of exploding grenades. The soldiers of the Wehrmacht, tired and humiliated, trudge along the side of the road, dragging themselves through the ditches of the country-side, weighed down by the mud and their loads of useless weap-ons and ammunition. Defeat is in their eyes. The earth beneath their feet trembles and shakes with the heavy vehicles. And the air is filled with noise like that of a far-off earthquake: it is artillery fire at the advancing front—there are already Ameri-can tanks down in the valley. But amid the din, you can also hear birds chirping, and in the sea of mud that extends over the whole countryside, the first flowers of spring are just pok-ing through.

Outside the fence of a concentration camp not far from the road, some German soldiers, assisted by a group of conscripted civilians, are getting the prisoners in line to drag them off with the retreating army. Before leaving, the Germans have set fire to the shacks in the camp, and above the crackling of the flames

[1] 1957-58. An original treatment by Antonioni and Tonino Guerra. Serialized in *Cinema Nuovo* 163 (May-June 1963): 219-228; *Cinema Nuovo* 164 (July 1963): 299-308; and *Cinema Nuovo* 165 (August 1963): 382-389.

you can hear the heartrending cries of sick prisoners left inside. One of them, covered in flames, manages to drag himself, screaming, up to the fence. With a desperate effort, he hurls himself toward the other prisoners and throws them into confusion: some people try to smother the flames with a blanket, others try to run away. The soldiers come running.

Taking advantage of the confusion, two prisoners at the end of the line get down on hands and knees and crawl into the ditch. It is full of muddy water, and the two of them dive in and remain still. Then there are some shouts and some orders and the column marches off again. With a leap, the two are on their feet and across the hedge, onto a path that meanders among the fields. Meanwhile, it is obvious that the soldiers have realized that some prisoners have escaped. Shots are heard close by. Four civilians, led by a sergeant, run after them through the fields. They shower the bushes, trees, and ditches with bullets. The two escapees carry on running until they make their way into the woods. They are literally covered with mud, both their faces and their clothes. They are now short of breath. They can't make it any further; they are too weak to continue running, and they fall down on the wet grass, exhausted. The shooting gets close again. It will soon be all over. But then suddenly it stops, and you can clearly hear the sergeant's voice and snatches of conversation that make the prisoners start: the woods where they are hiding contain a huge munitions dump which is going to be blown up at any moment.

So the two men, with the strength that is born of desperation, get up again and start running madly along the path that can be seen through the thorny undergrowth. They pass by enormous piles of bombs, heaped up under the trees. Their faces are scratched, their hands covered with blood, but they keep running until they reach a clearing. In the middle of it, they see a solitary house, apparently deserted. They reach it, open the door, and to their great surprise, in the center of the room there is a table laid for dinner, complete with steaming bowls of soup. It seems the owners just left. But the two men don't waste time speculating about their whereabouts. Without a second thought, they go straight for the soup and start to devour it.

One is about thirty, strong and with an intelligent gaze. Although he's quite weak, his movements are smooth and graceful. While the other prisoners, all Italian civilians deported to Germany in the summer of 1944, had, judging from their bowed heads and hunched shoulders, all been completely overwhelmed and resigned to their fates, Roberto's face (for that is the young man's name) still shows a certain vigilance, a certain attention to what is going on around him. It is precisely that wariness that allowed him to escape. The other man is Erio, and he is younger than Roberto. He has a typically Italian face, kind and sentimental.

Suddenly, the door is thrown open and several young German airmen walk into the room. They are wearing dark leather jackets and long white silk scarves around their necks. So this is who the soup belonged to! The Germans react very calmly. They laugh and even make signs to Roberto and Erio to finish eating, which the two Italians quickly do so they can get out of the house as fast as possible. But outside, they get a nasty surprise: a lieutenant in the SS calls them over and sends them to help another group of prisoners who are wheeling two small fighter planes out of the woods. They belong to the famous Richthofen squadron. Roberto and Erio proceed to remove the branches that camouflage the planes and then push them out into the open. There is another Italian among the prisoners, but they hardly have a chance to exchange more than a few words with him.

Meanwhile, the airmen have come out, still laughing and joking, and they climb into the pilots' seats. In a flash, the planes disappear in the sky, heading toward the hills, skimming the treetops. Then, one of the German soldiers barks out some orders, and the group of prisoners set off behind the officer's black motorcycle as it bumps along the road that leads into the woods. "Where are they taking us?" asks Erio, who seems exhausted. "To the Grand Hotel," Roberto answers with black humor. Every so often, the officer turns around to look at them with his cold, hard stare. His face is expressionless, his gestures few and precise.

At last, the platoon reaches an old camp in another clearing beyond the woods. There are a few barracks and a command post where the officer stops his motorcycle. Exhausted, the prisoners fall down on the hard ground, or prop themselves up along the walls of the first barrack, next to the other prisoners in the camp.

Erio bends down to shake a prisoner who seems to have fallen asleep with his head in the mud, a huge brute with beady eyes and the head of a bull. There's a strange kind of animal vigor about him, as if the suffering inflicted on him had not been able to beat him down. One has the impression he is one of those people who will always come out on top in any situation, even if he has to be a little ruthless and do it at other people's expenses. Unbeknownst to Erio, he has already picked the Italian's pocket, looking for something he can steal. Roberto has sat a little way off, in the shelter of the first barrack. He pulls a muddy potato out of his pocket, cleans it off a bit, and starts to eat it.

He's engrossed in this activity when he notices something odd. He raises his eyes and sees a blonde girl, leaning against the wall of the opposite barrack, wearing a black apron with more patches on it than you'd think possible. The girl makes signs to him that she would like a piece of his potato. Roberto is about to turn away when she pulls up her skirt to show him her thighs. They are lean and pale and, in this context, seem almost absurd. And since Roberto just stares at her in amazement, not able to decide whether to give her what she wants or not, she bares her breasts; they too are small and white and almost lifeless. All these gestures are done with complete indifference, as if this is completely normal behavior and she is used to doing it. Then the young man gets up as if to go over to her and give her the potato, but she stops him with a gesture. "Throw it," she seems to say. "It's forbidden to come anywhere near the women's barrack." Roberto hesitates for a moment and then throws the potato, which the girl catches in mid-flight, and then she disappears.

Right then, a whistle blows and the camp comes to life. Tired but hurrying as quickly as they can, the prisoners gather on the patch of hard ground. The SS officer stands in front of them with several German soldiers by his side. He seems to be the camp commandant. Only now can we see that he has one arm missing. In the distance, you can hear the shooting at the front. Some crows are sitting on the fence around the camp, watching the proceedings. With the sergeant translating, the officer says that his watch has been stolen and orders the thief to step forward immediately. The prisoners listen in amazement. His watch? It seems ridiculous to everyone to think about a watch at that particular moment.

No one moves. The officer waits a few moments, and then speaks again, this time with greater spite: "You will stand here at attention until the guilty man owns up to his crime!" Roberto steps forward and speaks directly to the officer: "May I remind you that my companions and I have only just arrived in the camp and that would make it impossible for any of us . . ." He has hardly finished speaking before one of the German guards hits him on the back with the butt of his rifle making him fall down, winded. Another kick forces him back on his feet and into line. Then an enormous explosion rumbles in the distance: obviously the munitions dump has been blown up. It begins to rain.

It is still raining when darkness falls over the camp. The prisoners are still out in the open, soaking wet. Some have fallen unconscious, their heads lying in the mud. Roberto's eyes are closed; he seems to be asleep on his feet. Despite his weariness, Erio is watching a crane flying low over the camp, diving and then soaring high again as light as a feather. "You could make about ten pounds of risotto with that," he exclaims and everybody looks up, as if they were expecting to see a huge plate of risotto in the sky. They are roused from their dreams by the camp sergeant, a man in his fifties with an honest gaze, who orders the prisoners back into their barrack.

As soon as they're inside, Roberto and Erio turn everything

upside down, rummaging through the straw pallets, in back-packs, shaking even those prisoners who don't have the strength to resist. They search every nook and cranny for the watch. Erio even wants to make a search of the latrines, where he finds Alvaro in a corner doing something suspicious. He jumps on him and grabs a little packet that the prisoner had hurriedly tried to conceal beneath his jacket. Finally, he gets it away from him and opens the wrapping. Inside, there are a few pieces of hard bread. Mortified, he is about to give him back his packet when there's a furious barking sound as the Germans let the dogs off the leash in the yard outside. In a flash, Alvaro is out of the latrine and back in the barrack. Erio is slower and unaware of the danger, so he shuts the door and presses himself against the planks of the wall, looking out through the cracks at the dogs running about in the shadows around the barracks.

Several times he tries to get out, but every time he does, he has to come back in again, breathless. His heart is in his mouth. The dogs never go away, always ready to jump on him. Finally, the right moment arrives; he runs out and quickly reaches the barrack, throwing himself through the door and shutting it behind him just in time. Trembling, he listens to the yelping of the dogs outside as they scratch angrily at the door, prolonging his fear and anxiety. The other prisoners, including Roberto, are so tired they don't even notice this little drama.

Meanwhile, total silence falls over the camp. This goes on for a long time, but just when the calm and the quiet seem to have made everybody fall asleep, the door bursts open and the dark profile of the German officer appears in the half-light of the doorway. Something glints in his hand: his revolver. Nobody has time to realize what's happening, nor the strength to move. The officer randomly fires three shots into the dark room, then shuts the door behind him and goes away. There are some shouts and cries from inside the barrack, quickly drowned out by other noises: snoring.

At dawn, four of the prisoners, including Roberto, carry out the bodies of the two men who were killed by the German officer. The radio in the command post is playing a military march that echoes throughout the camp. The makeshift under-takers are ordered to march in time to the music, and the arms of their dead burdens, dangling over the sides of the stretchers, also seem to swing to the beat. A long ditch, almost full of water, acts as the camp cemetery. It is located on the other side of the latrines, near the perimeter fence, behind the women's quarters. Roberto and his companions throw the dead men into the ditch and cover them up as best they can with heaps of mud and rusty tin cans that are lying nearby. Meanwhile, the guard who accompanied them has stopped outside the win-dow of the women's barrack. He's amusing himself with Jolanda, the girl Roberto saw before. The German soldier offers her a cigarette, but he wants to see her legs. Inside the room, the other girls indifferently watch this spectacle.

Meanwhile, Roberto has seen a large blackbird perched on the barbed wire a few feet away. He picks up a stone and cau-tiously approaches the bird, but someone frightens it and it flies away from him. Annoyed, Roberto walks off and sees a girl with large, dark eyes and an almost aristocratic bearing. "What's your name?" he asks her angrily. "Elly," she answers. "Elly? What sort of name is that?" "Greek." "Oh, Greek. How do you say 'hungry' in Greek?" The girl walks off without saying anything.

The four men are soon back in line with the others, stand-ing in the middle of the yard. The air is damp. Finally, one of the guards appears with large heads of cabbage under his arms. He stands in front of the lines, strips off one leaf at a time, and throws them to the prisoners, who dive after them, one on top of the other, fighting to get hold of a few morsels. At the end of the fight, one of them lies dead on the ground. At an order from the guard, two prisoners seize the inert body and drag it toward the ditch behind the latrines.

Alvaro, who fought like an animal, has several leaves in his hands and is chewing them greedily. Erio goes up to him as, at the guard's order, the lines form again. "Where are you from?" he asks him. "Rome," the other answers. "Wouldn't you like to eat some linguini as long as the Rome-Viterbo turnpike?"

"How long is that?" "About sixty-two miles." "Yeah, I'd eat that," Alvaro answers. Roberto, wrapped up in his own thoughts, turns toward the women's barrack, as if he couldn't care less about eating. Elly is standing there watching him.

The prisoners go back inside the barrack after night has already fallen. The air is full of distant artillery fire. Everything suggests that the war is almost over. But this is precisely what makes the German officer's spiteful action all the more frightening. For his part, he looks at the prisoners as if he can already see in their faces the contempt of the victor and the joy of the avenger: that is why his ferocity now knows no bounds. By now it's clear that the thief won't give himself up, and so every night, the camp commandant plans to come and fire a few shots into the darkness of the barrack, bringing death to someone. "They're losing the war and he's worried about losing his watch!" Alvaro says to Roberto.

The two friends try to joke about it, but by now the stress is getting to them both. All the other prisoners are fixing up little barricades; some are even thinking of spending the whole night standing along the wall of the barrack, others of lying on the ground or holding onto the beams in the roof. Roberto is more fatalistic: he just watches Alvaro and Erio busying themselves, trying to do whatever they can to defend themselves.

The hours pass, though the waiting is not uninterrupted. Everybody listens for the slightest noise in the silence that surrounds the barrack. Suddenly, a young prisoner starts shouting, throws open the door, and goes out into the yard. His cries are scarcely human. Roberto makes as if he's going to go and get him, but Erio holds him back, and soon the dogs are on the young man. When silence returns, it is a silence that weighs on the prisoners lying in their bunks. They all lie still, except for Alvaro. He has gone over to the bunk of the prisoner who went outside and has set about rummaging through his straw pallet: he pulls out a piece of hard bread and hurriedly hides it inside his pants.

Suddenly, there comes the distinct squeaking sound of the

command post's doors opening, and then slow footsteps, muffled by the watery ground of the yard. Roberto is gazing into space as if not thinking about anything in particular. Alvaro and Erio crouch down behind the defenses they've put up between them and the door to the barrack. But this time, the footsteps don't stop at the door but go round the perimeter of the barrack, as everybody follows the sound with their eyes. What's going on? Suddenly, one of the windows on the opposite side of the barrack is flung open, and the officer's arm thrusts into the barrack and fires the revolver into the darkness. More anguished cries, then nothing.

At dawn, the prisoners are lined up once again in the yard. In front of them, the officer once more invites the thief to come forward. No one moves. The only thing you can hear is the croaking of the crows. The women, grouped in front of their barrack, are watching the scene carefully. Only Jolanda sits by herself, calm and indifferent. At a certain point, Elly amazes everyone by leaving her companions and going over to the SS officer. "It was me who stole the watch," she confesses very calmly.

The prisoners' attentions are now focused entirely on her and the officer. But to everybody's surprise, the officer bursts out laughing and shows the watch on his wrist that no one had even dreamed of stealing from him. "Liar!" he shouts in Elly's face, suddenly growing angry again. Then he orders the sergeant to strip the women and have them parade naked in front of all the men in the camp. Jolanda is the only one who greets the order with a laugh. She is the first to undress, with that indifference and lack of modesty that characterizes the "aborigines," that is, the prisoners who have regressed to a primitive state.

When the group of women starts to march past the men, some of their faces are taut with shame, their eyes fixed straight ahead and full of tears. Elly is one of them. Seeing her like that, Roberto does an about-face and stands at attention, and all the others follow him. Only Alvaro tries to catch a glimpse out of the corner of his eye. The officer, amused by the spectacle of the naked women, turns around to involve the prisoners in his game and is confronted with rows of turned backs. Irritated, he gets on his motorcycle and drives off toward the camp gates. Later, the sergeant dismisses the parade. As he moves away, Roberto catches Elly's glance—she's already dressed and leaning against the wall of the barrack. He goes up to her, and the two embrace amidst the crowds of prisoners heading off toward their different barracks. But immediately, several sharp whistles force them to separate.

It is night. Everybody is waiting for the German officer. They are certain he'll come again, but by now there is just an immense feeling of resignation. The only one who is still working away is Alvaro. Along all four sides of his bed he has built a kind of barricade out of tin cans, stones, and bits of wood that he picked up God knows where. And now he's curled up behind his defenses, smoking a long cigarette made from a piece of newspaper. Roberto seems to be lost in his own thoughts and stands apart from everything that's going on around him. Apparently, he is thinking about Elly. Minutes pass and then hours. Slowly, everybody's eyes close and they all fall asleep. Even the officer's shooting seems normal, something that shouldn't disturb one's sleep, even if it becomes an everlasting sleep.

The pale dawn filters through the windows, and the prisoners begin to wake up in the semi-darkness inside the barrack. What has happened? Who died last night? How can it be that no one heard it or remembers anything? The camp and the surrounding countryside are immersed in an enigmatic silence. There is not a single voice nor a single shot to be heard. The first ones to take a look out the door stare in amazement at some white sheets of paper blown around by the wind in the yard. There is no guard. The women have also awakened. Jolanda is the first outside, as if she had nothing to fear. Across the other side of the yard, she slowly goes up the steps of the command post and walks through the rooms. Everything is a mess. She tries switching on the radio and immediately music comes out of it, the most incredible music in the world: "I Can't Give You Anything But Love," an American song that echoes round the camp, inside the barracks and inside people's heads and hearts. Some people hug their companions; others go off by themselves and cry. Some throw themselves down on the ground and stay there, looking at the sky, drinking in the air that suddenly seems sweetly perfumed.

Once the initial surprise has worn off, something new causes everyone to worry. Isolated shots break the silence, coming from the town and the woods, causing the prisoners to tremble once more in fear of their lives. The most terrible kind of death is that which comes at the last moment when one is almost free. The prisoners all crowd against the fence, looking at the landscape that stretches before their eyes, not yet daring to go out into the open. The most anybody does is go fifty yards beyond the fence and sit down on the grass: just being outside the camp is exhilarating enough.

At midday, the prisoners are all still there. The first ones to make a move are Roberto, Erio, Alvaro, and several others. Elly and Jolanda join them, and the group leaves the camp under the hesitant but envious gaze of their fellow prisoners. The friends walk cautiously towards the woods, looking around them every step of the way. As they slowly make their way forward, they begin to feel more at ease and they quicken their pace. Alvaro walks behind the group and every so often stops to rummage in the backpacks left by the departing Germans or to weigh their guns in his hands. But the slightest noise is enough to make him run to join the tail end of the group. At one point, he peers into a large crater that was probably made during an air raid and discovers some dead Germans at the bottom. At first, this frightens him enough to take a few steps back, but then the sight of something glittering leads him forward. Even though his eyes are full of disgust, he gently runs his hands over the dead men, slipping off their watches and gold chains.

Roberto and the others stop at the edge of a clearing to stare in amazement at a freight train that's just standing there on the tracks. There's not a living soul anywhere around. They go towards it and force open the doors of the cars. The train has come from France and is loaded with everything one could possibly want: perfume, clothes, uniforms, jars of honey, sugar. There are sacks of flour, beans, and corn, and they even find two tankers full of olive oil and one car loaded with antique chairs and beds and mirrors. First, the friends have a really good meal. When they're finished, their bellies are almost bursting. Then they set about searching the train and, in a short while, much of the goods are spread about on the ground; the prisoners hardly know what to take. Roberto has found some perfume and he takes it over to Elly who sniffs it as if she could get drunk on it. Jolanda nearly goes mad for the fabric she has found, wrapping her body in long swathes of it and dancing around. Then suddenly, something distracts them: a small crowd of German civilians has stopped to watch them, fifty yards away at the edge of the woods. They have suitcases, sacks, and bags, and one of them even has a small cart.

For a split second, all the suffering the prisoners have endured at the Germans' hands passes before their eyes. Their first instinct is to chase off those families who are just as hungry as they are. Several of them are openly in favor of this course of action; if they could, they would have the train sealed and held there as a store of food for the days ahead. But Roberto isn't listening to them. The Germans at the bottom of the field, waiting silently for a gesture of goodwill, move him to pity. Suddenly, a group of perhaps twenty, thirty, or forty children detaches itself from the rest of the group and comes running towards the prisoners; they are blonde and beautiful, and their arms are full of flowers that they hold out towards them. The prisoners are touched and hug the children while the German women move towards the train and begin to plunder it, at first silently and orderly, then gradually more desperately, until they raid the freight cars and empty them out, ruining most of the goods as they fight among themselves. The sacks of flour, pulled by a thousand hands, stretch and break into a cloud of white powder, the tins of jam roll under foot, and the packets of butter are squashed against people's chests as they clutch them greedily. Precious little of that cargo actually ends up in people's hands.

Alvaro doesn't go along with his friends. He can't stomach the idea of some of the goods ending up in German hands, so he tries to grab as much as he can in a furious, savage race against the Germans. When they have left and quiet descends once more on the clearing, you can still see Alvaro, rummaging among the pathetic remains on the ground, like a dog foraging through garbage.

Our group of prisoners has stopped at the top of a hill to look down on a deserted town, full of white sheets hanging out the windows. Another sheet, attached to a flag pole, flaps over the roof of a building, like a banner of surrender. It is almost a show of fear. When the group reaches the first houses, their footsteps begin to echo on the pavement and their movement takes on an eerie quality. The sheets fluttering in the breeze above their heads give a strange feeling of freshness to the whole place.

Suddenly, someone appears in front of the group, in the middle of the road; it is the young SS officer who was in command of the camp. His machine gun is aimed at them, and he stops a few paces away from them. In turn, they come to a halt, petrified. The officer, with his usual sharp tone that will not tolerate any argument, orders them to remove the sheets from the windows immediately. There is madness in his eyes. Since there is no one else around to do it, our prisoners have to do what he says. Roberto and the others are perfectly aware that this is no time for joking, and they begin to climb onto the window sills, followed by the officer threatening them with his machine gun. Still, by one means or another, they all manage to give him the slip, leaving him trying to hunt them down mercilessly. Erio, who has backed into a closed doorway, holds his breath as the officer's shadow appears on the road in front of him. But he can feel the door at his back opening and someone pulls him inside, into a dark hallway. Next to him, a young German woman is looking at him with kind eyes, almost tenderly.

Now, with a mounting sense of terror, Elly and Roberto hear the officer's footsteps coming closer. They would like to run away, but they hear other footsteps echoing at the entrance to the town. Jolanda also hears them from where she is hiding beneath an archway. Roberto leans out to look past the corner of the wall where he and Elly are hiding. A small platoon of soldiers, retreating from the front lines, is coming down the main street of the town. Their faces are covered with dust, their boots are worn out, and they are exhausted, dragging along a cart with their wounded stretched out on it. Seeing them, the SS officer runs towards them. He would like to organize them to defend the little town, but the soldiers don't even seem to be listening. So the officer insults them, shows them the stump of his arm, and talks about the greatness of Germany. These are the words of a madman and they arouse only pity. Indeed, there is something compassionate about the burst of machine gun fire that hits him in the chest: nobody knows who summoned the strength to fire his gun just one last time, but the officer falls to the ground.

The officer in charge of the group, a man of about forty, his face battered and unrecognizable, orders a soldier to give the officer the *coup de grâce*. And while the ragged platoon continues on into the distance beyond the town, a German soldier kneels beside the officer and places his revolver against the back of his head. The sharp, loud noise of the shot makes Jolanda jump as she watches the terrifying scene. Her strangled cry makes one of the soldiers turn his dusty, hopeless face towards her, and as he sees her, he seems amazed and approaches her like an automaton. Jolanda shrinks back, staring at the weapon that the soldier still carries in his hand. Then she quickly turns around and runs trembling into the courtyard of an old factory building. But here the walls surround her cutting off any means of escape, and she flattens herself against a wall with her face buried in her hands so as not to see the German as he comes closer.

The soldier stops a few feet from her. He calls her by name, and Jolanda slowly takes her hands away from her face, still staring at him. Ancient memories flash before her eyes. She and Franz, that was the soldier's name, had come to Germany together. They were supposed to get married. That's why she had come with him. But then, for a thousand different reasons, he had been sent back to the front, and she had ended up in a concentration camp. Now she doesn't love him any more. She is afraid of all Germans, even him. She shouts at him to go away and leave her in peace. Terrified, she tries to edge her way along the wall. "Don't kill me, please don't kill me . . ." She is almost screaming, fear is so deeply rooted in her.

It's only now that Franz realizes he still has his revolver in his hand, and he hurls it far away from him, into the middle of the courtyard. Then he goes towards Jolanda, begging her to forgive him—him but not Germany. They are both victims of forces more powerful than they are. But Jolanda can't understand that Franz is different from the rest of the Germans. She just can't do it. She asks him to let her go back to the camp where she'll be safe and can wait for the arrival of the Allies. She hasn't got the strength to forgive him. She has forgotten what the word even means. Franz falls down exhausted against the wall and watches Jolanda drag herself off towards the open factory gate.

Meanwhile, Elly and Roberto, holding hands, are tentatively moving along the walls of the houses, watchful, as if every alley might be an ambush. Night is falling over the deserted gardens, the streets littered with abandoned rubbish, the black roofs of the houses, and above everything there is a gray sky, heavy with dirty black clouds. The two young people cross the square that separates them from the little church, hoping to find a safe, calm refuge there. Slowly and fearfully, they open the dark, heavy door, and in front of them they find a touching scene—a crowd of people kneeling, quietly praying. Roberto and Elly stand in the doorway looking at the prostrate people in the light of a few candles around the altar at the back of the church. In the darkened nave, the muffled, age-old murmur of prayer rises up to greet them.

Meanwhile, two old, severe looking Germans have stood

up and come towards the door. Kindly but firmly, they ask Elly and Roberto to leave. Only women, children, and old people can take sanctuary in the church—no prisoners: they are afraid of reprisals. Roberto gets them to understand that Elly is a woman and that they aren't prisoners any more. But the others won't agree. Roberto gets angry and raises his voice: people turn around to stare at him severely. Elly turns away, pulling Roberto by the arm. Outside, it is now dark, and it is a terrifying darkness. They have just huddled against one of the pillars adorning the facade of the church when an old man comes out to tell Elly that she can come in and stay the whole night if she wishes. The girl doesn't want to leave Roberto, but he tells her that she should by all means accept. It'll make him feel better. "Let's go back to the camp," Elly suggests, but Roberto won't hear of it. He has had enough of that place. Once he's alone again, he huddles next to the pillar, ready to face the long, restless night, his first night of freedom. Every now and then, the sky is lit up by reddish flashes, and terrifying small-arms fire rips through the silence.

Meanwhile, Erio feels safe in the German girl's house. Heidi—that's the name of the girl who had saved him—had been married at a very young age to a man who belonged to a fighter squadron, and she has been widowed. Her feeling for the Italian is both maternal and sensual. She's full of concern and anxious to understand what Erio wants, even if their conversation is largely conducted through gesture, for Erio has only learned a few German words. He is so tired he ends up falling asleep in a comfortable armchair, leaving Heidi with nothing to do except watch over him tenderly. When a strange noise comes in from the street, Heidi quickly closes the window so that Erio won't wake up.

The same noise has also made Roberto jump. It sounds as if there is a tank at the back of the square, where the darkness is deepest. Or a creaky old truck. Or maybe soldiers running. Roberto leaps to his feet, but he can't make out anything in the darkness. No, it's not soldiers. It's just a horse that has somehow gotten free and is frightened, galloping around the deserted streets of the town. Now it rushes toward the front of the church, as if it would hurl itself against the building. Roberto feels as if it is coming to get him and flattens himself behind the pillar. But the horse suddenly stops and the night swallows up the echoes of its footsteps. Roberto can hear the horse snorting not far from him and can make out its outline as it lies on the ground. So he goes over to it, strokes it, and finally curls up against it, resting his head on its warm flank as if it were an old friend.

At dawn, two German peasant women arrive at the church dragging a small cart full of straw. Half asleep, Roberto watches them approach. He is still lying curled up next to the horse. He realizes that the women are lifting two big milk churns out from under the hay. He carefully follows their movements. Then he makes the connection between the cart and the horse that has suddenly come his way: perhaps he should get Elly and put her in the cart and leave. Having decided to do this, he gets the horse up and harnesses him to the cart, without even asking the German women who look at him in amazement. When they try to protest, Roberto just stares at them without even deigning to reply. Meanwhile, some people have come out of the church: old women with bottles in their hands. Elly is with them, and Roberto goes over to her and encourages her to drink some of the milk too. But when the peasants refuse to share it, he loses his temper and upsets the milk churns, spilling their contents all over the pavement. Then he gets Elly into the cart and the two go off together towards the outskirts of the town. Along the way they run into Erio who had been looking for them. Roberto drives the cart past a long line of German women outside a grocery store. Heidi is there too with a bag in her arms. As soon as he sees her, Erio wants to get down and tell her that they're leaving, but Roberto advises him not to—it's better not to make a scene and just disappear. Heidi hardly glances at the cart as it passes, noticing nothing.

They have just turned off onto a side street crowded with deportees, refugees, and the usual bustle of back street traffic when they hear the stuttering noise of an airplane flying low overhead, and they turn to look up at it. It looks as if it's going to crash on the town, and the passersby scatter desperately, so that in a flash the whole street is deserted with everyone lying on the ground, along the walls, or behind any shelter they can find. Roberto, Elly, and Erio also hurriedly get down from the cart and run underneath an archway. The airplane is a German Stuka bomber and it skims over the roofs of the houses leaving a long trail of smoke. Its black shadow passes over the prostrate forms on the ground as it continues to lose altitude, finally crashing beyond the houses with a horrible splintering sound.

Our three friends heave a sigh of relief. They start to go back to the cart when they realize that other prisoners have already taken possession of it to make their own escape. Roberto is amazed to see that Alvaro is one of them. The young man was wandering around the town until just when the plane crashlanded; he saw the cart with his friends leaving, and they were leaving without him! At first, he was overwhelmed with bitterness, but he is not one to take things lying down. The feeling only lasted a few seconds, until rage got the better of him. When he saw the cart standing all by itself in the middle of the road, he jumped on it and got his revenge by shouting that anyone else who wanted to hitch a ride could do so. Roberto and Erio start to throw some of them off, but too many people have heeded Alvaro's invitation. So Roberto furiously begins looking for something among the ruins, and finally he finds what he is looking for: a revolver. Clutching the weapon, he runs towards the cart, fully prepared to kill someone, but he finds Alvaro in front of him, looking more surprised than scared. For a moment, Roberto stops in his tracks and returns Alvaro's gaze. Erio stops too, just as angry, though he can't believe Roberto would shoot his friend. But at that moment the cart begins to move, and Roberto decides he must stop it; so he takes aim at the horse and shoots. The horse crashes to the ground.

Elly has followed all of this, terrified. Roberto takes her by the arm and pulls her away. As he follows them, Erio hears someone calling him: it's Heidi. The young man stops next to her, breathing hard. She wants to know what's going on. "Nothing," says Erio, "nothing." And he goes off with her, concealing his attempt to run back to Italy without even saying goodbye to her.

Meanwhile, Roberto and Elly have run all the way to the woods. Now they are safe, and they walk slowly along a path until they come to a large, blue pond with a border of white sand. They go towards the water, enchanted by the peacefulness and the sweet little bridge over it; then they spy a wooden building that juts out over the pond on stilts, but they are interrupted by the sound of women's voices. Four girls are taking a bath, and they have also undoubtedly escaped from a camp somewhere nearby. One of them, the prettiest one, does a little dance on the landing. She is tall and well-proportioned; Roberto's eyes follow her sinuous body to her breasts which are almost bare. He looks at her for a long time, and there is a single thought running through his mind: he is looking at a woman's breasts. Then, suddenly, a wave of memory wells up inside him, and he remembers what "Woman" truly is: for the last year and a half since he's been in prison, he hasn't even thought about such things. Hunger had wiped any other thoughts out of his head.

He turns to look at Elly and her gaze is warm, intense. Now he seems to understand something: up to now he has been fond of her without actually physically desiring her. But now things are different. Tenderly, he takes her hand and leads her behind a sand dune. They lie in the soft sand and make love for a long time, passionately. Everything around them is quiet: the buzzing of insects, the songs of the birds, and the clear sky over the pond. Later on, they wander about, following any little whim, almost like children. They chase a butterfly and a lizard, and they stop to smell the flowers until it is nearly evening. They find themselves on the outskirts of a town, on a wide avenue with little houses surrounded by gardens with flowers in them. It seems as if the war had never even touched this place. And this is where Roberto gets the idea that he would like to have a house to give to Elly.

The two young friends choose the last villa on the street, the most secluded as well as the most luxurious, with a swimming pool and tennis court on the grounds. Roberto opens the gate and finds himself in front of an austere looking woman in her fifties who is watering the flowers. It seems the most absurd thing in the world: only steps away from so many tragedies, someone is watering flowers. But what angers Roberto even more is the fact that the woman brusquely motions him to go away. So Roberto begins to shout, walks into the villa, and drags out another woman and her son, a fat boy about fifteen years old, plus two maids. His rage is so great that the Germans actually leave the villa. But as soon as they are outside, a new hope suddenly emerges for them: they see a German soldier passing the villa and they ask him to help them defend their property. After some hesitation, he comes over to them. It is Franz, Jolanda's soldier friend. The women soon make him aware of the situation and beg him to help them chase the prisoners out of their house. The soldier sets off towards the door without saying anything.

Elly and Roberto are terrified to realize that there is a German soldier, probably armed, coming straight towards the villa. They run and hide behind a big wardrobe in the bedroom. They can hear the German's footsteps in the hall below, getting closer and closer to the bedroom. He comes in. Roberto and Elly hold their breaths while Franz actually opens the wardrobe and rummages inside it. Then there are other noises, as if he is changing out of his uniform. And indeed, from the window they soon see him in civilian clothes, passing through the garden gate right under the noses of the German women who watch him angrily.

Now that the house is all theirs, Roberto and Elly go through the rooms which are furnished with hefty but high-quality pieces of furniture, reminding themselves of the comfort of armchairs and what it feels like to have a beautiful vase of flowers in the room. Elly seems perfectly at ease. She puts on a silk robe that she digs out of the wardrobe, and suddenly she is transformed: she has rediscovered the look and the manners of her aristocratic upbringing. Roberto looks at her in amazement. Then he calls her to him, onto the soft bed on which he is lying. Through the window, they can see that night is falling over the woods. There is no shooting any more. "You can hear the crickets!" Roberto exclaims, in a voice that suggests he's found something very precious after it's been lost for a long time.

They stay there sitting on the bed, delighted to be able to enjoy the sounds of the woods, and the sounds of the town in the distance. That night in fact, the square is full of people, most of them drunk. In one corner—who knows where it came from—a barrel organ is playing. However beaten up it is, it still makes its thin, discordant sounds, and Alvaro sits there listening to it and winding it up again and again. Then he gets bored of it and gives it a kick. With more kicks he trashes it completely and hurls the broken remains down a well. Now Alvaro is wandering round the town, arm-in-arm with an old Russian, asking him about Stalin and what it's like in Russia and whether it's true that everybody is equal there. Then they quarrel because they can't agree whether it was Marconi or Popov who invented the radio.

Meanwhile, in the courtyard of an abandoned factory, Jolanda is sitting next to a group of ex-prisoners. Near her, a pale, thin young man is reciting the rosary in a quiet voice. He is doing it with great dignity, and Jolanda looks at him with surprise. The young man stops praying and quietly addresses her. He is thanking God, he says, for sending him to Germany and thus enabling him to become less wicked. "The important thing is to become holy," he keeps saying. Then he goes off to talk to other people, but Jolanda looks after him for a long time, unsure whether to admire him or pity him.

Later, when she lies down in a secluded part of the factory, someone comes knocking at the window. Jolanda goes to see who it is and is amazed to see Franz, her German ex-fiancé. "What are you doing here? What do you want?" The young man doesn't know where to go anymore and asks to be allowed to stay, but Jolanda won't hear of it. She offers him a packet of chocolates and tells him to go away and not come near her any more. Isn't he satisfied enough with what he's already done to her? She will never be able to forgive him.

Another gray dawn and the sky seems covered with soot. Down the street that leads into the town from the hill, a white ambulance approaches and stops at the first houses. The German soldier driving it gets out and cautiously looks around him. Then he starts running towards the wood, disappearing into them. From a window in Heidi's house, Erio has witnessed the whole thing. When he sees the driver run off, he rushes outside, jumps into the ambulance, and urgently presses the starter button. But the engine won't start. Erio quickly checks everything and realizes that there is no gasoline. Desperately, he gets out, looks around, and sees two Italian former interns coming towards him. He calls them over and persuades them to help him push the vehicle into the garden of the house. "This will get us back to Italy in less than a day," he says, promising to take the other two with him that very day.

Then he goes back into the house and asks Heidi if she has any gasoline. When she says no, he starts searching everywhere and loses his temper because Heidi doesn't help him with much enthusiasm. Then he goes out in search of his friends. Heidi follows behind him, but after a while he says good-bye to her. He's seen Alvaro in one of the stores and goes in after him, then they both come out again; they have to find Roberto and Elly. The group of friends starts looking for gasoline all over the town, in every house. They even look in the church, and then they go to the town hall where there might be some gasoline hidden somewhere.

They turn all the offices upside down, rummaging about the shelves and through the cabinets full of files and papers. Roberto can't control himself any more: he'd like to destroy the whole lot, as if those papers represented something old and orderly that no longer has any reason to exist. Now there is freedom, every individual is his own master, no more lists or files. Elly is the only one of the group not to let herself get carried away by this frenzy of freedom. She knows that the most important thing at the moment is to get out of the chaos and start rebuilding a quiet, normal life. So with some difficulty, she manages to drag Roberto and the others away, just as they set fire to the papers that they have thrown out the windows onto the street.

Shortly afterwards, they are wandering around the edge of the town again. Perhaps they can find some gasoline in one of the vehicles the Germans abandoned as they retreated. So they reach the countryside, and, after crossing over a bridge, they come to a stop: a curious, festive scene greets their gaze. Some Russian prisoners are cycling madly around in a field. They're going round and round, waving their arms about like an infernal sort of carousel, wild and joyous like a cossack dance. A lot of women are watching them and laughing, and an old man with a beard is playing the accordion. The Russians are pedaling furiously and splashing up mud from the water-logged ground, but if anyone gets soaked he doesn't seem to mind and shouts all the louder. Roberto goes towards the Russians and starts talking to one of them as he watches the show with great curiosity, almost greedily. He likes to observe everything and try and understand it. Elly can't manage to drag him away from it all.

Not far away, Alvaro has seen a man digging the soil in his little garden without even bothering to look at the Russians. From the look of him he's Italian, and Alvaro goes over to him, his curiosity aroused. Indeed, he's from Romagna, and Alvaro tells him he must be mad, digging the ground at a moment like this. Why would he want to do a thing like that? And he drags him away to a haystack where Erio and Elly have stopped. Then Roberto arrives with some Russian women to get some straw to spread on the muddy ground so that the bicycle wheels won't get stuck. The women go off with armfuls of straw, but Alvaro lets out a loud shout. He's noticed something sticking out of the haystack, the bumper of a car. Everybody throws themselves on the haystack and soon they can see the whole car. It's an old Mercedes, a black convertible though it also has a back seat. Roberto sits in the driver's seat and, just for a laugh, tries to start the engine: it's all in perfect working order. It's even got gasoline in it. In a flash, Elly, Alvaro, Erio, and Forlimpopoli (that's the nickname they've given to the guy from Romagna) all jump in the Mercedes and the car races off towards the town.

Everybody is excited, Forlimpopoli more than the others, for he's sitting in the back seat laughing and shouting as the wind blows through his hair. It's a mad race and it upsets Elly. She can't understand why they must waste gas in such a stupid way. "Stupid?" says Roberto in excitement. "I haven't been in a car for two years!" And he drives like a man possessed. When he gets to the town, he's doing fifty miles an hour and sending everyone in front of him scattering out of the way. Groups of escaped prisoners are running in all directions and soon the streets are deserted. Roberto feels as if he's the master of the whole town, the whole situation, the whole of Europe.

Then the Mercedes makes its way back up the hill along a road with lots of dangerous curves, when suddenly, Alvaro notices that Forlimpopoli isn't there any more. More than anything else, this makes Elly lose her temper, especially because Roberto has greeted this piece of news with a huge laugh, which Alvaro immediately echoes. They're both laughing so much that Roberto has to stop, and Elly immediately gets out and walks away, indignant and alarmed, to see what has happened to the poor guy. Roberto and Alvaro just keep on laughing, they can't contain themselves any longer, and soon Erio also feels uncomfortable and walks off after Elly. Roberto and Alvaro stay where they are and, little by little, calm down.

It's the middle of the afternoon now; it's neither hot nor cold. The air is still, and there's not a sound to be heard except for the chirping of the birds and the mooing of a cow somewhere. Alvaro pricks up his ears. A cow? Where there's a cow there's also steak, and the two men discover that they're really hungry; hungry for the smell of proper roast meat, of steak. They get back into the car and take a dusty little road that leads off the main road towards the woods, in the direction where the mooing sound came from. The woods are dark as if it is already evening, and Roberto switches on the headlights. The road winds through the trees which are getting more and more dense. Suddenly, a little animal jumps out from a bush and stops in the middle of the road, dazzled by the headlights: it's a rabbit. "Come on, let's kill it!" shouts Alvaro.

Roberto presses the accelerator and the car lurches forward, but the rabbit manages to jump out of the way a split second before it gets run over by the wheel. The two of them decide to wait in ambush with the headlights switched off. After a while they hear the noise of twigs snapping and see a shadow appear on the road. Roberto switches on the headlights, and a few feet away they can see a deer, standing there petrified with fright. Roberto hurls the Mercedes towards the animal as it jumps about, steering the wheel quite sharply in order to follow it, but he's very good and he nearly manages to catch the animal. It's only a couple of feet in front of them now. But then the deer makes a big leap sideways into the trees, and as he tries to follow it, Roberto steers too sharply and hits a tree. The two friends get out and look at the crumpled hood of the car with concern. That's the end of the Mercedes, and they can also forget about the deer! Disillusioned and bitter, they retrace their steps and reach the edge of the woods. They're just about to come out into the open when a bullet whistles over their heads followed by another one. They throw themselves to the ground just in time to avoid a burst of machine gun fire that riddles the ground all around them.

Roberto starts cursing. Who the hell is shooting at them? Are they crazy? He crawls on his hands and knees to a bush and looks down the road. What he sees makes him let out a cry that soon has Alvaro by his side, despite his fear. An American patrol is coming down the road. They move forward slowly, shooting at every noise, at the faintest shadow. "Americans!" shouts Alvaro, and he goes to stand up but another burst of gunfire soon has him back on the ground. So they both wait there and remain perfectly still, watching the patrol as it proceeds to the town and disappears around a bend in the road.

Roberto comments that it's a strange encounter with their liberators. Then slowly and making certain not to catch up to them, they too set off towards the town.

When they arrive in the town square, Roberto and Alvaro are confronted with an amazing sight. An impromptu orchestra is playing to more than two hundred ex-prisoners as they dance happily around the square. There are very few men among them, and those who are there seem almost intimidated. By contrast, the women are nearly out of control. Roberto stops to take in the scene and is almost overwhelmed by it. It makes his head spin. Then he starts to dance too, embracing one of the women, then another and another, and they let him do it; they'd let him do anything. Nearly all of them are quite young and they have a mad desire to enjoy themselves and make up for lost time.

Alvaro too is caught up in the wave of liveliness. He takes the arm of a young Czechoslovakian girl dressed in rags, even though she's with one of her own countrymen, and starts to lead her away to dance. But the Czechoslovakian guy, seeing that Alvaro is an Italian, holds him back. He says that he's been to Italy many times and has wonderful memories of it, until Alvaro, in order to get rid of him, says that he knows Czechoslovakia very well and has wonderful memories of it too. At that, the other guy's face lights up and he smiles, and Alvaro smiles too, and finally he can go off with the girl and waves good-bye to him. "Viva l'Italia," says the Czech, as he shakes him by the hand and bows politely. "Viva Czechoslovakia," says Alvaro, no less politely as he holds tight to the Czech girl

After a while, Roberto and Alvaro have rounded up about a dozen girls: a brunette; a blonde; a tall, wiry type; a sexy, feline type; a home-body type girl; and all other kinds of women. They lead them out of the crowd into a grocery store and take whatever they can find, and then they go and find a place where they can sit down, somewhere comfortable to eat in peace and make love.

Meanwhile, Elly, accompanied by Jolanda, is looking for Roberto. Elly is getting more and more concerned; she thought the young man would have caught up with her immediately, but the whole day has gone by and she hasn't even seen him. The two women turn a corner and realize that there's a large crowd running towards the pharmacy. "What's going on?" they ask anxiously. "Someone died. He drank three pints of alcohol."

Elly leans against the wall so as not to fall down. She can feel in her bones that it's Roberto. Trembling, she moves towards the pharmacy, her eyes fixed on the group of onlookers crowding round the door to the shop. But Jolanda's voice forces her to turn around: "That's where he is!" she shouts and points to a lighted window above them. In the rectangle of light, a man and a woman have appeared, with other people behind them all cheering happily. The man is Roberto and he's holding two women in his arms, looking down at the square and the huge party. But he doesn't see Elly. She's right underneath him, incredulous, and you can see the humiliation in her face. Jolanda tries to make a joke of the whole thing. She drags her friend towards the doorway of the building, inviting her to go up with her, but Elly doesn't feel like it: her embarrassment and her disgust are so great that she doesn't even want to go near the place. She prefers to wait for her friend outside on the steps in the darkness.

Jolanda goes into the room where Roberto and his friends are. Their search for a place to spend the night has come to an end in a natural history museum, full of stuffed animals and exotic plants. There's a lot of confusion and everybody is out of control. The men are chasing semi-naked women who show absolutely no modesty in allowing themselves to be hugged and kissed. One couple is making out behind a group of plants, there's another couple dancing in the other corner, and Roberto has come away from the window to sit astride an armchair with a stuffed goat's head atop his own head. He's got three women grouped around him laughing like hyenas. He's laughing too, out of his mind, completely unaware of where he is.

He's living in a dreamland, with no rules, no order, no limits. Absolute liberty. As soon as he recognizes Jolanda, he get up to embrace her, as if he hasn't seen her for years. "Elly is downstairs," she tells him. "She's downstairs waiting for you." "Then why doesn't she come up?" says Roberto. "Bring her up, she should be having a good time too, enjoying life now that it's suddenly gotten better again."

He lurches towards the stairs, calling several times for Elly. But he gets no answer. So he goes down into the square, followed by Jolanda, still calling for Elly. Now it's his turn to look for the girl among those partying in the streets. The town seems to have been swept by a wave of excitement. No one wants to go to sleep. In the darkness you can hear voices and laughter and shouting, and Roberto's cry gets lost in all the confusion: "Elly! . . . Elly!" But she hears him. She's stopped in an alley, hiding in the shadows; she's crying and sees Roberto go by but doesn't stop him, so the young man carries on until he arrives at the villa. But the villa is wrapped in total darkness and nobody answers his call.

So Roberto goes back to the town. He meets two Allied soldiers leading a captured German soldier towards the woods, God only knows where they found him. They are followed by a woman shouting desperately, and Roberto feels enormous pity for her and follows behind her without really knowing why. He's just so full of curiosity about everything that he wants to see it all. The prisoner is shoved into a shack at the very edge of the woods. There are others in there too, watched over by a guard patrol of soldiers. Roberto stops to talk to a sergeant. He notices that the Allies seem to have more sympathy for the Germans than they do for the Italians, and they mention di Carnera[2] with contempt.

Roberto leaves them and sees a small villa with lighted windows and a lot of people around it, talking. Among them is Alvaro, talking to a black man. The little villa is occupied by

---

[2] An Italian boxing champion whose popularity was exploited by the Fascists, his short-lived fame demolished by Joe Louis. [Editor]

several prostitutes. There's an enormous bouncer at the entrance, barring the way, and inside two women are playing cards. Obviously, they haven't been working tonight; there are too many women around. The black guy talking to Alvaro would like to go inside but the bouncer won't let him. Finally, he pushes him back so hard that he lands flat on the ground. Alvaro helps him get up and tells him that he can find a woman for him, but he'd like a tank of gasoline in exchange. Roberto joins in, trying to persuade the black guy, and they arrange to meet the next evening at the edge of the woods. They'll bring the woman and he'll bring the gasoline. Then the two friends go off to try and find a woman to give to the black guy. Alvaro immediately thinks of Jolanda. In fact, they go looking for her in the warehouse at the factory, but unfortunately she's not there. So they stop in a huge room that's been taken over by about thirty guys from Naples and they listen to them singing songs. Alvaro and Roberto sing some too. Some people are moved, others laugh, and others try to sleep on the straw pallets arranged along the walls. There's even someone playing cards by candlelight, and Roberto ends up joining in too, for a long time.

The morning afterwards, two soldiers from the army medical corps, accompanied by an Italian officer, walk into the big room. The ex-prisoners from Naples are still sleeping soundly. Roberto and Alvaro are also sleeping on a straw mattress right under the window. The Italian officer is a man in his forties wearing a wonderfully well-preserved uniform, and he walks past the sleeping figures and orders everyone to get up. He says that the Americans have given him command of all the Italian prisoners, and the first thing he's going to do is disinfect both them and the place they're living in. After a bit of hesitation, many of the men from Naples stand up. Being former soldiers, they haven't forgotten what rank means: it applies in peace as well as war, in defeat as well as victory. Roberto and Alvaro watch them while they get undressed and march off in line to another wing of the factory.

When the lieutenant notices the two of them still lying on

their bed, he comes over to them. "How come you're not getting up?" he asks, visibly annoyed. "We are civilians," Roberto nonchalantly says to him. "That may be, but you've still got to go and get disinfected." At that, Roberto explodes. He's not taking orders from anyone. He's had enough. He's a free man. Who put him in command anyway? The Americans? Who cares what the Americans say. Just leave him alone. If you really insist, bring a couple of packets of disinfectant over here and he'll do it himself, back in the villa, when he feels like it. The officer walks off, annoyed.

Only now do Roberto and Alvaro get up, taking their time about it. They leave the big room and stop for a moment to watch the guys from Naples getting disinfected: they look as if they're in the middle of a big cloud of white flour. Someone says it's DDT, a wonderful new disinfectant. Roberto goes up to the lieutenant who's writing the prisoners' personal details down in a big register and asks him for some packets of disinfectant. He wants them partly out of curiosity and partly just to annoy this guy who's taken it on himself to restore order just when the rest of Europe is in chaos. Then, with two packets under their arms, the two friends walk back to Elly's villa.

Unfortunately, they find something there that they weren't expecting. On the terrace of the villa, several American officers are talking to Elly, who is moving among them with perfect, well-bred grace, as if she were the lady of the house. Roberto is annoyed by the whole thing and stops in the middle of the garden to call to her. Elly leans on the balustrade of the terrace and motions to him to come up with a slight gesture that has a certain coolness about it. "So you're doing it with the Americans now, are you?" Roberto asks her, with a hard edge in his voice.

Elly is taken aback for a moment. Her faces darkens, but she quickly recovers herself. "Yes," she says, with complete calm. "Well then, make sure you disinfect yourself," Roberto replies, showing her the packets of DDT. And he puts them down on the steps of the terrace and leaves, followed by Elly's heart-wrenching gaze.

That same evening, Roberto and Alvaro keep their appointment with the black guy who can get them the gasoline. Except that he doesn't have it. "No gas, no girl," Alvaro tells him. The guy promises he'll bring it tomorrow but says he'd still like the girl today. Everybody's got a girl, some have two or three or ten; he's the only one who doesn't. "You're too black," Alvaro explains to him, but he lets him tag along behind, and the three of them go back to a warehouse where Alvaro is living. There are other black men already inside and Jolanda is kneeling in front of one of them, waiting for him to finish getting drunk. The others are all sprawled on the ground along the walls, knocked out by lots of whisky. "Are you going to go to sleep or aren't you?" Jolanda asks him, offering him a glass of liquor for the umpteenth time.

Alvaro immediately starts to take the men's clothes, first their shoes, then their pants, and finally their shirts. Having done that, they all put on the American uniforms, telling the guy who was supposed to bring the gasoline to stay there and watch his fellow countrymen. Otherwise, he'll get no girl. They leave and head for the center of town; given the cautious way they walk, it's clear they've got a plan in mind. The square is full of soldiers. Some frenetic jazz music is coming from the schoolroom, whose blacked-out windows glow indicating there must be a light on inside.

Roberto, Alvaro, Erio and the others come to a halt in front of a large doorway. They're a bit worried because the two Americans who are guarding it are throwing out an Italian in civilian clothes who tried to go inside. "They treat us like Negroes," he protests as he walks away. Then, one at a time, they make up their minds. First Alvaro goes inside, walking behind three other Allied soldiers, next Roberto and Erio, then the others. All it takes is a half-salute in the American style or a muttered "Hi Joe" to the guards and they find themselves in a wide entrance hall, pleased that they've made it, despite all the prohibitions. Indeed, Italians are not allowed inside.

The corridor leads to a large room decorated with paper

streamers, mirrored balls that reflect the lights, silver balls, etc. A small band is playing the boogie-woogie, and in the middle of the floor, a solitary couple is dancing away. Everyone around them is clapping their hands in time, cheering the two of them on with shouts and whistles. The girl is beautiful and a good dancer too. Roberto stares intently at her and gets a nod of greeting in return. Then he turns around as if he's looking for someone and finds her immediately: Elly. The girl is on the other side of a group of officers. She jumps slightly when she sees Roberto but carries on talking to the captain standing next to her. The captain has his hair cut in the German style: very short. He has gold-rimmed glasses and is thin, barely thirty years old, and looks like a scientist in the way that only Americans can (in fact, he took a course on nuclear physics with Enrico Fermi). He wears a uniform that is elegant in its very nonchalance. His name is Gregory.

Alvaro immediately throws himself at one of the girls he saw on his way in. Erio takes an interest in the band, and Roberto moves closer to Elly. He asks her to dance, but she doesn't answer him immediately. She looks at him with a serious expression, and when Roberto is about to repeat himself, she says no. "Why not?" says the young man. "I'm tired," she replies. Roberto walks off with an ironic look on his face; he's not the slightest bit upset. Right behind him is the beautiful dancer, and without even worrying about all the men hanging around her waiting for a chance to dance, he drags her to the center of the room, holding her tightly around the waist. Then Elly gets up and starts dancing with the captain.

The officer is happy to see that Elly is finally prepared to be so generous to him, and at a certain point he leaves the center of the room to lead her out onto the shady terrace that runs along the first floor of the school. He tries several times to kiss her, but she seems to have lost all the passion she showed when she was dancing and won't let him put his arms around her. The officer doesn't insist. Suddenly, at the sound of a voice, Elly turns sharply around: it's Roberto, smiling at her from a corner of the terrace and telling her to go ahead and kiss the captain, she should lean her head a little to one side so that she can offer her mouth to him more prettily. Elly tries to master her indignation and is about to say something when the young man walks off laughing. He goes back into the room and sits by himself to watch the couples dancing the boogie-woogie with greater and greater abandon. Even Alvaro is having a go at it and is making some very strange moves with a short, fat, Danish girl.

By midnight, almost all of them are drunk and the party quickly goes downhill. Many of them just roll underneath a table, others pour bottles of liquor all over themselves, but most just carry on dancing. At one point, the soldiers get the women to do strange acrobatics, opening their legs and sliding them through underneath them, then dropping them on the floor. Several of the girls are willing enough to do this—in fact, they're having a ball—but others try to wriggle out of it. But the soldiers won't let them. One is after Jolanda and won't leave her alone. She doesn't know what to do to get rid of him, and although Roberto at first is amused by it all, he finally catches Jolanda's imploring eyes as she tries to give her partner a slap. The soldier pours a bottle of beer all over her and that brings Roberto to his feet. He grabs the officer by the lapels, and giving him a shake, tells him to leave Jolanda alone. The soldier gives him a shove, and Roberto responds by throwing him to the ground, where he lands right next to Elly's table.

Elly has followed the whole thing with absolute amazement, and now she apprehensively watches what will happen next. The soldier gets to his feet in a fury and starts throwing punches at Roberto, who again responds with savage force. A huge fight ensues with chairs and bottles flying all over the room. Alvaro is kicking like a mule, and Erio is locked in a struggle with a short guy who's punching him like crazy. A cavalry officer grabs an American tank commander and pulls his hair out. The fight degenerates, dragging everyone in and becoming ridiculous. Meanwhile, someone goes over to speak quietly to the band leader. The guy takes the microphone and asks for silence. When he doesn't get it, he makes it an order. Everyone stops, and when there is quiet, the band leader announces that Germany has asked for an armistice: the war is over.

A huge cheer erupts in the room. But the Italians don't know what to do. "Should we be happy or not?" Alvaro asks Roberto. "After all, we've just lost the war." "Let's get out of here," says Roberto, glaring at him, and he heads off with the others towards the exit. Elly follows him with her gaze and looks worried.

The announcement of the end of the war has electrified everyone. The square echoes with the sound of singing. The church bells are pealing madly and almost by magic all the street lights come on; the windows are thrown open so that light pours out onto the streets where all the black guys are dancing as if they were possessed. Roberto, Alvaro and Erio move through the general hubbub without really taking part in it. They're cut and bruised and they walk slowly towards the old factory.

Roberto sits down by himself on some steps and holds his head in his hands. He's got a dreamy look on his face and doesn't seem to notice what's going on around him. Suddenly he's forced to take notice of a woman's legs that appear in front of him. He looks up and discovers it's Elly: she smiles at him and offers him her hand, helps him up and then embraces him with emotion. "The war is over," she says in a gentle voice. When two people have suffered through something together, they only need the briefest glance to understand one another, and at that moment, both Roberto and Elly feel that what's happening around them is so important that their own personal issues are irrelevant. And besides, everyone in the square is kissing and hugging each other: how could they not be affected by such spontaneous happiness?

Slowly, they move off towards the outskirts of the town. The town is quiet here but the night is full of the sounds of partying. They pause for a moment to admire some huge bonfires that the Russians have built in the fields next to the railway. A few people are shooting into the air but it's a happy sound. And then, just as Roberto and Elly are approaching their villa, Roberto feels something strike him in the back of the leg and he collapses on the ground. He touches his calf and realizes that he's bleeding. "They've shot me," he says, clutching Elly, who helps him drag himself to the villa and gets him onto the bed. She disinfects the wound and carefully bandages it. "You never know when death is going to creep up on you!" she says as she undresses. "You live through a thousand trials, and then when you least expect it, you catch a bullet that wasn't even meant for you, shot by some guy in a moment of celebration." Roberto looks at her tenderly. "I love you so much," he says.

Roberto's bandaged leg keeps him laid up in the villa's soft bed for several delightful days. Elly is constantly near him, affectionate, patient and understanding. She keeps him well supplied with cigarettes, chocolate, biscuits, and jars of preserved fruit. There's even a wonderful gramophone. And their friends are constantly dropping in. Alvaro comes to tell him about his business dealings, Erio brings Heidi along, and Jolanda has lots of new boyfriends to introduce him to. Elly and Roberto finally feel as if they could never live without each other. Roberto is very affectionate towards her, passionately in love. And when he's finally able to get up and walk, the first thing he says is that he wants to marry Elly immediately, without waiting to get back to Italy. In fact, he's heard that there's an Italian priest in the neighborhood who had also been deported by the Germans, and he's already married some other Italians to some Polish girls. Elly is so happy that morning that she runs to the bedroom and bursts into tears.

Roberto starts looking for the Italian priest with Alvaro, who's managed to get them two bicycles. There's a warm breeze over the fields and roads indicating that summer is fast approaching. The prisoners are walking around in shorts, and the Russian girls have short black skirts and white blouses while the Americans are in their undershirts. Roberto and Alvaro look around them in wonderment; they go in the direction of Bergen, at least that's the name of the place where they've been told the Italian chaplain is.

Then, after a couple of hours, they catch sight of a large town hidden in the middle of the countryside. They stop and look at it, and while they are there a man comes up to them, another ex-prisoner wearing a light-colored uniform. "Bergen?" says Roberto, gesturing at the town. The other nods. He's a Hungarian officer, and he explains that there are ninety other Hungarians around. "The Americans sent us to live here." Roberto asks him whether there are any Italians in the neighborhood, apart from themselves, and if there is a chaplain among them. The man says yes, there are Italians; the few of them who were in the area had been rounded up with others of various nationalities, and then there's a small Allied garrison that runs everything. All in all, there are about a thousand men and fifteen thousand women.

Alvaro opens his eyes wide: "Fifteen thousand women?" Yes, that's right; Jewish women from all over Europe: Dutch, Yugoslavian, Bulgarian, Ukrainian, and so on. The Allies had sent the Germans away and put them in prison while they waited to be repatriated. So only the women are left. Roberto and Alvaro don't inquire any further. They say good-bye to the Hungarian guy and set off towards the town, whose dark, pointed roofs are sticking up into the pale, clear blue sky, grouped around the central church tower.

As soon as they reach the first houses, Roberto and Alvaro realize they are being watched by thousands of pairs of eyes from behind closed windows. A group of women is walking down the street ahead of them, and they immediately turn around and take the two men into their circle. "What language do you speak?" asks one of them. "Italian," says Alvaro. "I only speak Neapolitan," says the girl, which the two men think is very funny.

Here too, almost all the women are young, with attractive faces, well-combed hair, and pretty dresses. Obviously the Germans had killed their parents but decided their children might be good for something. None of them smile. "Of course they're sad, they're Jews," Roberto explains, and he turns away from them suddenly as if it hurts his eyes to look at them, like when you get a blinding flash of sunlight in your face. Then he looks up and sees that there is a girl standing at an upstairs window who indeed has a mirror and is trying to shine the sun straight into his eyes. She's beautiful, and she makes signs to him, inviting him to come inside. Roberto runs towards the door of her house but his friend holds him back. "This place is a paradise!" he shouts, and he starts running like a madman through the streets, blowing kisses to any woman who appears at the window.

Several days have gone by and Elly doesn't know what to think. Roberto has disappeared without saying anything to her, and she doesn't even know the name of the town where the young man was headed to look for the priest. She talks about these things with Jolanda who has come to the office to see her and to get some medicine. She's not feeling well but she won't go and see the doctor: she's afraid they'll find something really wrong, so she carries on, trusting that a few pills, vitamins, or some such thing will see her through. "Roberto is in Bergen," she says. "Erio told me." A little later, Elly sets off for Bergen too, in an American jeep.

Elly is blind to the thousand men who live in Bergen and sees only the women, looking at her with hostility. She tries to question some of them and ask about Roberto—an Italian who looks like an Italian—but they are all very vague. It's obvious that they remember the young man; they've met him and know him well, but they won't admit it. After a while, Elly feels uncomfortable surrounded by all these women talking in strange languages. She's never seen anywhere like this place. She feels in her bones that Roberto must have had some unbelievable experiences here, and perhaps he's still around. Why won't they tell her where he is? She continues through the town and suddenly comes to a small swimming pool, located in a meadow full of flowers, with an iron gate outside. Alvaro is in the water, surrounded by about forty women—perhaps Roberto is there too. She goes up to Alvaro who comes to meet her, wrapping himself in a long white bath robe. Elly asks him about

Roberto, and he also hesitates before he answers. At length, he tells her that Roberto isn't there any more, that he had been in the town but has left, and now, as far as he knows, he's in a hotel near the lake, not far away. "Is he alone?" Elly asks. Alvaro hesitates again. Then Elly gets mad and he's forced to blurt out the truth: "He's got a French girl with him."

Elly now knows what she came to find out, and she says good-bye to Alvaro and leaves. She feels like her heart has stopped and she can't wait to get away from that place, the town that seems heavenly, but a ridiculous sort of heaven with women who talk in strange tongues and have hair and eyes of every shade, women who can do anything they want and hardly let a man walk down the street without calling him into their houses. They're all there, leading the same lives whether it's inside or outside, in the gardens or under the trees. Women who have suffered as much as her, and more than her, who think that all they have to do is put on a bit of make-up and some lipstick and they'll be able to blot out the atrocities of the past. What this town is, is a paradise full of she-devils, bitter and twisted. In other words, a hell. Certainly, this is the reason that Roberto came here. Elly gets back into the jeep and drives speedily away. She doesn't even ask Alvaro where to find Roberto. She goes straight back home, throws herself down on the bed, and cries. Just a few days before, on that same bed, she had been weeping for joy.

The hotel that Alvaro was talking about is a small building with an aged and respectable appearance in the middle of an estate that has a fine view of the lake. Down below, there's the lake shore, and above, the road that winds its way up there from the woods. All together, it's enchanting. There's a lot of confusion on the road. A line of about twenty taxis has stopped in front of the main gates, and a crowd of about twenty girls is loading their belongings onto the roofs of the cars, with a bit of help from the cab drivers. The taxis have come from France— the border is only about twenty miles away—and they are going to bring home the French prisoners. They are all excited and touched by this display of national unity.

In one of the salons of the hotel, Roberto is talking to a girl. She's a beautiful creature with a really great figure: she's a ballerina by profession. It's obvious that the two have had a love affair, even if that's now coming to an end. The girl is insisting that Roberto come with her. But the young man won't go and she can't understand why. "Why don't you come to France and you can go on to Italy from there? What do you want to hang around here for?" "Just to have a look around," says Roberto, almost as if he's talking to himself. He's leaning against the window and watching the line of taxis—it's been so long since he saw a taxi! "You're off to Paris now," Roberto continues, "and you'll be able to take taxis every day there. You'll have a job, a house . . . And I'll have all that too. I really think we'll never see each other again, you know. It's sad, but don't you find it a little beautiful too? I think it's lovely. And yet, I don't want not to see you again."

The girl is listening to him without understanding what he's saying. Then she hugs him tightly, and Roberto smiles and kisses her. And he stands at the window and watches her running across the lawn towards the taxis which are just beginning to move off in the direction of the woods, back to France. Then he drags himself away from that scene, goes out of the hotel, and heads toward the lake shore. There are girls bathing in the water as well as three or four men, and everyone is laughing and splashing about in the water. Roberto takes his fishing tackle from a hut, and he's about to load everything into a boat that's tied up on the shore when he sees Elly driving down the road that circles the estate; she's got her American captain with her.

Roberto puts his fishing things down and watches the two of them. Elly takes off her summer dress and she's got her bathing suit on underneath. The captain has his on too. They dive in and laugh and shiver because the water is so cold. As she gets to the shore again, Elly notices Roberto. She looks at him for a long time, quite seriously. Then, as the captain stretches out in the sunshine, she comes towards the boat where Roberto is sitting, holding a stick that she's picked up off the ground. She stops about twenty feet away from the young man, looks at him again, and then writes something in the sand so that it's clearly visible. Then she goes back to her captain and lies down in the sun. After a minute, Roberto gets up and goes over to see what she wrote. There's just a single word: *Makaroni.* If Elly had been hoping for a reaction, then she must have been disappointed. Roberto doesn't even blink an eye. He just scuffs out the letters with his foot, then picks up his fishing gear, and slowly, without turning around, he climbs back up towards the hotel with Elly looking after him.

Back at the abandoned factory, in the large room where Jolanda lives, a group of Italians is listening to one of their companions singing songs as he accompanies himself on the guitar. Roberto, looks at them from his corner with a bored expression on his face. What irritates him most is his comrades' emotion, the incurable homesickness that seems to weigh them down. So he gets up and leaves the room and walks around the streets for a while. He only came back yesterday and already he wants to get out again. He feels constantly restless, and when he hears the murmuring of a crowd in the town square and waves of booing and jeering, he heads off to see what it's all about.

In the square, a crowd of ex-prisoners all leaning against the wall is watching the departure of the Germans, dressed in civilian clothes now, who had voluntarily given themselves up to the Allied command post or had been rounded up from where they were hiding in the countryside. The jeering is directed at them, and there's a line of military police between the trucks and the prisoners to make sure there are no reprisals against the defeated Germans. Roberto stops to watch and is so absorbed by his thoughts that he doesn't shout or curse at them along with everybody else. Jolanda too, whom we can see standing in the shadow of one of the houses around the square, seems to be preoccupied by her own private concerns.

From behind the half-closed shutters of the houses, the families of the Germans watch their young relatives, huddled with their heads bowed inside the trucks. And one of them suddenly opens a window and throws a flower onto the trucks, making the ex-prisoners explode with rage. In the lines of German prisoners climbing into the trucks, we can also see Franz. The young man looks around him hopefully, as if looking for someone. As soon as she sees him, Jolanda quickly tries to hide. She didn't know that Franz was still in the town. Unfortunately, he's still there, just a few steps away from her. And she looks out again, peering around the corner of the house, hoping that he hasn't seen her. But Franz is staring straight at her, smiling with affection, as if asking her forgiveness.

Jolanda is touched. Almost against her will she walks over to the truck, alone, to the amazement of her former inmates from the camp. She passes through the line of Allied soldiers who hardly notice her and walks right up to the truck. Suddenly, there's silence in the square as if everyone is waiting for something momentous. But instead, it's very simple: Franz and Jolanda merely look at each other, as if sharing the same, deep feelings. Then Jolanda holds out her hand: "Good luck, Franz," she whispers to him with emotion. "Good luck, Jolanda." They both have tears in their eyes as the truck moves off and their hands separate forever.

At this point, many of the former prisoners invade the square and surround Jolanda, insulting her, pushing her about, and ripping at her clothes. Only Roberto protests this display of unruly behavior. He hurries Jolanda into a doorway, but the young girl suddenly falls down in a faint. Roberto bends over his poor friend and soon realizes that Elly is beside him, having run up to help Jolanda too. Their eyes meet, but this is no time for private quarrels and there is no tension between them. Jolanda is more sick than she had seemed, and when they get her into the jeep that Elly has brought up, they realize that it's not just a passing faint. Imprisonment has done serious damage to Jolanda's health, and suddenly, it's too much for her. A trickle of blood comes from her mouth.

Elly and Roberto watch the car drive away with their hearts in their mouths. Then they are forced to look at each other again, and they feel ashamed of their own little squabbles and arguments: in the presence of death, everything seems petty. They walk out of the town in silence until Elly stops to lean against a tree. "I'm leaving tomorrow," she says softly. "They're giving me a ride in a jeep." Roberto feels the ground give way beneath his feet. He knows that it would take a lot to express what he's feeling right now. But he also knows that there is something that still stops him from saying what's in his heart, so he simply shrugs his shoulders.

Slowly, they leave the crowd and walk towards the woods, arm in arm. They look more like brother and sister than two lovers. They look around them, at the leaves, the flowers, a baby rabbit that has somehow gotten onto the path, and the birds that are flying back to their nests, warning of the coming rain. And so they arrive at the train that had been abandoned in the clearing and was the first stop on their journey to freedom. They pause to look at it. Jokingly, Roberto begins to question Elly. For example, that American captain that's always hanging around her, what does he mean to her? Elly laughs. "Why should you care? Are you jealous?" Roberto goes red in the face. "Who me? Jealous?" And suddenly, they are once more a man and a woman, struggling with their feelings. Still, everything is quite good-humored. "The captain wants to marry me, take me back to America." "That would be a good move for you," says Roberto, as he stretches out his palm, testing for the first drops of rain. "America is a great country."

Since the rain is getting stronger, the two young people take refuge in one of the freight cars. They are silent for a little while, listening to the sound of raindrops falling on the roof. Roberto feels as if the rest of the world doesn't exist; the war was a kind of second flood that swept everything else away. Nothing will ever be the same again, only mankind and animals are left, and the two of them, who are a bit like animals themselves as they sit in that freight car. That's why one can't just behave as one would have before; one can't go back to the old ways, to old feelings. But Elly can't stand the silence any more and says: "Please, Roberto . . . say something . . . please!" But Roberto doesn't even turn around to look at her; he's so wrapped up in his own thoughts. He almost seems to be speaking to himself when he finally says: "You know what I've always been afraid of? Of saying things before I've gotten them sorted out in my head . . . So it's better for me not to say anything. Elly, believe me, I really mustn't. Go to America with your captain. If that's what you feel like, do it. What could I give you? We've been through two wars: one general and one personal. We've all changed. I certainly feel completely different from what I was before. That's what I feel right now, and what are you going to do with someone who feels like that?"

His voice begins to break, and so he stops talking; to cover his embarrassment, he starts hunting in his pockets for a cigarette. He tries to light it, but the matches are damp, and that simple glitch is enough to humiliate him completely. He sits there with his head bowed, in silence. After a short pause, Elly says timidly, "What are you thinking about?" There are tears in her eyes. While Roberto was talking, a few tears had fallen, but he hadn't noticed. Now he takes refuge in sarcasm. "I'm thinking about matches," he says. "Doesn't your American ever use matches? Do you want me to ask you in American English, 'Got a match, baby?'" Without a word, Elly stands up and steps out of the car. "Where are you going?" Roberto asks her, weakly. But Elly just keeps walking away into the rain, quickening her pace as she goes.

A steam train is traveling the stretch of track that runs through the woods. The conductor rests his elbow on the window of the car as he carefully slows the speed of the train. Along the embankment, several workers greet the reopening of the line with satisfaction. In fact, the locomotive is going to be linked to the cars that had been abandoned in the clearing. A series of jolts wakes Roberto up: he's spent the night sleeping in the car and now he looks out, curious to see what's going on. He's happy to see that the train is moving slowly forward. He dangles his legs out of the car and lets himself be carried along. Unfortunately, the journey is very brief because the train immediately slows down and pulls into the village station.

There is a crowd of people in the station yard, and they surge towards the train as it draws to a halt. They are mostly Italian prisoners, and they come forward waving flags, cheering, and letting off firecrackers. They jostle each other, and some of them make flying leaps onto the steps of the cars or climb up onto the roofs. In the space of a few moments, before it has even stopped moving, the train is filled with ex-prisoners. Roberto is almost squashed in the rush. "What's going on?" he asks the person nearest him. "We're going home to Italy." But instead of cheering him up, the news seems to upset Roberto. He looks at all those excited faces and can't find it in himself to share their happiness. He feels empty, spent. How many times during his imprisonment had he dreamed that this would be the most beautiful day of his life? And yet here he is, assailed by a thousand feelings and fears, overcome by an infinite sadness.

But there is Erio, shaking him by the shoulder, for he had seen Roberto and climbed up next to him. Erio is happy and in the mood for fun. "Look at Alvaro," he says pointing to their friend who is dragging a little cart full of stuff he acquired in his "business" dealings over the last few months. Now he's trying to get the stuff into the car and take it home to Italy. But it's absurd to even think of such a thing—the train is crammed full of people and there's no room. So Alvaro starts arguing and loses his temper, but his shouts are lost in the general hubbub. It's a hot, sunny day. Along the length of the train there are a lot of women saying good-bye to relatives. This is the final, definitive farewell. Suddenly, Roberto jumps down to the ground. Erio calls him again and again, but Roberto doesn't even turn around. He's heading towards the village. In a field by the roadside, he stops to pick some flowers and then makes straight for Elly's house. But here, he gets a bitter disappointment. They tell him that she's just left; she's going away too. She was heading for the town square where there were some trucks that would take people to the North.

Roberto starts running, but as he gets nearer the square he slows down. Once again, he feels ashamed, as if what he is doing is a useless gesture, and when he gets to the square, he's seized by a sense of futility again. Still, he starts searching the faces of the crowd around the trucks. Finally, he sees Elly's friend the captain standing by a jeep. There's a mechanic fiddling with the engine. Roberto recognizes Elly's suitcase, but she's not there. Looking at the captain who is so elegant in his uniform, with his well-mannered gestures and his steady gaze that indicates such a different way of thinking from his own, Roberto suddenly realizes that he's still dressed like a tramp. He takes refuge in rummaging through his pockets for a cigarette: bits of candles and scraps of paper, shoelaces and a dirty handkerchief, and finally, a cigarette butt. He goes to light it, but the captain forestalls him by offering him one of his own Chesterfields. Roberto says no thanks and lights up his own instead.

After a moment, they hear Elly's voice as she waves good-bye to the American major at the command post where she'd just been to make her farewells. Roberto moves off a little ways and leans against a wall watching Elly get into the jeep. She sees him and looks at him sternly and very seriously. But then she seems to melt and is almost overcome with emotion as she approaches Roberto. "Aren't we even going to shake hands?" she asks him. Reluctantly, Roberto shakes her by the hand. "So now that we've got that out of the way . . ." he says. Elly makes a sad little gesture. "I just don't understand you, Roberto . . ." she whispers. And then, after a moment, she says sadly: "But I'm sure you love me."

Roberto is sitting there on the wall, his eyes cast down and his arms hanging limply between his knees: a man with no will-power. "Apparently, loving someone isn't enough," he says. And he doesn't even look up at Elly as the tears run down her face. Then, with a sudden movement, he gets up from the wall and walks away. Elly just looks at him. "I was going to give you some flowers," he says, turning around and showing her the tulips. Then he throws them on the ground and turns the corner, walking off to where he can see the train in the distance, literally covered with prisoners, all waving and shouting.

But before he can get to the station, he sees someone running along a side street. It's Jolanda. She's waving, as if to get someone's attention. She comes towards him, stumbling in her haste. You can see that she's trying to shout, but she's hoarse and out of breath. She's run away from the hospital where they had admitted her because she wants to go back to Italy with everybody else. Roberto runs up to her, but she has already fallen to the ground and her hands are clutching at the grass. He picks her up and makes her as comfortable as he can, but her face looks drained; she's gasping for breath and her eyes are dull and tired. You can see that she has no more strength. But the strange thing is, this look suits her; it seems to be just an extension of what she looked like when she was a prisoner, one of the brutalized women in the camp. And her eyes light up once they see Roberto, and he strokes her hair and tries to comfort her. For the second time that day he feels something inside him that amazes him and is almost a rebellion against his own nature: a sudden flash of feeling and emotion.

Roberto turns to look at the train. Miraculously, everyone seems to have gotten on board, and in a few moments it will leave. He can see Heidi running up to it and Erio happily leaning out to help her get in. He sees them embrace and again feels something melt inside him. Jolanda's feeble voice gets his attention as she says: "Leave me here, leave me . . . at least you go." But Roberto shakes his head. "I'll wait for you," he says. "We'll take another train tomorrow . . . or next week . . . I'm staying right here with you, Jolanda. We'll go home together, I'll take you back to your own village." Then he pauses and goes on: "And when you're in your own town you can get married . . . I've always said that you should marry someone from your own country. Then you'll see that we'll forget everything that's happened. At least, I hope we will."

But he stops again because he can hear Erio and Alvaro calling him over the noise of the crowd. However, he doesn't even turn around. His gaze is focused on the woods. "Jolanda," he says, his voice breaking with emotion, "I'm ashamed of what I'm about to tell you, especially at a moment like this. But I'm afraid of going back to being a normal person, with a peaceful, tidy life after all this horror and then all this freedom. I'm afraid of everything that we'll have to do to live in peacetime, having a family and normal, social routines. I'm afraid it's too difficult, and I don't even know who I could live with like that. I'm a wreck, rotten. I'm afraid that everything we've been through will turn out to be the only thing that ever happens to us in our lives. Do you know what I mean?"

As he looks down at her, he sees that she has closed her eyes and doesn't appear to be listening. He puts his hand in her lap, and he instinctively feels that while he was talking, Jolanda has died. He touches her and knows that he is right. Feeling lost, he turns around, looking for help. With a loud, deafening shriek, the train begins to move. Erio is there, waving to him, calling to him desperately. If Roberto gets up now and runs he can still make it to the train in time. But he doesn't move a muscle, and suddenly, that shame that he had told Jolanda about crushes him like a house knocked flat by a bomb. Trembling, he bends over Jolanda and kisses her cheek, calling her name, saying over and over: "Forgive me, forgive me!" He doesn't even notice the train that's leaving right in front of him, carrying away a chorus of shouts that echo down the valley. He turns around to look at it only when it's almost out of sight, and then he jumps up and starts running like the wind towards the town.

In the square, the trucks have already left. Only the jeep is still there, and the mechanic has just finished making his repairs and is closing the hood. After one last glance towards the point where Roberto had disappeared, Elly gets in, the captain by her side. She smiles, a little sadly. A German woman comes up to her and hands her a package of cakes. Elly thanks her but she's embarrassed. She has so many conflicting emotions. Then the jeep moves off, rapidly disappearing in the dust from the street. Now the square is empty and silent. The only sound is the engine of the jeep as it roars away into the distance. And then slowly, another sound is heard above it: Roberto's voice calling out, "Elly! . . . Elly!"

His voice gets louder and louder and now you can hear his footsteps. Roberto bursts into the square and stops to look around him. The only thing he can see is the cloud of dust left by the jeep slowly dissipating into the air. Roberto is devastated as if he only now realizes the value of what he has just lost. He will never see her again, never. He doesn't even have her address or her surname. It's ridiculous, but he doesn't even know her full name. He starts walking like a robot, and the town around him seems to have settled into a deep silence. The soldiers have disappeared. A German man raises the iron gate at the front of his store and greets a woman standing at an upstairs window. The postman walks by delivering his letters. A street-sweeper is cleaning the sidewalk. The windows of the houses are open, and inside you can see little children playing, women busying themselves in the kitchen.

Roberto stops in front of the garden of a particular house. Seeing him there, the woman inside sends her little boy to shut the gate, as if she is afraid of him. And then he realizes that he's the only one left who is dressed in rags; his face and his thoughts are out of place here. He starts walking again, more hurriedly now. The square is full of sunlight and it gives the place a party-like atmosphere. It's actually a Sunday, and he realizes that it's become important again to make a distinction between Sundays and the other days of the week. He follows some women who are going into church, and he hears from inside the sweet voices of a choir. Walking around the streets of the town again, he notices a soldier's metal helmet, upturned and filled with water, serving as a drinking trough for some hens. And he notices too the American signs posted all over the village, which, together with the small garrison that's left, regulate the life of the town and its citizens with their warnings and information.

Then he begins to run and run, until he reaches the woods and the clearing and beyond it the countryside with its fields of unripe corn. It's as if he can't believe his eyes: there's not a single sign of the terrible camp that once was there. Fresh, bright green grass has covered the earth, blending it in with the rest of the surroundings. The ruined barracks seem like innocent heaps of wood. There's nothing left of all the suffering of the past, and Roberto is overcome by a wave of weariness. He sees a German girl coming towards him, a beautiful girl who smiles at him as she passes. Roberto stops her with a gesture and looks at her. They are alone in the middle of a field; a few days before he would have taken advantage of the situation without another thought. But now he just waves his hand at the huts and says: "I wonder what happened to all the rats?" The girl, of course, doesn't understand and laughs and goes on her way. Roberto lays down on the ground and stares up at the sky, with the air of a man who wants to be left in peace.[3]

---

[3] In *Cinema Nuovo* 163 (1963), the publication of this treatment was prefaced by a letter from Antonioni to the critic Guido Aristarco:

Dear Aristarco, In a few days' time I will begin work on Red Desert; *in other words, this is a moment when I can't think about an old screenplay, not even about one of my other films. Every time, we begin all over again from scratch; this is the characteristic of our profession. Whether it's good or not, I don't know. But that's the way it is. Nothing is more quickly dated than an idea for a film.*

What I can say about Makaroni *is that we did some investigation among survivors of the war in order to write it. To the question, "What was the worst time of your life?" they all replied, "The concentration camp." And to the question, "What was the most beautiful time?" they all said, "Immediately afterwards." They meant by this the time in Germany that followed the end of the war. The Germans were in retreat, the Americans hadn't arrived yet, there was disorder, chaos, freedom in its raw state. Those who happened to live through it remember it with nostalgia. That is a sign that in our life today, with our social duties on the one hand and our morality on the other, there is no room for adventure. That's all I remember about* Makaroni.

Affectionately, M. A.

A DOCUMENTARY ON WOMEN[1]

I had gotten tired of seeing the same things all the time. The abbey at Pomposa, the castles of the Val d'Elsa, the chapel of the Scrovegni, the drawings of Leonardo da Vinci, the eruption of Mount Etna—there wasn't a single Italian documentary that showed anything except works of art or places of outstanding natural beauty. Why do they always show only these things? While I don't think I ever asked myself this question in such clear-cut terms, I certainly felt this way. What I was interested in was people, and I wrote screenplays about people. One was called *Stairs*. It was more a series of short sequences than a documentary—comic and dramatic scenes that occurred on stairs, depicting life's upward and downward movements—through which I hoped to communicate the anxiety of our times. But I didn't make that documentary, and so I never communicated this anxiety.

But I did make one about the boatmen on the Po River. It was called *Gento del Po* (*People of the Po Valley*). People, with their feelings, joys and sorrows, and their problems. And then I did one about the street sweepers in Rome. People thought it was poetic and it won a prize. Another one I made about

[1] 1966. In *TVC* 1 (July-August-September 1966): 26–30.

cartoon characters. People thought it was funny and gave it a prize too. (Afterwards, I also wrote a screenplay for a film about cartoons: *The White Sheik*. It was Fellini who directed that one.)

I could have continued down this road for a long time. I had enough ideas: the clerks in the telegraph office, the women who used to clean the trains when they got into the station, hostesses, prostitutes . . . I prepared the documentary about prostitutes with meticulous care, making in-depth investigations and scouting out locations. But the producer got scared off when he saw the material I had collected. It was just after the war and Rome was in complete chaos. It was an extraordinary atmosphere. In the evenings there was a party-like mood, excitement and women everywhere. People had just woken up from a nightmare and they wanted to give free reign to their natural impulses—even the lowest impulses. That's why there were so many women in prostitution: they were taking advantage of a particularly favorable climate. But I found things that would make your blood run cold: under-age prostitutes, some as young as seven or eight years old. Their territory was the Villa Borghese area.

My producer was a small, blonde young man with very gentlemanly manners. I always thought he was a bit of a sex maniac. His two, small blue eyes looked at you fastidiously and slightly lasciviously. When I gave him my screenplay about prostitution his gaze became softer than ever. He got up, went over to the window and opened it. Perhaps he needed a breath of fresh air. Then he turned to me and said: "I don't believe it." And so the game became one of convincing him that Rome was full of loose women. I had to take him to some houses in the suburbs and other hangouts in the city and introduce him to the prostitutes my inquiries had led me to: the madams, the pimps, a sordid underworld, greedy, barren, and scary. That was the very word that my producer used. "Too scary." But from that day forth, he changed his business hours. Before, he used to make appointments for the early evening, and meetings would drag on until late at night,

112

but from that moment onwards, you could only get to see him in the morning. After lunch he disappeared, and no one knew where he went. He lost weight too, about which his wife was very happy.

One morning, I said to him: "Let's make a documentary about women." His tired face suddenly brightened up. He got to his feet and went to open the window: I then understood that this was his instinctive reaction whenever he was excited. He asked me to bring him the screenplay as soon as I could.

That was how it came about that I started thinking about women, not as we men usually think of them, but "Woman" as a topic of discussion, as a theme to represent.

I have never bothered to ask myself why the screenplays I have written since then have mostly been about women or are centered around women more than they are around men (or so they tell me). As far as I'm concerned, it was an instinctive choice. But perhaps now, going back over things in my mind, I can make out two basic motives. One is material, the other is moral. Circumstances have always arranged things so that I have always lived surrounded by women. When I was little, I had three aunts and four female cousins. Three of them, in turn, had about another ten female cousins. When we went to the countryside, one of our favorite games was to shut ourselves in a barn full of hemp and pile on top of each other in a really big heap so that we were all squashed tightly together; a human pyramid of legs and arms, heads and thighs. I remember my aunt used to be very suspicious of these games, which were obviously unconscious, childish demonstrations of sensuality.

And I have always found myself in the thick of women's issues. It's useless to repeat how and why. Little crises over clothes, hair, shoes, bags, boyfriends, husbands, children, and lovers. But I liked that atmosphere. It enabled me to hear people talking about the world in a different way than I was used to, and I realized that it wasn't at all a silly way to look at things. And this is where we come to the second reason. Women perhaps have a more subtle, more sincere way of filtering reality. Women instinctively possess an acumen that men don't. They're less hypocritical. Men are forced by their jobs, and by the daily relationships that they have with other men, to control themselves, to tone down their reactions, to hide their feelings. Women, less so. Of course, I could be wrong. Nevertheless, as a man, every day I am forced, often with a certain amount of surprise, to note how much more clear-sighted women are than men, and often how much braver they are too.

The documentary I wanted to make was complex. But I remember the screenplay came out rather well. I spread my net wide. Women of all different countries and all different types: Swedish, American, Chilean, French, English, African, Italian, Russian, Chinese, etc. And then there were swimmers, shop assistants, nuns, school girls, clerks, domestic servants, widows, pregnant women, college students, fiancées, etc. Then the inquiry turned to consider women according to their most natural and inevitable classifications: the beautiful ones and the ugly ones.

There would be a lot to say, and a lot has already been said, about beautiful women. For example, as I walk along beside a beautiful woman I have often felt a sense of shame. Really beautiful women are full of a sort of frightening, unapologetic exhibitionism, not demonstrating the slightest regard for anyone who happens to be with them. As for the ugly ones, it was my intention to write a proper screenplay or treatment about them. A memory of my youth. I used to live in Ferrara, a city that is famous for its cult of beauty, and not only feminine beauty. My group of friends decided one day that we would start flirting with the ugly girls. You cannot imagine what happened. It was as if a wave of madness swept through the whole city, a new breeze freshened the spring air, a strange excitement, upsetting people's values, an affront to their sense of propriety: the ugly girls had taken possession of the city. Proud of being courted by us, they walked down the streets with their heads held high, boldly looking the men straight in the eye. The shop assistants all deserted their posts on the flimsiest of excuses, students cut school; they all wore flashy, bright colored outfits and had color in their cheeks as if they were enjoying a marvelous party. In short, they behaved as if they were beautiful. But the more distressing this sight became, the more we encouraged them and led them on with the cruelty that's typical of youth.

My documentary ended with an analysis that was very detailed. My aim was to deal with the theme in an abstract manner: Woman, *tout court*. To deconstruct her gestures, mannerisms and her gaze. To get down to the essence of femininity, identify it in its most recondite sense, fix it in images.

When my producer read the script he was enthusiastic. This time, he opened both the windows in his office. He was dripping with sweat and his hands were trembling. I had gone a bit overboard, I admit, in my description of the "eternal feminine," but I hadn't anticipated that he would react like this. He was literally in a frenzy. The thought of being in the middle of so many representatives of the fairer sex made him dizzy. And yet, the documentary was never made. Do you know why? Because of a woman. My producer met her right at this time and fell madly in love with her: he disappeared, changed his lifestyle, left his wife and children . . .

I met him some time ago and we reminisced about our old project. His comment was: "What an opportunity I lost!" But then his attention immediately wandered to a woman who was passing by. I noticed that he almost seemed inclined to follow her. It was more an impulse than an actual movement I sensed, and he immediately repressed it. Nowadays, he has gray hair and an almost tired face. His eyes have lost that look of lasciviousness and their old sparkle, and instead you can read in them the bitterness of a life full of regrets.

THE COLOR OF JEALOUSY[1]

*(The opening credits roll against a backdrop of dense traf-
fic and the chaotic street life of Rome.)*

A street in Rome at dusk. A man in his car, stuck at a red
light, his fingers drumming on the passenger seat. He looks
impatient and checks his watch. He's surrounded by a lot of
yellow taxis, and in the taxis there are all sorts of people: a
very calm guy who is waiting patiently, another who is reading
the newspaper, a fat man who is constantly fidgeting, someone
who is smiling to himself, someone who is talking to a female
companion and making her laugh, a nervous woman who is
taking such deep drags on her cigarette that she almost gets
through half of it in one breath, etc. The taxi drivers all look
depressed and have the same indifferent pose.

The man turns around to look at the passengers in the taxis,
and they too turn to look out of their own windows; when
people's gazes meet, some seem embarrassed to see someone
up close like that. But everybody ends up looking at the impatient man, the only one in a private car. The man is embarrassed by it, and he becomes even more uncomfortable when

---

[1] 1971. Screenplay.

he realizes there is a long-haired young man next to him who is sketching and looking up at him every two seconds as if drawing his portrait. The man changes his position and turns his head away, but the other guy carries on regardless. So the man hides his face behind his hand and sneaks a look at the time. Then he checks the light. It is still red.

Everybody is watching the light, and each person sees the red circle differently. To those who are farther away from it, it seems small, and to those who are near, it seems bigger. It's biggest of all to the impatient man, and it seems to get larger and larger until it becomes a big red sun, staining the yellow hoods of the taxis red. In fact, evening is falling rapidly. How much time has passed? It seems like hours to the impatient man. The sun that is the red light seems to be setting over the yellow hoods of the taxis until it disappears beneath the horizon and a pale green light shines upon them. The taxis and the man's car all set off together; but the space they leave behind is soon taken by other cars.

Another street in Rome. Like the first one, this street looks like an unfinished drawing, set against a uniform beige background. But there are lots of realistic episodes to be seen against this background, typical street incidents in realistic colors: people gesticulating as they walk along or sit at tables outside a bar. One of these individuals sitting down particularly stands out because the impatient man's gaze falls on him. But then a horse and buggy crosses the street with a deafening clatter of hooves and wheels: it is full of tourists and their laughter echoes into the distance.

Matteo—that's the man's name—looks at his watch. He checks the clock in the dashboard against his wristwatch. He does this while recklessly but calmly continuing to drive on. In fact, he's a very calm sort of guy, about thirty-five, with longish hair that he sometimes runs his fingers through. But despite his self-control, it's obvious he's in a hurry and in a state of mental turmoil. His self-control comes from his tendency to be self-critical, and this quality keeps his fits of jealousy—which we shall shortly see—from becoming foolish or ridiculous. For example, he starts to shout at someone who manages to miss his car by a hair but then immediately breaks into laughter and makes a gesture of apology to the other driver. He's easily distracted: now he has to brake hard because a gorgeous woman in black steps in front of him and blocks his line of vision. Matteo stares after her, lost in thought, and is only brought back to reality by the sound of car horns honking behind him.

The road takes him out of town onto a tree-lined avenue. Overhead, the tallest branches are intertwined to form a kind of green roof, and at the sides there are green bushes. Traveling through this greenery Matteo should be reassured, but it is just too much green, especially when lit up by his headlights which are also a sickly greenish color. In fact, they make the green plants look false, as if they were made of plastic. Matteo drives on, wrapped up in his own thoughts, without taking any further notice of the outside world whose colors are slowly fading into darkness.

As the street lights get fewer and farther between, finally disappearing altogether, Matteo settles into driving and concentrates on going as fast as possible. In the darkness, the windshield seems like a blackboard with warning signs, traffic lights, and oncoming cars sketched on it. But Matteo goes faster and concentrates only on the dull gray of the pavement. He can't see a thing and leans forward towards the windshield. The headlights of the oncoming cars make him blink and he mutters to himself. He almost knocks over a trash can by the side of the road. He really can't see a thing. What's the matter with him? Finally he realizes he hasn't switched on his own headlights, so he puts them on, merrily cursing himself. White stripes and arrows appear in the light of the headlights, painted on the road surface. A huge array of straight and curvy signs. Matteo stares straight ahead of him.

MATTEO (*voice-over*): What's the point of calling each other every day, loving each other, if we can never get beyond these same old issues, these stupid arguments . . . Each time I promise myself this will be the last time, that I'm not going to stand for it anymore. And yet, every few weeks or so, every month, when it seems that everything is going along just fine, something sets us off and our hang-ups start to get on each other's nerves, we don't get along anymore and we have a fight. (*Pause.*) I didn't want to go and see her this evening. But we said some pretty serious things.

Yvonne's face appears against a pink background. The background seems to be a bedroom wall; we can recognize this from some furniture in one corner. Later we will see that the house is furnished in the same style throughout, but now Yvonne is talking on the phone.

MATTEO (*voice-over*): If you ever think you can beat me . . .

YVONNE: And if you ever think you're unbeatable . . . You have no top-spin, you can't even do a proper smash or a volley . . . You can't volley. Whenever you're up against someone who can volley, like Gigo, then you never score anything.

MATTEO (*voice-over*): Gigo?

YVONNE: You know, Arrigo.

Backview of Matteo with his ear glued to the phone. He doesn't seem to be in any particular place. He turns slightly and one eye comes into the picture; he's sarcastic, biting.

MATTEO: Well, he's a pro!

YVONNE (*voice-over*): Oh sure, a pro!

MATTEO: At least, he's pretty good; I mean really good. Not like you. You just think that all you need to do is train a bit harder and you'll be able to beat me. Go on, admit it; you'd give your right arm to be able to do that.

YVONNE: My right arm, eh? Well, I don't know about that.

Frontview of Matteo, talking happily, now that he's gotten to the heart of the matter.

MATTEO: Yes you would. As far as you're concerned, I'm just someone you want to beat, your number one adversary. And not just in table tennis; in everything.

Yvonne makes a gesture of protest and Matteo wags his finger at her.

MATTEO: Yes you do. You really see me like that.

YVONNE: Like crows.

MATTEO: What have crows got to do with it?

YVONNE: Crows don't see things like we do, you know. They see black birds as white. And white pigeons look pink to them and seagulls look yellow. Didn't you know that? Why is that, do you think?

MATTEO: I don't know. I'm not a crow.

YVONNE: No, I mean why do I see you as my adversary?

MATTEO: That's just how you are. You're the sort of person who prefers to destroy other people, humiliate them, instead of the usual tendency in love, which is to destroy oneself, merge your own identity into someone else's. It's not easy to be with a woman who's always trying to humiliate you, you know.

Yvonne, looking very calm.

YVONNE: What about you? Don't you always want to win too? Perhaps what I want to defeat is your doggedness, your absurd competitiveness . . . I'd like to put a check on your aggressiveness. There's nothing wrong with wanting to win, provided that it's in the context of a game. But the way you carry on, our whole relationship gets dragged into things, and I don't like that.

MATTEO: What don't you like?

YVONNE: I don't like the way it was when we were in the mountains, when I'd look at you in the evenings . . . well it was the morning by that time since we always went to bed at four or five o'clock . . . and you were still thinking about the game. You don't know the sort of mood you get into. There was one night when I wanted to go and block up the door to that stationery store with bricks and cement, just wall them all up inside because it would make you feel better for having lost to them.

MATTEO (*voice-over, amused*): Can you imagine that guy's face if he'd come to open his store in the morning and couldn't find the door anymore?

He laughs at the thought.

YVONNE: It may well be funny as a joke but it's still crazy. It's not easy to be around someone as obsessive as you.

Before he answers, Matteo lets a moment go by during which he tries to control a sudden sense of irritation.

MATTEO: Listen, Yvonne. I don't like feeling I'm always on trial.

YVONNE: You can't do anything about that; it's just the way it is when you're with someone.

MATTEO: Oh really? Well then, tell me, what standards am I being judged by?

YVONNE: I'm judging you in comparison to myself.

Matteo is slowly getting worked up.

MATTEO: Oh no. You've got to take me the way I am, Yvonne . . . and the rest of life the way it is: fear and pain, dreams and madness . . . In books they've been talking about nothing else for centuries, so what makes you think you are going to change human nature? You know, this is what I do for a living from nine in the morning until five at night, and I'm telling you that it's not easy to tell if someone's normal or mad or a little mad or a lot mad. Words are ambiguous things . . . Who's normal anyway?

He makes a vague gesture.

MATTEO: But that's not good enough for you. You think I'm mad; funny but mad. (*Shouting.*) Well then, see how mad I can be!

Yvonne holds the receiver away from her ear; the loud voice hurts her eardrums.

YVONNE: Don't shout. You cannot imagine how shrill your voice is over the phone.

We see Matteo again from the front. He looks absolutely toxic, but he's under control.
MATTEO: Perhaps you should change the way you're talking too, Yvonne. After all, no one is forcing you to carry on with this.
YVONNE (*coldly*): Very true, no one's forcing me.

A pause. Yvonne lets it go on while she thinks about her reply.
YVONNE: Now that I think about it, Arrigo's voice has quite a nice sound to it.

Matteo gets worked up again.
MATTEO: That's more like it. Call Arrigo, why don't you? He's normal. Just think how many nice games you could have against him.

Yvonne's face is completely in shadow. The receiver is still held slightly away from her ear. Silence.

Matteo doesn't say anything, and neither does Yvonne. After a moment of apparent conviction but in reality of deep uncertainty, Matteo makes the decision to put down the receiver and cut off the conversation.

Yvonne hears the telephone click, and in turn, she slowly lowers the receiver with a sigh that suggests her patience is stretched to the limit.

Matteo is standing next to the little table where the phone is standing. He looks as if he doesn't know what to do and makes a meaningless little gesture. Then he goes over to another table but has no reason to be there either; as he raises his arm to pick something up, he realizes that his hand is trembling.

He raises his other hand: same story. He smiles contemptuously at himself and then assumes a nonchalant air, walking as if he knows exactly where he is going. But as he passes the phone table, he can't resist the temptation and picks it up to dial a number. Then he pauses, the receiver halfway to his ear and his hand resting on the dial, thinking about something.

The images look less real now. Matteo is on the phone talking to Yvonne.
MATTEO: How are you then?

Yvonne is very serious, with a long-suffering look about her.
YVONNE: Bad, very bad. How do you think I am?

Matteo smiles in satisfaction.

The color of the image changes, and the phone call starts over.
MATTEO: How are you then?

Yvonne is smiling and appears calm.
YVONNE: Fine. How about you? What are you calling back for? Didn't you say . . .

Matteo frowns . . . and hangs up. Suddenly the images take on their original, true colors because the gesture of hanging up belongs with the scene that had been interrupted before these two possible outcomes.

Matteo drops into a chair sighing wearily, but it's a nervous weariness. He stretches his arms and, in the heat, unbuttons his shirt. Someone rings the doorbell and he goes to answer it. It's the concierge with a letter for him. Matteo takes it, shuts the door, and then drops it on the floor. The envelope is a pale shadow on the equally pale white floor.

Matteo goes back into the living room. He switches on the TV: there's a sort of film with people in a room talking about jewel robberies. The phone rings, and thinking it was his phone, Matteo runs to pick up the receiver; but no, it was a phone in the movie. Matteo changes the channel; on the state TV network there's a news item that manages to distract him from his own thoughts. They've uncovered a coup d'état and some people—nobody of any importance—have been arrested. It is the second coup in nearly three years, but the government doesn't seem very worried. Even the announcer makes light of it, though the details of what he's saying belie this levity: extra police in the capital, the army is being held in barracks in a state of alert, a small arsenal has been found at the villa of a very high ranking official, etc. The broadcast isn't very long, and as soon as it's over, Matteo goes to the window. Below, the street seems completely normal. The same old traffic, the traffic signal at the corner with the policeman directing as usual, and people walking along the sidewalk perfectly calm, or at least that's how they seem. Around him, other windows are lit as the people inside go about their everyday business. You can even hear some bells in the distance.

In the bathroom, there's a blue and brown butterfly flying about which finally comes to rest on the mirror. But it immediately takes off again and alights on the soap.

Matteo comes in and stretches out his hand for the soap, nearly squashing the butterfly as he does so. He picks it up and tries to get the soap off the butterfly's wings and wash it clean, but the butterfly shows no signs of life; so he puts it on the washstand and starts to comb his hair.

MATTEO (*voice-over*): It was right not to call Yvonne. You can't sort these things out over the phone. There's only one way to do it: make a trip to Pescara . . . a trip to Pescara . . . Pescara . . .

He keeps on like this until he's fixed his hair the way he wants it.

MATTEO (*voice-over*): . . . and then I can explain things to her face-to-face.

He takes a close look at his reflection in the mirror: his beard isn't too long; it'll do. The butterfly has started flying around again and brushes past his face.

Matteo's car is flying along the freeway. It's really dark and the headlights illuminate a bend in the road through the mountains. The radio is playing classical music.

The same car on the same freeway, with the same bend in the road, but in daylight. It's a cloudy dawn on an autumn day and the radio is broadcasting the political news.

Matteo in a different car, but the same freeway and bend in the road. It's midday in summer. The radio is playing pop music.

Matteo in the car we saw at the beginning. Matteo is driving, holding the wheel with two fingers. The white line down the center of the road seems to run along with a life of its own, curving and twisting through the turns in the road. Matteo stares at the line which gradually gets wider and wider until it becomes the whole glistening white road. Signs pass with directions to various towns and mile markers indicating the distance left to go. The car's dashboard is lit up and you can see the miles fly by on the odometer.

The headlights of other cars catching up to him are like yellow dots in the rearview mirror which get larger and larger until they fill it completely and cast a yellow glow inside the car. The headlights of oncoming cars are two blinding white spots shooting their beams into his windshield like bullets. The brake lights of cars that Matteo manages to overtake are like two red dots that light up for a moment as he passes them and then go out. Matteo is a bit dazed by it all.

He glances at the odometer and speedometer. They're just more numbers on a blackboard that's already full of sums. They are the display screen of a calculator, or the voice of an astronaut chanting numbers and more numbers.

Matteo's face seems to focus on a single thought.

MATTEO (*voice-over*): I wonder what Yvonne is doing right now? What's she thinking about? Did she really mean it when she said she'd call Arrigo . . . or was that just a threat to get back at me? If she was serious, did she do it straight after I hung up, or did she wait a little to make up her mind? If she phoned him, I'll bet he went straight over to Pescara in his car. Which would mean he's on this freeway too, somewhere. Any of these cars overtaking me could be him, or any of the ones that I'm overtaking. Perhaps he's in this one here . . .

Meanwhile, we see Yvonne on the phone to Arrigo. She's naked, having just stepped out of the bath, and she has a towel in her hand. He looks happy, while she seems a bit cold but decisive. We don't hear what they say to each other because their words are covered by Matteo's voice-over, but it's clear that Yvonne has invited Arrigo to come and see her. In fact, as soon as he hangs up, Arrigo slips on a sort of jacket—he dresses really well—goes out of his apartment and gets into his car.

The car in front of Matteo isn't going very fast and over-taking it is easy: obviously, the guy driving it isn't in any particular hurry.

After passing the car, Matteo goes back to staring straight ahead of him, scanning the area lit up by his headlights.

MATTEO (*voice-over*): There's only one thing to do: I mustn't let Arrigo pass me, whatever car he's in. This car has four people in it, so it can't be him.

And a car overtakes him with four people in it.

MATTEO (*voice-over*): The problem is that cars with just one person in them account for most of the traffic on the freeway.

What make of car does he drive? Something sporty, I seem to remember.

While he hasn't been concentrating, the car has drifted into the middle of the roadway, and another car behind him now flashes its headlights to be allowed to pass. Matteo laughs as if to say, "Not on your life, buddy," and he moves farther into the middle of the road and turns around to try and see who this impatient driver might be. But the headlights of the other car dazzle him. The other guy begins to honk his horn and tries to overtake him, using all sorts of maneuvers to force Matteo to move over. Some of these tricks are so dangerous that Matteo is indeed forced to give in and move over. The driver is a woman, and she makes angry gestures at him through the window. Matteo laughs and answers by opening and shutting his mouth without making any sounds. But then suddenly, he makes an angry movement, accelerates, catches up to the other car and overtakes it. Now the two cars are locked in a furious and dangerous race. Matteo has the advantage on the turns, but the woman, having the more powerful engine, has the advantage on the straightaways. In the end, Matteo gives in with a grimace, as if the driver and the whole situation has begun to bore him. Making a big show of indifference, he switches on the radio: they're broadcasting one of the usual game shows. The presenter, a guy who sounds like Corrado,[2] or maybe even Corrado himself, is interviewing one of the contestants.

PRESENTER: And you Miss Patterson, what do you do?

CONTESTANT: Peterson, not Patterson.

PRESENTER: Oh I'm sorry. I guess I didn't have that down as "pat" as I thought.[3] (*Laughter.*) Anyway, what do you do for a living?

CONTESTANT: I'm a driver.

PRESENTER: A driver? What sort of driver? With a private family or a limousine service?

---

[2] A famous Italian game-show host. [Translator]

[3] The Italian original includes an equally weak pun, typical of game-show humor. [Translator]

CONTESTANT: A taxi driver.

PRESENTER: Oh, a taxi driver! Well then Miss Peterson, you must get all sorts of people in your cab, eh?

CONTESTANT: Sure!

PRESENTER: And tell me, do you get more, er, "business," from men or from women?

CONTESTANT: More from men.

PRESENTER: More from men, eh? Now, among these men— and this is a bit of an impertinent question, but don't worry, there's no one listening (*laughter*) so you can tell me the truth— among these men, have you ever had any that, ahem, when they find themselves in a cab with an attractive young lady like you, try to give you a nice big tip, shall we say?

CONTESTANT: Oh sure, plenty.

PRESENTER: And what do you do? Hold out your hand and grab it . . .

Matteo turns off the radio with annoyance. The human voice is replaced by the hum of the engine: smooth and steady, a bland sort of noise that merges with the shapeless, colorless monotony beyond the windshield.

Matteo can't manage to control a sudden enraged impulse. He presses the pedal to the metal and grips the steering wheel tighter. There's a bend in the road, and he takes it without slowing down, feeling the car slipping away from him towards the guardrail at the right-hand side of the road. He tries to straighten it out, but there's nothing he can do about it; the car sideswipes the rail and begins to careen alongside it, and try as he might, there's nothing that Matteo can do to get it back on the road. The car spins, and after a long skid comes to a halt in the middle of the road, facing the opposite direction of the way it was going before.

Matteo didn't have time to let in the clutch and the engine has stalled. There's deep silence all around. Matteo gets out and realizes that the road is wet; that's why he skidded. It's been raining recently. Matteo sits down on the guardrail, a little shaken. Everything is pitch black around him except for a few lights, far away in the mountains, and of course, his car headlights. The stretch of road in front of him is not only wet but stained with oil and grease, and the raindrops that fall on it make it shine with iridescent colors. One of these drops seems to be shaped like a face, like Yvonne's face, and its colors are her colors.

After a moment, Matteo sees two other headlights coming up the freeway. He gets up, opens the car door of his vehicle, and puts on the hazard warning lights.

The other vehicle is a big truck with a sign on its rear: *CAUTION: Race Horses In Transit.* Two men get out of it. One of them, the driver, is a stocky man with a beard. The other is a small guy, about fifty years old, with a half-comical, half-gloomy appearance; he looks like an ex-jockey.

TRUCK DRIVER: Something wrong?

Matteo gestures at his car as if to say, "See for yourself." Together, the three of them push the car to the side of the road.

TRUCK DRIVER: Let's have a look at it then.

Matteo opens the hood and the driver starts to fiddle with the engine. The other little man looks at his watch as if worried about the delay. Nobody speaks. The silence is broken by a neighing sound from inside the truck. The little man jumps and glances at the truck. There's another neigh and another. The little man makes a sign to the driver who has stopped fiddling under the hood, and they open the rear door of the truck, with Matteo behind them.

Inside the truck is a beautiful, shining black horse. On the ground, in a pool of blood, there's a little dog that the horse has trampled. The little man looks at the scene in horror. It's as if he's witnessing an enormous tragedy, and the driver is also shocked. Matteo looks inside the truck and at the two men without fully understanding, although he feels the horror and the shock of that scene with them.

DRIVER: Perhaps it was when we were in the bar.

Matteo turns to the little man.

MATTEO: How come there was a dog in there? Did you know he was there?

The jockey doesn't answer him, and the driver makes a gesture as if to say, "Of course we did."

DRIVER: He's a dog from the stables.

The jockey opens his mouth and says, almost to himself:

JOCKEY: And how's he supposed to run on Sunday?

MATTEO: What?

DRIVER: He wouldn't even get in the truck unless the dog was there, he won't eat . . . let alone race.

There's a pause. Everybody looks at the horse which has taken a step towards the dog and raised its hoof as if to touch him, but doesn't quite dare.

DRIVER: What the hell got into him?

Then he turns to the jockey and points at the dog.

DRIVER: Shall we take him away?

The other guy's face seems to say, we can give it a try, and he takes a handful of oats and gives them to the horse who won't touch them. The driver meanwhile has gotten the dog out and then he goes to the driver's cab.

A car with its brights on tears past them in the outside lane and Matteo follows it with his gaze: as before, the red taillights grow smaller and vanish into the distance.

The driver has come back with a pistol, and he carries the

dog to the edge of the road and fires two shots. Inside the truck, the horse nervously shifts and starts to pull on its halter. The jockey jumps into the truck, strokes its neck, and gives it a lump of sugar, but the horse still refuses to eat. Then he gets down, and the driver closes the door before turning to Matteo.

DRIVER: Well then, shall we try and get you started?

Matteo tries the starter and the engine fires. After revving it a little, Matteo switches it off.

MATTEO: It's fine, thank you.

He nods at the dog.

MATTEO: I'm really sorry . . .

The driver shrugs his shoulders and then points at the jockey, who is walking slowly towards the driver's cab as if to say, "He is the one you should feel bad for." After a moment, the truck moves off, and the roar of the engine can't drown out one last neigh.

It's raining harder now, and Matteo turns toward his car to see the headlights' beams striking the dog's body just in front of his bumper. To move the car he will first have to move the dog. Matteo does so with a certain amount of distaste, trying not to get blood on himself. But he can't avoid it. The headlights of another car quickly overtake him and seem to make the blood even redder as it stains his hands. Remembering his haste, Matteo gets into the car again and looks at the time.

We see the vehicle on the freeway again. It's pouring, and all we can see is the square of the windshield, swept clean by the wipers. The rest is darkness. The yellow and red lights of other cars appear through a whirlwind of raindrops that lash the car.

MATTEO (voice-over): I can't see a damn thing . . . and maybe Arrigo is in one of these cars. The only thing to do is try and pass them all.

He overtakes one of them with two people in it; Matteo speeds away. His headlights reveal snatches of the mountainous landscape, until gradually the light increases as if the dawn has suddenly appeared, and the car seems to slow down. There are mountains, white, jagged peaks all around, and the landscape is covered in snow. It's a view from the window of a house.

In a rather large room—a basement or garage or attic—Yvonne is playing table tennis with a tall, slim young man; he's not good-looking, and he has a strange, almost vulgar face. He's playing very well; there's a considerable difference in ability between him and the young girl. But she seems happy, because even with this really good opponent, she's playing far above her usual standard.

Matteo walks into the room just as Yvonne aims a powerful shot that not even Arrigo—the young man in question—can hit back.
ARRIGO: Wow!

Yvonne laughs excitedly. She starts playing again, and this time it's Arrigo's turn to smash an unbeatable shot over the net. Yvonne throws her paddle on the table with a shout of disappointment, and the young man goes over to her.
ARRIGO: If you hold it like that, you'll never hit it straight.

And he rearranges her hand on the handle of the paddle.
ARRIGO: It's not that there's any one way of doing it properly; people hold it however they find most comfortable. The Japanese hold it one way, and the Chinese in another . . . but having said that . . .

Matteo looks at them, slightly annoyed. Remembering him standing there, Yvonne turns around.
YVONNE: Come on, let's have a game, you and me.

Matteo doesn't move. Arrigo leaves the room and holds out the paddle as he passes Matteo. But before he disappears, he asks Yvonne:

ARRIGO: Is he any good?

YVONNE: Well . . . he's kind of violent . . . very . . .

ARRIGO: Like the Hungarians. In fact, you look a bit Hungarian Matteo . . .

He walks off, stopping to talk to another girl in the corridor, putting his arm around her. You can see them laugh together and start to walk off. Yvonne moves over to Matteo.

MATTEO: I don't feel like playing.

He's in a bad mood and walks down the corridor, up (or down) a staircase and into a bedroom. Yvonne comes behind him. She's staring at him, wondering what can have irritated him. She goes over to him again and he looks at her a little strangely.

MATTEO: Why did you go and play while I was still up in the bedroom?

Yvonne is honestly surprised.

YVONNE: Why shouldn't I have?

MATTEO: Because you should have waited for me.

YVONNE: Look, Matteo, why don't you take a shower?

MATTEO: Because I don't want to have a shower. I want to play table tennis.

YVONNE: Well, first you don't and now you do. Did you want to play with me or with Arrigo?

Now it's Matteo's turn to be surprised.

MATTEO: What's Arrigo got to do with it? . . . Why would I want to play him?

YVONNE: Oh, I don't know . . . just to pick up a few tips.

MATTEO: What's that supposed to mean? That I'm not good enough for you now you've had some lessons from him?

134

Yvonne doesn't answer. Her expression seems to say that it's not worth the fuss, but Matteo keeps looking at her, challenging her.

YVONNE: OK then, the two of us will play.

They set off back down the stairs and the corridor until Matteo stops. There's a book on a shelf fixed to the wall, and Matteo picks it up as if weighing it in his hands.

MATTEO: What's my book doing here?

YVONNE: Did you finish reading it?

MATTEO: Of course not.

He seems unhappy, worried. Yvonne looks at him with concern.

MATTEO: And I don't know how many more days I can keep waiting here for a phone call that never comes.

YVONNE: Well, why don't you call them?

Matteo snaps.

MATTEO: Just like that, I'm supposed to call them? The clinic doesn't call so I'm supposed to call them.

He makes a gesture as if to say, "That's wonderful logic," but his expression contradicts him: he's ironic and bitter.

MATTEO: You know Yvonne, there are moments when I can't stand the good points about you and I prefer the bad ones.

He says this with the book in his hand as he retraces his steps back up the corridor with Yvonne trailing along behind.

YVONNE: What good points can't you stand?

MATTEO: This ruthless logic of yours, your bluntness. You make things too simple. I might have a thousand reasons for not calling them, or just the flimsiest pretext, but to me it's still a valid decision.

YVONNE: And my bad points?

135

Matteo makes another gesture, as if her bad points are too many to describe. But it's obvious that, in the meantime, he's had another thought, and he fidgets nervously. However, his voice is steady when he says:

MATTEO: To hell with vacations and enjoying oneself . . . this idea of getting away from it all and relaxing . . . I don't want to relax. I don't want to be always spinning in neutral. Relaxation is inertia, death.

They've come to the stairs, and here they pass Arrigo in the corridor, who raises his hand as if he's going to touch her breasts or waist, but instead he raises it all the way to his head and strokes her hair. But he does it in such a familiar way that Matteo almost might not be there, and he's very put out by it. Still, he says nothing, and Yvonne doesn't even notice. She moves in front of Matteo into the bedroom and goes into the bathroom. Matteo sits down in an armchair and starts flipping through his book, as if this is the only thing in the world he wants to do at the moment. But after a while he raises his eyes and looks around him. Mechanically, he picks up a newspaper from the floor and starts to read one of the articles. The first few lines say: "Dissatisfied with the bill that has already been approved by the House and has just been passed to the Senate, teachers in high schools and middle schools are threatening to give the go-ahead for action in the fall semester unless Parliament changes the plans under discussion."

Yvonne walks by him, naked.

Matteo in his car on the freeway again. Trying to fake an ironic expression, he shakes his head as if he disapproved of himself. With a roar that makes him jump, a sports car speeds by and in a flash disappears in front of him. Matteo can't help recognizing the driver as Arrigo. He immediately accelerates to catch the other car, but the two red lights in front of him are steadily pulling away. Matteo speeds up even more, but it's useless; the distance between them is increasing. Matteo is doing

70, 80, 90 miles an hour . . . it's hopeless. With a chilling inevitability, the two red taillights grow smaller and smaller. But Matteo doesn't take his eyes off the road. His headlights show a white line in front of him which disappears into the darkness beyond the cone of light from his car. Beyond the line, the two red lights grow dimmer and dimmer until they finally disappear. Then Matteo pulls out a cigarette and lights up. Meanwhile, he overtakes another car with a man in it; Matteo slows down enough so he can see who it is. The other guy turns around and makes a gesture as if to say, "What are you looking at?" so Matteo accelerates ahead.

MATTEO (*voice-over*): All I need is to be a few minutes ahead of him. If she sees that I've rushed over to her, Yvonne will forget the reasons for our quarrel, and everything will go back to being the way it was before. And that prick, Arrigo, will know she only called him over because of what had gone on between the two of us, and he'll feel so out of it he won't want to hang around. In fact . . .

Matteo's expression suddenly changes as he gets a new idea.
MATTEO (*voice-over*): In fact, at this very moment, Yvonne might be regretting what she said to me; she might be trying to call me back . . . or maybe she had the same idea as me and thought the best thing to do would be to come in person, and she got behind the wheel and right now is headed in the opposite direction.

As Matteo is sitting at the steering wheel thinking this over, a car comes around the curve towards him. As they cross paths, there is an explosion of light as the headlights are reflected off windshields and side windows, the wet asphalt and then . . . total darkness. The sound of the rain and the car itself drown out the sound of the other car which seems to be a shadow, the merest puff of a breeze. Matteo makes a sad little gesture. After a few moments he sees another car coming towards him. He stops, gets out, and leaning out the window to get a better look at whoever it is, he waits for the car to overtake him. But the only thing he gets is a splash of water.

It's not raining anymore, and through a gap in the clouds the moon has come up. You can see some strange fires in the mountains. Matteo sits down on the guardrail by the edge of the freeway to look at the moon: it's full and very bright.

MATTEO (*voice-over*): The moon!

He shakes his head, laughing and looks up at it. A pause.

The mountains stand out sharper now against the slowly clearing sky. They are white with snow and lit up by the moon.

It's in one of these mountain valleys that the house is situated. Seated around a table in the living room are Yvonne, Matteo, Arrigo, and his girlfriend, the same girl we saw him talking to in the corridor in the previous sequence, plus another older man and a young woman with brown hair and a dark expression: her name is Anita. Anita has a nervous habit of twisting her wedding ring around her finger when she's particularly tense.

The game they are playing is called "Racing Demon," and it consists of laying down the cards in little piles and rows in front of oneself. You have to get rid of your cards as fast as possible, and the first person to be left without any is the winner. It's a game that calls for quick wits, fast reflexes, good eyesight, and intense concentration: getting to a pile of cards just seconds after someone else beats you to it causes shouts of rage. There's not a moment's pause, and everybody's nerves are stretched right until the end of the game.

So that's the situation. There's no conversation, only exclamations of triumph or frustration, broken words, monosyllables, and sighs. Yvonne is the quickest. Matteo does his best, but he's hampered by his glasses (he doesn't usually wear them), and he can't keep up with her. He's given up on winning by now, but he still wants to avoid coming in last. He manages to come in second to last, not without some arguing, because he's put down a two and a three simultaneously using both hands and that's against the rules.

ARRIGO: It's not allowed, it's not allowed . . . you can't use both hands together.

Matteo's reaction is completely out of all proportion.

MATTEO: Well how the devil am I supposed to put down two cards with one hand?

ARRIGO: I don't know, it's an English game so why don't you call the Queen of England and ask her?

MATTEO: See! You can't answer that one!

ARRIGO: The rule is that you can only use one hand; you just have slow reflexes. Once you're off the phone with the Queen you'd better call a neurologist and have them checked out.

Matteo is furious and Yvonne has to intervene.

YVONNE: You should both go to the neurologist and have your brains checked out.

ARRIGO: *He's* my doctor. Do you think he's any good?

He points at Matteo who shrugs his shoulders in a sulk. Everyone around him is wearing a very forced smile. You can sense the rancor and resentment, the dislike beneath these exchanges, as the conversation quickly widens to include everybody. People are saying things like: "What matters is the cards in the pile on your left"; "What's the point of playing if you don't follow the rules?"; "Games are a serious business you know"; "Oh, don't be so stupid"; "That's typical of a doctor." This last comment is directed at Matteo who is the angriest of all. Only Anita is calm, and Yvonne is glowing because she won. Anita goes up to her:

ANITA: You are so good . . . I don't know how you do it.

Yvonne smiles with pleasure and, in gratitude, holds out her hand towards Anita, who immediately gives it a squeeze. Yvonne pulls away and moves towards the others. The forty-year-old guy, who has followed the whole thing with amusement, smiles at her with affectionate understanding and kisses her on the cheek. Anita is smiling too, a little sadly but with affection.

Matteo too has witnessed this episode. He's very quick and catches onto almost everything. But he's immediately distracted by Arrigo's girlfriend who's standing right in front of him.

GIRLFRIEND: So what shall we play tomorrow night?

ARRIGO: Yes, tell us. What argument will we have tomorrow? It always ends up like that . . .

The girl goes over to Arrigo and whispers something to him. Arrigo bursts out laughing, and she slips her hand under his shirt and strokes his chest.

FORTY-YEAR-OLD: I have an idea of what to play, but we'll have to drink a bit more before I tell you.

YVONNE: Good idea . . . Will you help me Anita?

Together the two women go over to a liquor cabinet and begin to fix something to drink.

MATTEO: How about a downhill ski race?

A chorus of "Yes . . . what a good idea? . . . After lunch though, how about one o'clock?"

FORTY-YEAR-OLD: Count me in, provided we can do it in teams of two.

More voices saying, "Yes, it's less tiring that way . . . No, why do we have to have teams?"

ARRIGO: Yvonne, how about you and me?

YVONNE: I don't know if that's a good idea. Matteo is much faster downhill; he's more reckless.

ARRIGO: Exactly. He'll leave us so far behind it'll just be you and me in the woods together . . . won't that be nice?

FORTY-YEAR-OLD: At least three runs, eh? Give me a piece of paper and I'll draw up a table so we can keep score. Matteo . . . Matteo! Have you got a bit of paper?
MATTEO: Go see the guy at the stationery store.

He's talking almost angrily. He looks very sulky and nervous. He throws open the window but it's cold outside and a strong wind whips around the room so that there are shrieks of protest: "Shut the window! Are you nuts? Matteooo . . . Matteooooo!"

Matteo looks down at the street. Opposite there's a stationery store, a modest little business and quite old; Matteo is staring at it as if seeing it for the first time. Suddenly his face brightens with an idea that puts him in a completely different mood. He turns towards the others who are going off to bed.
MATTEO: Hold it everyone. I have a suggestion to make. Come here and look at the stationery store.

Everyone goes to the window, shivering. They look down.
MATTEO: See it?
VOICES: Of course we can see it . . . we're not blind . . .
Yvonne starts to feel a bit worried.
YVONNE: Come on Matteo, why don't we go to bed?
MATTEO: I propose that we make that store disappear.

Everybody looks at him stunned. Yvonne, with a sort of compassion.
GIRLFRIEND: What do you want to do that for?
MATTEO: Because he's an idiot. He's an ill-mannered old . . .

His voice fades out, and we see Matteo going into the stationery store. It's morning and there are other people in the store dressed in ski outfits. The stationer is a typical South Tyroller, slightly red in the face, coughing up into his handkerchief and then folding it carefully over and putting it back into his pocket. On one of the shelves, pinned up among other things, there's a picture of Hitler. The stationer turns towards Matteo, who is closest to the counter.

STATIONER: Can I help you?

Matteo stares straight into his eyes for a long time. Then he says very naturally:

MATTEO: No.

The other man looks at him without understanding but already is quite angry since he's getting even redder in the face.

Next, Matteo is in the living room of a house in the mountains, with the rest of the group. It's the same scene as before. He's explaining his idea to his friends, but we don't hear his voice. Everybody is reluctantly listening to him while the wind coming in through the window ruffles their hair, scatters the newspapers around, and makes the doors slam . . .

Yvonne and Matteo are in their bedroom now. Matteo literally drops into an armchair: he's exhausted. His arms are dangling limply and his eyes are closed. Yvonne is switching the lighting in the room on and off so that it's left in a sort of half-light. Then she pauses in front of her lover, looking down at him. Matteo is the first to speak, but without opening his eyes.

MATTEO: What's the matter?

YVONNE: Nothing . . . that's why I wish you would *do* something. I feel just really empty inside. Don't you?

MATTEO: No, I feel completely full. Filled with rage and frustration . . . noise and shouts of anger.

YVONNE: About the stationer's store? But how could you possibly think . . .

She stops, seeing that Matteo is shaking his head.

YVONNE: Because you lost, then?

An unhappy nod from Matteo.

YVONNE: Well, then, how come I won and I'm not full of happiness?

MATTEO: It's a mystery. Will you pass me a cigarette?

Yvonne gets a cigarette and is about to throw it to him.

YVONNE: If you don't open your eyes . . .

MATTEO: I can't . . . they won't open . . . they really won't . . .

He forces them open with his fingers and Yvonne throws him the cigarette which he catches in mid-flight. He puts it in his mouth and then giggles with exaggerated glee.

MATTEO: He came in last.

YVONNE: Who?

MATTEO: Arrigo. He lost.

YVONNE: Oh thank God. Finally something makes you happy.

A pause.

YVONNE: I still can't decide whether you're actually envious or just jealous?

MATTEO: Why should I be jealous? Is he flirting with you?

YVONNE: Flirting . . . he's in love, or that's what he says.

Matteo looks at her incredulously, trying not to show that he's taken aback.

MATTEO: Has he said that often?

YVONNE: When he feels like saying it . . . and when I feel like listening to it.

MATTEO: And what does he say? I love you? Oh, get out of here!

YVONNE: No, not in those words, but with a gesture or a sign . . . a word said in a certain way . . .

Matteo keeps looking at her, but with a certain amount of curiosity now. Then he bursts out.

MATTEO: So you're telling me I'm up here in the mountains, on vacation, in this beautiful house with geraniums at the windows, everything nice and tidy . . . and we're actually immersed in filth.

Yvonne makes a little gesture of protest and Matteo corrects himself.

MATTEO: Well, you'll admit it's at best a bit questionable. What a nice discovery to make this evening.

He looks around him with a sort of bitter smile, a little forced.

MATTEO: Things seem to have changed their meaning . . . words don't mean the same as they've always meant ever since language was invented . . . there are actions and signs going on behind my back . . .

YVONNE: Right in front of you too, except that you don't notice them.

MATTEO: Well, that's normal. Can you imagine how embarrassing it would be if I *did* notice them? (*A pause.*) You understand that everything changes from this moment on, my whole system of communication is fucked . . . That scarf you've just put on might mean that your neck is cold, or that you like the scarf or . . . it may mean "I love you."

And he emphasizes these last words with an emphatic gesture. Yvonne smiles. Matteo's hand grips an ashtray.

MATTEO: This ashtray is an ashtray for everybody else, but who knows what it might be to you two.

He drops it on the ground, but the ashtray doesn't break. He picks up a vase of flowers.

MATTEO: Now to me, this is a vase. But what is it to you? . . . What might a vase mean to you? . . . A vase equals flowers, flowers equal color, color equals beauty, beauty equals love . . .

He drops it too, and the vase is smashed to smithereens.

Yvonne takes two steps towards him and slightly raises her voice.
YVONNE: Cut it out, Matteo!
MATTEO: It seems so stupid to me . . . Love is so stupid, let's just admit it . . . because it's a mystery, a deception, and that's the secret because even deceit has a sense of mystery about it; that's why we all fall for it.

A pause. Yvonne picks up the bits of the broken vase.
MATTEO: Sorry, but you seem to be enjoying this situation.
YVONNE: Well, it amuses me.

Matteo squirms in his chair, shaking his head as if to say that he's had enough.
MATTEO: Tell me something . . . are you screwing behind my back too? I mean, Christ, I would have noticed if you did that in front of me.
YVONNE: He would like to, but I said no.
MATTEO: But he would like to.
YVONNE: Oh yes.
MATTEO: And you said no.
YVONNE: Well, yes.
MATTEO: Did you say yes or did you say no?
YVONNE: I said no.

Matteo can't contain himself any longer and jumps up, shouting.
MATTEO: Damn it, I'll bash his brains out! I'll crack his skull for him! I'll make his stupid smash at table tennis look like a slap on the wrist!

But in a second, he's recovered his self-control and his normal tone.
MATTEO: I'm sorry, I'm sorry . . . A fuck here, a fuck there . . . What difference does it make?
YVONNE: Well, if that's the attitude you're going to take, no difference at all.

Matteo starts walking up and down. Yvonne has finished undressing and is naked. She raises the covers, but before lying down she looks for something and starts talking again.

YVONNE: Anita too, you know.

MATTEO: Anita?

YVONNE: Yep . . . and she'd pay to do it.

MATTEO: Well, as for her . . .

Meanwhile, Yvonne has found what she's looking for—a magazine—but now she turns to him with interest.

YVONNE: As for her, what?

MATTEO: A bit of therapy would do her the world of good. You should tell her so.

YVONNE: There, you see? Arrigo, makes you mad but Anita doesn't. How do you explain that? It's just the same if she wants to go to bed with me.

Instead of answering, Matteo takes a seat and looks her up and down from head to toe.

MATTEO: You know what you are?

YVONNE: What?

MATTEO: A pathological liar.

They both look at each other in silence.

Back to Matteo in his car on the freeway. He's nodding his head in a half-serious gesture of assent.

MATTEO (*voice-over*): Yes my dear: a pathological liar. You should see a shrink . . . get over this tendency to confuse your fantasies for reality. My dear, you really are confused.

He screws up his eyes, looking at something that's hardly distinguishable from the rest of the darkness, as he talks to himself.

MATTEO: Now I'm getting all mixed up . . . What the hell is that out there?

We can see some lights and someone signaling: it's the reflective armband of a policeman. Matteo slows down.

There are some cars stopped next to a highway patrol car. They're checking people's IDs. The cars all have Pescara license plates. Matteo pulls up at walking pace and makes as if he's going to stop, but the policeman waves him on. Matteo does as he's told, but as soon as he's passed through the road block, he stops next to the guardrail and goes back to peer into the stationary cars to see if by chance Yvonne is in any of them. He had spotted a Fiat 127 that was the same color as hers. But it's not Yvonne. Matteo goes back to his car while other cars begin to pull up and are all forced to stop. For Matteo, this is a stroke of luck; this way he can check on everybody that goes through. He leans on the hood of his car and lights a cigarette.

After a while, a policeman come up to him.
POLICEMAN: Sir, you can't stop here.
MATTEO: Why not?
POLICEMAN: Because you can only stop in designated areas on the freeway—there's one about three miles from here.
MATTEO: Sure, but that's not on the route, it's easier here, you see.
POLICEMAN: What's easier?

Matteo smiles and starts to explain with the attitude of someone who thinks that everybody already knows this.
MATTEO: Well, you see, I'm waiting for someone . . . that is someone who's going to Rome, to my house, and if I don't see her, don't stop her, she'll get away from me. I don't know if I've made myself clear.
POLICEMAN: Very clear, but you still can't stop here. In any case, why don't you wait for her at home?

Matteo looks at him, shocked.
MATTEO: Well, I'll be . . . I hadn't thought of that.

He shakes his head as if to say, "How stupid," and the policeman looks at him pityingly.

POLICEMAN: So then, what are you going to do?

MATTEO: I don't know, what do you think?

The policeman loses his temper.

POLICEMAN: Show me your driver's license and registration.

Matteo gives them to him and the policeman checks them.

POLICEMAN: Apart from stopping in an unauthorized area, you've got two other infractions: against Article 117 and Article 123.

MATTEO: And what do they say?

POLICEMAN: They say that if you stop at night on the freeway you have to leave your lights on, and that if you're supposed to wear glasses for driving then they should be on your nose and not on the dashboard or in your pocket or at home.

MATTEO: I'm sorry, but doesn't the highway code say anything about when glasses don't suit you? Because mine make me look awful, they take away from my nice dark eyes, you know.

POLICEMAN: That'll be 10,000 lire.

MATTEO: Is that all?

POLICEMAN: It'll be 40,000 if you don't cut out the witticisms; that's Article 123.

The headlights of a car are approaching up the hill. The car is on the other side of the slope on the freeway and its headlights are angled high into the sky. They catch a cloud that's pure white and dirt black; then they slip down to illuminate a cliff and slide over that to illuminate some trees, a house, and a warning sign, then they fall suddenly on a wall and then directly on Matteo's car.

MATTEO (*voice-over*): Any of these lights could be Yvonne, coming to see me. There's not much to say, that's her message for me, otherwise I wouldn't be feeling what I am . . . That's her little love letter she's come to deliver just for me. And even if it gets mixed up with all the other messages people are carrying back and forth on this freeway, at the end of the day, it's enough for me.

Now we see Matteo's face, his gaze fixed on the windshield. The drops of rain slide down the glass and are swept away by the wipers. But on the side windows, the drops hold still for a while before they slide downwards. One of these drops is magnified until it becomes an eye, Yvonne's eye. A ray of light that slides over the glass becomes a caress, stroking Yvonne's face. A squeal of brakes or a slippery curve become her laughter, and as her mouth opens to laugh, her teeth seem to take over the whole windshield. Then her mouth disappears; the roadway reappears with the shaft of light on the asphalt. Another shaft of light shines in the opposite direction, and as the two cars cross each other, the shafts of light seem to kiss.

Now we see Yvonne and Matteo in bed. Dawn is visible through the window as Matteo looks at the time: it's six o'clock, and he turns to Yvonne to wake her.

MATTEO: Yvonne . . .

YVONNE (*with a start*): What is it?

MATTEO: What do you want to do with your life?

YVONNE: How the fuck should I know?

MATTEO: Well, you should think about it.

YVONNE: At this time of the morning?

And she goes back to sleep.

Matteo's car is driving along at a steady speed through the rain. At the wheel, Matteo glances at the fuel gauge and at the clock.

MATTEO (*voice-over*): The more I think about it, the more I have to admit I don't care whether I do find Yvonne waiting for me at her place. I want her to come running to me. What I mean is, I want her to know that I came running to her, but at the same time I also want her to have come running to me. So that every time she sees the headlights of a car going towards

Pescara, she'll wonder whether it might be me; she'll want it to be me, but she won't be sure.

Yvonne, in her car, going in the opposite direction of Matteo. Some headlights are coming towards her; she slows down, stops, tries to see who's in the other car but can't see anything. And she's upset about it. Sighing anxiously, she sets off again.

Matteo's car, seen from above on the freeway.

Yvonne's car, traveling towards Matteo's; they are about to cross but they don't slow down. They pass side by side without stopping. Their headlights cross and there's a swish of rain.

The same scene again. As he drives by, Matteo turns to look at Yvonne's car as it passes but sees nothing and drives on.

Another repetition. Yvonne doesn't notice Matteo passing by.

Another repetition. The two cars are about to cross; we still see them from above. They draw closer and there's a moment's pause. They're stopped right next to each other. Yvonne turns to look at Matteo, but there's only a shadow visible inside his car. Matteo turns to look at Yvonne and also sees only a shadow. The two cars continue on their journey leaving the empty road and tire tracks in the rain.

MATTEO (*voice-over*): For a fraction of a second we were next to each other; perhaps that was us. At least, it was certainly me, if that means anything, and the other car could have been her, or the person I wish she was, the sign that I might recognize her by, although it's exactly that sort of symbolism . . . the randomness of a passing shadow . . . that makes her unrecognizable to me.

Yvonne's car on the freeway: it's a shadow, a vague outline, a blur of light.

Matteo's car traveling in the opposite direction; it looks the same.

MATTEO (*voice-over*): Traveling by freeway is the only way that she and I have left to express what we have to say to each other.

Matteo's face, isolated on a black background, lit up by the feeble light from the dashboard. Everything around him is dark.

Arrigo's face appears to him two or three times, emerging from out of the darkness, each time a bigger and more obsessive image.

And the same thing happens with Yvonne's image.

Yvonne and Arrigo's silhouette, cast onto the wall of the living room of the house in the mountains. It's evening and the shadows are cast by some candles which Yvonne and Anita are placing around the room. The candles are shaped exactly like a penis, but the only person to notice this strange fact is the forty-year-old man who approaches Yvonne as she puts one of the candles into a holder.

FORTY-YEAR-OLD: Nice.

YVONNE: Yes, aren't they?

Then all the women sit in a circle and the game begins. (It's an erotic game.)

When the game is over, the group has split up into couples, scattering throughout the room, lying on the ground or on couches. Each couple is as hidden as possible from the others. Matteo's gaze is focused on one of the candles as it burns down: the flame seems huge to him and is a blue-green color. Yvonne is leaning against him, and every so often she caresses him, becoming more and more passionate. The others are doing exactly the same.

Outside the window, with the candles reduced to flickering stumps, it is dawn. Nobody has moved; they are all in a deep sleep.

In Matteo's car, the cassette player comes to the end of a song leaving only the hum of the engine.

MATTEO (*voice-over*): I got behind the wheel to get to Yvonne's house as fast as I could, but the more I go on, the more I realize that I'm not looking forward to the actual moment of arrival. What will be waiting for me in Pescara?

Matteo's car arrives and stops on a street in Pescara, in front of Yvonne's house. Matteo gets out, pulls his keys out of his pocket, and opens the front door. He goes up the stairs and opens the door to the apartment, very softly so that no one will hear. He steps into the hallway. There are lights on in every room of the house. It's a middle-class house that's trying to look sophisticated. There are certain curious things: a lamp that throws shadows onto the wall, a very comfortable, inviting three-seater couch of questionable purpose. Matteo looks into the living room. There's thick carpet on the floor so his footsteps are silent. The living room is empty, and from there Matteo goes into a passage with more doors leading off it. Matteo opens the first one: it's an empty closet. Still on tiptoe, he gets to the bedroom door. A squeak and a rustle make him flatten himself against the wall. (*The image fades out.*)

In the bedroom, naked on her bed, Yvonne is lying next to Arrigo, who is also naked. Yvonne seems to go wild at his touch. Her eyes are closed and she is close to having an orgasm.

Instead of Arrigo, it's Anita, but Yvonne reacts to her in exactly the same way as with Arrigo.

(*The image fades in again.*) Upset, Matteo walks into the bedroom, but there's no one here either. He goes into the bathroom, no sign of her here too. He goes back out into the passage and opens another door; there's a little office that leads into the kitchen. Both rooms are empty, and he retraces his steps back to the living room. Then he hears the door click open, and the light is turned off. He takes a few steps towards the hall, groping his way through the darkness, bumping into the furniture and making some noise. The lights spring back on, and in the half-open doorway, Yvonne gives a small cry of fright as she sees Matteo. But she quickly recovers, walks inside, and goes towards him.

YVONNE: What are you doing here?

MATTEO: Nothing, I was looking for you.

YVONNE: I was in the bedroom . . .

MATTEO: How can you have been in the bedroom if you only just walked through the front door?

YVONNE: I was going out, not coming in. I was just turning out the lights.

Matteo doesn't seem to follow.

YVONNE: I came through the kitchen and through the living room to the front door.

MATTEO: I was in the kitchen too, and you weren't there.

YVONNE: Well, you must have been in the bedroom while I was in the kitchen, and while I was in the bedroom you were in here . . . Or while I was in here, you were in the kitchen . . . Anyway, what are trying to get at?

She looks at him for a moment to try and figure out what mood he's in. Meanwhile, she takes off her gloves, her overcoat, and her scarf and throws them on a cushion on the ground. She's dressed conservatively, but there's always something about her that catches the eye. It's usually just a little thing, but it's enough to define her character. She's a girl of twenty-five or twenty-six, who doesn't want to be completely overwhelmed by the image of a well-brought up young lady, a teacher and a professional. Today, it's her blouse, of a very light, pale material, quite ordinary but almost see-through and quite low-cut, so that everybody can see her well-proportioned breasts. Matteo certainly can't help noticing it.

MATTEO: You were going out?

YVONNE: Yes, but it doesn't matter.

MATTEO: Don't let me stop you.

YVONNE: Come off it . . . you come all the way from Rome to see me . . . do you really think I'd go out?

MATTEO: I could go to the theater; I see they're doing *Il Trovatore*.

YVONNE: OK then, go see *Il Trovatore*.

Matteo knows that if he's going to maintain any credibility, he must go to the theater, but he just can't do it. So he sits down.

MATTEO: Who were you going out with?

YVONNE: I was going to a meeting with the students to discuss some of the problems at school.

MATTEO: You go to meet your students dressed like that?

YVONNE: They wouldn't even notice that I'm "dressed like this." They've got other things on their minds tonight.

MATTEO: Well then, if it's important, you shouldn't miss it.

He's still sitting down, and Yvonne stands in front of him, looking him straight in the eyes.

YVONNE: Matteo, do you want me to stay or do you want me to go?

Matteo, behind the wheel of his car on the freeway. He fidgets nervously in his seat, finishes one cigarette and immediately lights up another.

MATTEO (*voice-over*): The problem with a conversation, an exchange of words, is that some of it would certainly come out wrong, or ambiguous . . . and the things that she would say or I would say, they wouldn't be what we expect, and there would be unforeseen consequences involved in every gesture and every word, weaving such a web of confusion around the things that we would say (or rather the things that we want to hear) that communication between us would be even more difficult than it would be on the telephone.

Yvonne's living room. She's still standing there in front of Matteo.

YVONNE: Matteo, do you want me to stay or do you want me to go?

Matteo gets up and goes to lean his forehead against the window as if he wanted to cool himself by touching the cold glass.

MATTEO: I wish I could go, Yvonne; go to hell, that is.

Yvonne smiles with a look of tolerant compassion. She approaches him from behind and hugs him. She speaks softly to him, in an almost motherly tone.

YVONNE: We had a horrible vacation and we're both upset . . . all that time wasted, playing games . . . But perhaps it wasn't so bad, or it was but there was a reason for it. Don't you think there might be reasons? You should know.

She tries to draw him out of himself, to get him out of this mood, but Matteo is all wrapped up in himself. He only answers reluctantly.

MATTEO: We've got as many reasons as you want . . .

YVONNE: Such as?

A pause. Their embrace relaxes but they stay next to the window. We can see flashes of lightening revealing a fantastic, changing landscape, depending how long and in what direction the lightening flashes.

YVONNE: Such as?

Finally, Matteo allows himself to be drawn in: this is his field of expertise.

MATTEO: Well, games are a way to let off steam . . . a permissible way, a sanctioned release of tension. That's pretty significant. They're highly structured with rules; it's like working. In other words, games have the same meaning as work but they are directed towards an erotic end; obviously, underneath the competitive instinct there's a desire, a form of pleasure . . . Don't look like that: it's a symbolic pleasure, not a sexual one. People wouldn't play if they didn't work.

YVONNE: Then we've obviously been working too much.

Matteo nods in agreement.

MATTEO: Perhaps. All our aggression is pent up.

YVONNE: But if you are saying that people play in order to let off steam, how come you were so uptight?

MATTEO: Because I was losing and so I was frustrated . . . you get the idea.

YVONNE: So you take it out on me and hang up on me on the phone? How do you explain that?

MATTEO: Ask Arrigo.

YVONNE: What's Arrigo got to do with it? I don't understand.

MATTEO: Neither do I.

They burst out laughing and embrace.

They're in bed, naked under the sheets.

YVONNE: You hurt me, you know that?

MATTEO: I'm sorry.

YVONNE: I'm aching all over.

She feels her lower abdomen, getting up from the bed to go to the bathroom, as she continues:

YVONNE: I don't understand, you do it so angrily . . .

In the bathroom, Yvonne is using the bidet, looking at herself. Matteo comes to the doorway. He's affectionate.

MATTEO: You mustn't take me seriously when I hang up the phone on you, you know.

He goes over to Yvonne, who's still sitting on the bidet. She smiles at him and gives him a playful slap on his dick which is right in front of her face.

Matteo's face, as he's driving along in his car, still thinking about Yvonne.

Matteo and Yvonne in a bar. The room has very plain, faded, almost washed-out colors. But there's a couple sitting at a table who, in comparison, stand out quite distinctly. So does a tired waiter who is going back and forth with the orders or cleaning the floor. The couple is made up of two old married people, who exchange a few words now and again as they read different pages of the same newspaper and then swap.
YVONNE: I've got to tell you something.

She smiles, as if ashamed of the confession she's going to make.
YVONNE: I knew a man and woman once, they were married. I really liked them a lot and we saw a lot of each other and we slept together.
MATTEO: The three of you?
YVONNE: No, just him. I was in love with him and he loved me too, but he was very fond of his wife. It happens. But one evening she committed suicide, and he came running to me in a real state. We made love all night long . . .

She breaks off, thinking about the incident.
YVONNE: . . . and it was great.

Another pause.
YVONNE: Perhaps it's because love is deeper when there's desperation in it.

Matteo gives her a brotherly caress, and Yvonne smiles again.
MATTEO: You didn't have it easy either, did you?

Matteo, driving again.

Yvonne and Matteo, walking out of somewhere that we can only just see; it was brightly lit inside. There's a lot of people around them, coming and going. A lot of confusion. It could be a cinema in a mall, but it shouldn't be too obvious what it is: what counts are the people, their faces and expressions. Yvonne stops, looking around. She's nervous.

YVONNE: Sometimes I feel as if I have no excuse for being alive. Sure, our parents give us a reason by having us, but I never know who would accept that . . . Who? . . . These people here?

MATTEO: What's this all about?

YVONNE: I'm a poor, mixed-up kid, just like your patients.

She smiles, and meanwhile a few tears appear in her eyes.

YVONNE: My colleagues, the school principal, the pupils, my friends . . . you . . . I'm always busy . . . there's no time to get to know oneself.

She just manages to hold back the tears, as if she resents her own emotions.

YVONNE: What a stupid bitch . . . I'm taking myself too seriously . . .

Suddenly she turns to Matteo.

YVONNE: I don't really care, you know. I just want to have a good time and that's all.

Matteo nods; he understands, but obviously he doesn't believe her.

Some spots appear—they indicate the next scene in which Yvonne and Matteo are facing one another in Yvonne's living room. He's sitting on the couch, she's standing up. Matteo looks at her with a sardonic, somewhat bitter look. The colors of the scene are more harsh.

YVONNE: Do you want me to stay or do you want me to go?

MATTEO: Perhaps it would be more convenient for you if you were alone.

Yvonne is about to explode with rage.
YVONNE: Yes, it would be more convenient.

She picks up her clothes from the cushion.
YVONNE: So what are you going to do now? Are you going to the opera?

Matteo is undecided for a moment, then he looks deliberately casual.
MATTEO: Yeah . . . I think I will. I'll come down with you.

They move off, Yvonne trying to put her overcoat on and Matteo ostentatiously helping her. They go downstairs, she's two steps in front of him, walking rigidly upright, and he's behind her, apparently very confident. They go out to the street and Yvonne turns towards him.
YVONNE: Do you know the way? Take the first left, then go straight and you'll soon get to the theater.

Matteo's tone is dismissive.
MATTEO: Yeah, yeah . . . thanks . . . See you.

He goes off and Yvonne watches him. Then she too moves off in the opposite direction. But as soon as he's turned the corner, Matteo runs back and begins to follow her. Yvonne turns down an alley without turning around. Matteo hurries on, reaches the alley, stops, and cautiously pokes his head round the corner. Yvonne is there waiting for him. Matteo doesn't know what to do or say. Yvonne looks at him with sympathy and pity.

Matteo, in his car on the freeway. He rubs his hand over his brow as if he were tired. Tired of thinking, remembering, imagining.

MATTEO (*voice-over*): That's how it would end. That's why I feel such a need to travel, to become one with this car, to transform the things that I need to say into a beam of light, a shaft of brilliance from these headlights traveling at 90 miles-per-hour—much better than talking to her, especially on the phone.

The shaft of light from the headlights sweeps across the straight sections of road and around the turns. Finally, it pushes up a slope and then dives into the descent.

MATTEO (*voice-over*): Yvonne should have no more doubts. I have become this ray of light, traveling towards her. And the things that she needs to tell me, they are those other shafts of light, traveling in the opposite direction.

First Yvonne's car and then Matteo's seem to become shapeless, shiny objects, speeding through the darkness.

MATTEO (*voice-over*): What counts is getting across to her the important things, leaving all the rest out; but all the rest is who we are as people: the messy situations we get into, our expressions and gestures . . . It's all about defining ourselves in the simplest possible terms, like a beam of light traveling in a certain direction . . . Yvonne is that light over there. And I'm this one, flashing by another car just for love of her.

The shiny object that is Matteo's car takes shape again or goes back to being a normal car during this last monologue by Matteo. There's another car in front of him, and after uselessly flashing his brights to signal his intention of overtaking it, Matteo moves aggressively to pass it. The two cars squeeze past each other dangerously. The other slows down but soon regains its speed. Matteo continues driving, unperturbed.

Inside his car, Matteo lights a cigarette as he reflects. As he reflects, he starts to laugh.

MATTEO (*voice-over*): Even with Arrigo . . . I can only

establish the right kind of relationship with him if I think of him as two headlights following me or two red brake lights I'm following . . . Otherwise, if I start to think of him as a person . . .

Arrigo in the house in the mountains. A few shots of key gestures: a caress for Yvonne on the stairs, the table tennis lesson, etc.

MATTEO (*voice-over*): . . . there's something not quite right about him . . . it's the way he behaves as if he were best friends with everybody; you never know where that could end up. But as long as he keeps behaving like that it's fine with me: Arrigo trying to overtake me or letting me overtake him (though I don't know if that car *is* him), Yvonne running towards me to apologize (though I don't know if that other car is her), and me running towards her in a fit of jealousy (though I mustn't let her know that) . . . That's all fine with me.

During this last piece of dialogue we have seen the corresponding scenes: Arrigo's car being overtaken, though it isn't certain if he's inside it or not; Yvonne's car passing Matteo's in the opposite direction, though she too can't be seen very clearly in the driver's seat; and from the line "me running towards her in a fit of jealousy" on, we see a long piece of freeway, clearly lit up by the moon, seen from very high up. From that altitude, Matteo's car seems hardly distinguishable.

MATTEO (*voice-over*): Sure, if I were the only person on the freeway, and there were no other cars in either direction, then everything would be much clearer. Because then I could be absolutely sure that Yvonne is still in Pescara and never even dreamed of calling Arrigo on the phone, nor did Arrigo think of going to her from Rome. Just to be on the safe side, the best thing would be for there to be just three cars in this part of the world: mine, Yvonne's, and Arrigo's.

The same stretch of freeway (the same shot), but by day and deserted. From closer up you can see the rusty guardrails, the weeds growing through the pavement, the decrepit tollbooths at the entrance and exit to the freeway, with their broken windows and a sleepy old man standing inside.

Some city streets, by day. Futuristic streets, absolutely unreal. In one of them, a crowd of people is moving onto a side street that comes out into a square. In this square, there are more people with everybody assembling in one place to look at something: Matteo's car as it passes by. They point at it, and Matteo waves to them, smiling.

On another street, the same thing happens with Yvonne's car.

On a third street, or avenue or square, the same thing happens with Arrigo's car, but there are fewer people to see it.
MATTEO (*voice-over*): If that's how it was, then no other car could be going in my direction except for Arrigo's, and the only car traveling in the opposite direction would be Yvonne's car.

Then there's an outburst of roaring car engines, flashes of headlights, squalls of rain and distorted faces seen through car windows.
MATTEO (*voice-over*): But who can pick out one car from the hundreds of others, coming and going in this inferno of headlights and rain, let alone recognize who's in it? You'd have to have a really good vantage point from where you could check each of them individually.

The three cars—Matteo's, Yvonne's, and Arrigo's—are followed by the camera which closes in on them and blows-up the image so that you can see the three drivers through the windows. The camera follows Matteo's car as it stops in front of Yvonne's house in Pescara. Matteo gets out of it, tired, and goes towards the front door.
MATTEO (*voice-over*): At this stage, getting to Pescara and

Yvonne's house and finding that she'd stayed in with a head-ache, thinking over the reasons for the fight, would be small satisfaction.

In the bathroom, Yvonne takes a pill. Then she pauses thoughtfully, annoyed with herself and with everything. She touches various objects without picking them up. She comes out of the bathroom and then goes back in. She lifts her skirt to go to the toilet but doesn't and wipes herself with toilet paper. She throws it away after having looked at it to check for any signs of her period. Then she goes back into the living room where Matteo is. We can't hear what they say, but from their attitude and expressions, it seems to be just general remarks, a cold exchange.

MATTEO (*voice-over*): If Arrigo turned up, there'd be an enormous fuss.

Yvonne, Matteo, and Arrigo. A three-way conversation which we can still not hear. We follow their expressions and the rhythm of their gestures and remarks, the movement of their lips, the little smiles, frank laughs, and sarcastic com-ments. Yvonne's reactions are very lively and her gestures are quite theatrical. Matteo's behavior towards her is very differ-ent from Arrigo's, but at times it seems as if the two men have formed an alliance against her. At others, Yvonne seems allied with Arrigo against Matteo and vice versa. Finally, Arrigo leaves. Yvonne and Matteo flop to the ground, tired out. She takes his hand, and both look out the window: dawn is quickly creeping up from beneath the horizon. There's a breeze, dead leaves, and dust.

MATTEO (*voice-over*): But if on the other hand, I found out that Arrigo had been careful *not* to come and that Yvonne never acted on her threat to call him, then I'd feel like a fool.

The following scenes will have a very rapid, staccato rhythm and take place on stylized sets.

Yvonne opens a door with some plates in her hand; she's at home. She crosses the passageway, disappears, reappears immediately and goes into the living room where Matteo is, looking very embarrassed. So as not to humiliate him, Yvonne doesn't look at him while she busies herself setting two plates on the rug, next to two floor cushions. Then she goes out through the door again, Matteo watching her, still very uncomfortable.

MATTEO (*voice-over*): On the other hand, if I'd stayed at home and Yvonne had come to see me, that would have been embarrassing too . . .

Yvonne rings again and again at a door on the top floor of a building in Rome: Matteo's house. Nobody answers. Then she goes down the stairs, which seem to her—and to us—to be interminable, and at the end of the stairs she bumps into Matteo who's getting ready to climb up. Yvonne throws her arms around his neck saying frantically:

YVONNE: I'm sorry . . . I'm sorry . . . I'm sorry . . .

She's very different from what we know of her, and Matteo looks rather coldly at these exaggerated displays of emotion.

MATTEO (*voice-over*): I would have seen Yvonne in a new light, as a weak woman asking for help, and something would have changed . . .

A pause.

MATTEO (*voice-over*): And what about Arrigo? I'd die of shame if I seemed to be running to Yvonne because I was jealous of Arrigo . . .

Matteo runs to the school where Yvonne teaches: it's evening classes. The school is nearly falling down. Matteo is shown to the classroom. Yvonne comes out into the corridor, and Matteo immediately begins to make a scene, right there in front of the school janitor and some pupils who are peering out from behind the door.

MATTEO (*voice-over*): . . . or if Yvonne came running to me to apologize, just to get away from Arrigo . . .

Yvonne, behind the main entrance to her apartment building from the street. As soon as she hears footsteps receding from the other side of the door, she opens it, glances down the street, and slips out. She starts running, constantly turning to look over her shoulder. It seems as if there's someone following her and that someone might be Arrigo, but we can't be sure. At any rate, Yvonne goes into a department store full of goods and people and then exits by a side door.

Matteo is just getting home when Yvonne catches up with him. She gets out of her car and stands in front of him with an apologetic air, or looking like someone who wants to be forgiven.

MATTEO (*voice-over*): . . . though of course, Arrigo wouldn't dream of leaving his house . . .

Arrigo's studio. It's a big room with a pleasant untidiness about it. It looks like quite a successful studio. Arrigo is studying a model and is concentrating on what he's doing. The model is an enlargement of Rome, seen from the air, with several pieces of plastic, wood, and material over it: it's a different urbanization of Rome from the way it is in reality. There's a girl helping him to move certain bits of plastic. She's naked to the waist (Matteo is still imagining all this): she has beautiful breasts and thighs, and although she is very seductive, she moves about naturally, as if fully clothed.

In one of the streets that leads out of Rome, the model has an abstract version of a gas station.

In his car, Matteo shakes these thoughts away and gets into the exit lane to a real gas station.

Matteo goes into the bar and buys some tokens for the

telephone. He dials the area code for Pescara and then a number. Nobody answers. Matteo seems satisfied. He re-dials just to make sure and there's still no answer.

MATTEO (*voice-over*): Obviously, Yvonne couldn't resist the temptation and she's jumped into her car and driven to Rome.

Matteo hurriedly leaves the bar, gets into his car, and gets back on the freeway, but he exits at the first opportunity. In front of him, at a fork in the road, there's a signpost with the name of a town. Matteo takes the opposite direction, back onto the freeway, but in the other direction, back towards Rome.

Matteo, behind the wheel, in a thoughtful mood again.

MATTEO (*voice-over*): And so, all the cars that I overtake or that overtake me, might be Yvonne.

He overtakes a car and crosses another going in the opposite direction.

MATTEO (*voice-over*): In the other lane, all the cars traveling toward me could be Arrigo, thinking that he'll find Yvonne at home.

A pause.

MATTEO (*voice-over*): Unless Yvonne has stopped at a gas station . . .

Matteo seems shaken by this thought.

Yvonne is coming out of a bar, getting back into her car, going through the same motions as Matteo did. Except that she's leaving the freeway to go in the opposite direction, back towards Pescara.

Yvonne's car veering left to right.

Matteo's car veering right to left.

(*The following images are all highly stylized, throughout the sequence.*)

MATTEO (*voice-over*): Now we are traveling in opposite directions; we are going away from one another. Perhaps the car I am overtaking or that's overtaking me is Arrigo's, and he also got halfway there before he tried to call Yvonne . . .

Arrigo's car takes the exit ramp towards a service station. Arrigo gets out of the car and walks towards the bar. He takes some tokens out of his pocket and goes over to the phone.

Yvonne is also phoning from a bar at a gas station, but she's dialing Matteo's number.

At Matteo's house, nobody answers.

Arrigo finishes dialing the number and waits.

Yvonne's house: nobody answers.

Matteo is also on the phone, dialing Yvonne's number, but the line is busy. (It's busy because Arrigo is calling it.) Matteo frowns, darkly. He hangs up and dials Arrigo's number.

Arrigo's house: nobody answers.

Again Matteo dials Yvonne. This time, the line is free and Matteo cheers up again. But not completely.

Arrigo puts the phone down. Opposite the service station where he is, there is another one on the other side of the freeway.

Yvonne walks away from the telephone. Her service station is the one opposite Arrigo's, but they can't see each other. From where Yvonne is standing, you can't even see the second telephone in the same bar, and that is the one Matteo is using. So neither of them sees the other.

(*From this moment on, everything will become highly realistic again.*)

Matteo, in his car, slightly dazed by all these whirling possibilities. He looks tired and makes a few movements, exercises to stretch his body, just to get rid of his nervousness, his frustration, but gradually these movements become slower and finally cease. Matteo sighs deeply. He slows down and you can see him steadily relax. He's only doing about 40 miles-per-hour on the right hand side of the freeway so the other cars can easily pass him. He lights a cigarette, not because of stress, but just to enjoy the taste of it.

MATTEO (*voice-over*): Everything is still uncertain but I'm calmer now. I feel almost relaxed. As long as we keep calling each other's number and there is no one there, all three of us will keep going backwards and forwards like puppets on a string . . . I don't really know why I'm calmer, there is no reason. It's just idiotic to carry on like this. Love is a big fraud. No, it's not a fraud, but it's not the magical experience it's supposed to be either . . . It needs to be redefined. If Cleopatra had had a big nose . . . All great revolutionaries, from Che Guevara on down, they've all had a woman in their lives . . . Perhaps they kept her well out of sight . . . A woman on the side, something separate from their everyday lives . . . What would the feminists think of that?

White lines on the road.

MATTEO (*voice-over*): . . . they come from nowhere and they have nowhere to go.

His eyes are staring straight ahead of him but he's looking into emptiness. As he lowers his gaze to the dashboard, he realizes he's running low on gas. He stops at the first gas station and a girl comes up to him.

MATTEO: Fill it up, please.

As the girl starts to work the pump, Matteo takes a few steps to stretch his legs. There's the usual bar, lit up for the night, and Matteo's eyes immediately pick out the telephone inside. Slowly, Matteo walks in that direction, but when he gets to the bar, there's a sign saying "Out of Order" on the only available phone. (The other is occupied by a woman with her back to Matteo at whom he hardly even glances.) Matteo asks the barman for help and he points to another door. Matteo goes in and finds an office, dimly illuminated by a weak, greenish sort of light. There's something so funereal about that light that Matteo feels uncomfortable. He picks up the receiver but then he seems to think better of it. He sees himself reflected in the window, in that spooky light, and he stands rooted to the spot. Gradually, the green light reflected in the window becomes a meadow, and in it there's a man standing quite still. His hand is thrust deep into one of the pockets of his jacket and his big eyes seem pitiful. (It's the same man from the beginning of the film, and this is the only unrealistic moment of the final sequence.) Matteo too stands quite still, staring at the green in the window, the field, and the man. It's as if this man is looking back at him and saying: "See? I wanted to save you from all this." The man and the field disappear and only Matteo is left, reflected in the glass of the window. It's the first time since the previous evening that Matteo *has seen himself.* His face still looks upset from the tensions of that night, and he feels a wave of shyness sweep over him. He puts down the receiver and goes back to the bar. He stops in front of the glass door and looks out.

A large truck has pulled into the gas station and is filling up with gas. There's also a little sports car with a young man getting out of it. While he waits, he leans into the car, talking and laughing with the girl inside it. She's very pretty, very young and natural looking. Matteo looks at these displays of affection with irritation and then shifts his attention to the truck.

A very skinny truck driver is chatting and joking with the

attendant with a sort of crude gallantry. Matteo turns back towards the interior of the bar. Next to the doorway, the window display is full of chocolates and candy with little scenes of lovers kissing. It bores Matteo and he goes out to his car. He pays the girl for the gas, starts the engine, and is about to drive off, but the truck has also started moving, and since he is not in a hurry any more, Matteo lets it pull in front of him. But the sports car then forces its way into the space left between Matteo and the truck, the two young people having started up again quickly. The man waves a hand out of the window in a gesture of apology towards Matteo.

Matteo doesn't even see him. He's distracted by a dull, deafening roar that's coming from the freeway. The freeway is empty; there aren't even any cars on it at this time and the effect of this silence, contrasted with that roaring sound approaching him, is really quite unnerving. After a few moments, the noise of a motorcycle overwhelms everything, and a motorcycle policeman draws up and stops on the exit ramp from the gas station, blocking the way out. The truck, the sports car, and Matteo's car, one behind the other, have nowhere to go.

An impressive convoy of military vehicles begins to roll by: howitzers, light armored tanks, ammunition transporters, trucks full of soldiers in combat gear, officers' cars, military ambulances, supply trucks, military engineers, etc. Matteo turns off his engine and gets out of his car to watch. Motorcycles are zipping up and down the length of the convoy; the policeman is talking on his walkie-talkie; an officer gets out of his car to wait for another one and then gets into that.

The skinny truck driver and his mate have also gotten out of their cab and approach Matteo.
TRUCK DRIVER: What the hell's all this?

Matteo shrugs his shoulders. The truck driver grumbles,

170

looks at the time, and exchanges a few words with his companion. They're obviously in a hurry.

By contrast, the two young people seem to be enjoying themselves. They get out of their little car and run to the edge of the freeway to watch the parade. They wave at the soldiers, who are gloomy and would rather do anything than joke around. But the two of them keep at it and even make faces at the soldiers, anything to get a reaction from them. But it's to no avail, and finally the policeman sends them back to their car. There they find another activity and hug and kiss each other passionately; they've forgotten all the other onlookers and don't even try to hide the desire they feel. Matteo tries not to look at them; the sight irritates him. So he concentrates on the convoy. A motorcycle rider pulls up to speak to the policeman, and both of them drive off at top speed. Meanwhile, a gap in the convoy appears and the truck driver immediately takes advantage of it, scrambling into his cab with his mate and heading off onto the freeway. But the sports car is faster and it recklessly overtakes the truck, hurling itself onto the freeway with a sudden burst of acceleration. Just as it's pulling out into the first lane, a military staff car emerges from behind one of the stopped howitzers, also accelerating hard. An accident is inevitable. The little sports car is rammed by the staff car and is hurled forward several yards with its mid-section practically ripped out.

The convoy suddenly comes to a halt. Matteo approaches the little car: inside you can see the bodies of the two young people, covered with blood. The girl is lifeless, but the young man is still alive, judging by the efforts he's making to move. What he's trying to do isn't clear. He's not moving towards the car door but the other way, and every movement must be agony for him. Matteo tries to come to his aid, but the door is twisted and jammed and he can do nothing but watch the harrowing agony of the young man as he still tries to move; finally he reaches the body of his girlfriend, rests his head on it, and tries to caress her, but he falls limp on top of her and just stays there motionless, though still breathing.

Then soldiers run over, officers, the employees from the gas station and the bar. An ambulance siren goes off and the auto mechanics' truck arrives on the scene. A non-commissioned officer approaches Matteo and asks him some questions, another takes the truck driver to one side. They are trying to get the crowd away from the vehicle. Lights are placed around the scene of the incident and the atmosphere becomes nightmarish. The skinny truck driver is in tears. But despite all this bustle, there's a strange silence and in this silence you can hear the noise of the blow torch they are using to cut the two young people out of the car. Matteo looks at that purplish flame as if he is somehow responsible for it.

When it's all over and the mechanics have even towed the wrecked car off the freeway, Matteo is still there, alone, seated on the guardrail. He feels very tired. The traffic on the freeway has started up again as per normal. Matteo gets up and goes towards his car.

Matteo's car, traveling at a moderate speed towards Rome. Other cars pass him, the usual sorts of cars you see on a freeway, most of them with engines roaring. But their headlights, which are still on, are less noticeable in the breaking daylight. The landscape around is also more recognizable, at least the outlines of boulders and other rigid shapes. The car radio is playing Bach's *Prelude No.8* as Matteo drives calmly along. He answers any car that signals it wants to overtake him with conventional signals; in short, he takes part in the dialogue of cars about curves and passing one another. But nothing more. His face is tired but serene, although if you looked closely you could probably see the traces of fright. He's re-entered the normal world where cars are just cars and the beams of the headlights are just beams of light, merging into the light of the dawn, and not cryptic signs of love, messages to be decoded only by those who are capable of receiving them and understanding them.

TWO TELEGRAMS:
I'll Tell You About a Film I Never Made[1]

She was born to and raised by a wealthy family, in the countryside. The countryside was humid and fertile, similar to northern Italy but harsher. Her childhood was full of restrictions,
and she grew up a silent little girl, with no sense of irony and
no girlfriends. In her own way she was sensitive. Sometimes
she was filled with a burning enthusiasm about herself and her
own potential. Now she is a grown woman who is sometimes
happy and sometimes sad—usually for the same reasons. She
is someone who craves struggle more than harmony. The indifference of Nature was the most dramatic discovery of her teens.
It wasn't enough for her merely to look at those immense landscapes of green and yellow; she would have liked somehow to
be a part of them, to upset their smooth undulations and
cadences. The erratic movement of the wind was also a source
of frustration for her, though she didn't know it. Today, at
forty, she feels betrayed when she thinks that there must be
somebody out there who is truly living life to the fullest.

She doesn't like people, especially if they are nice to her.
She hates sentimental people. The thing she likes most about

[1] In *Corriere della Sera*, 27 June 1976; reprinted in *Quel bowling sul Tevere* (Turin:
Einaudi, 1983).

her husband is his broad forehead because it gives an impression of toughness. She has a rather idiosyncratic and tender idea about ugliness as far as people and objects are concerned. She would prefer that her relationships with other people weren't quite so rigidly conventional. And she would prefer that other people were always a little bit drunk. But her husband is a teetotaler—in everything. He doesn't know what excitement is. He's even gloomy in bed, and that's why she cheats on him. The first time it was with a man who she left as soon as she realized she didn't love him, and the second time it was with a man who she left as soon as she realized she did. She is a woman who is modest about her own feelings. She hides them, masks them, and thus blocks them. She is not even sure that she really feels what she feels. Perhaps these emotions don't serve a purpose for her. So she substitutes different emotions for them, for example, going to private parties where the naked guests give themselves over to promiscuity, or introducing the thirteen-year-old son of one of her friends to the mysteries of sex.

This episode changes the boy's life and hers too. The boy's father is happy that he has had his first sexual experience. But not that it should be with a woman of her age. To get her away from his son he ends their friendship. And in trying to reclaim it, she makes the biggest mistake possible, offering herself to the father almost without knowing what she's doing. But the father knows quite well and gets a kick out of it. This is the very moment when she starts to back out of it, and to soothe her conscience, she confesses everything to his wife and thus loses that friendship too.

From that moment onwards she retreats into a circle of respectability from which lies, infidelity, and unconventionality are excluded. She looks for a job in which she can use her degree in chemistry, finds one, and performs it scrupulously. She works in a skyscraper. Prefabricated walls, aluminum, glass and neon. Perfect grayness.

The first time I see her, she is just a woman who has stopped

at a gas station. Those places always have a lot of shiny sur-
faces, and every time she sees her reflection she jumps. She
looks around her as if afraid of something or in a hurry. She
orders twenty liters of gas and then changes her mind to ten.
She doesn't want to get her windshield cleaned. She opens her
handbag, closes it, then opens it again. She fumbles as she hands
over the money. She really seems to have no sense of style
whatsoever.

The gas station is two minutes away from her office. She
parks in the lot reserved for the skyscraper, and after a dizzying climb in the elevator, she sits down at her desk. From the
big window, one can see—as if projected on a screen—an urban
landscape full of hard angles and the colors of skyscrapers. As
the sun shines down the street, thousands of windows that are
never opened are illuminated. The woman waits a little before
calling in her secretary or reading the afternoon mail or making phone calls. When she starts work, her actions come from
habit, and the familiar surroundings help her to regain her self-
control. Her colleagues and staff also help her do this, affectionately. They even manage to make her smile. Little by little
a glacial composure comes over her.

Before she had gone down to the gas station to fill up, her
secretary had knocked at the door with a telegram. She had
opened it with a pair of scissors which she had then placed on
the desk, in the exact spot where the approaching sun would
shine on them. Her telephone rang. When she finally answered
it, the ray of sunlight had passed over the scissors and was
nearing the edge of her desk. It was her husband on the phone,
asking if she got the telegram. Ah, so you're the one who sent
it? She was annoyed by the thought that the message would
probably contain some sort of expression of affection. She had
no reason to think so, but that was what came into her head,
the thought of another clash with reality. In fact, her husband
had something else to ask her, something that was not really
suitable for the metallic timber of a telephone line: he wants
a divorce.

The woman didn't say anything. She literally had nothing

to say. Words make sense when there's a face in front of you that you can say them to or avoid or *not* talk to. But instinctively, she had turned her head away, and her mouth was no longer near the receiver. The line to her husband had gone dead and what she was listening to was simply the sound of her own amazement. She hung up and let her gaze fall on the telegram. It repeated the same phrases she had just heard, with one ironic addition: "Hugs and kisses—these days, that's the only thing we do well or with any dignity or honesty."

That's when she went down to fill up with gas.

Inside the office, it's already evening, and soon it will be outside too. The colors of the day are fading fast. Outside, the difference in the level of light stops the windows from reflecting the interior of the room, and the landscape dominates: static and indifferent. The windows do not even reflect her own image.

The woman would willingly go out if only she could find a good reason to do so. But at home, her husband will be waiting for her, certainly worried about the scene that will follow their meeting. That is, if he is waiting for her. He is the last person she wants to see.

The clerks have all left. They came to say good-bye and then went away. In the silence that follows, she closes her eyes and listens to the noise of the traffic and the wind, buffeting the building.

High up, where she is, there is always wind. It carries the noise of the traffic as well as a drawn-out whistling. It is the wind that makes the skyscraper sway and makes her feel slightly dizzy.

The woman moves a few steps. She realizes that the direction she has taken leads to a small table near the window, and she hastens to switch on a small light under a lampshade. A cone of harsh light swamps the black of the little table. Now the grouping—table-armchair-lampshade-woman—is clearly reflected in the glass. The rest of the office is in shadow. The woman gets up and disappears into the shadows by the desk. From the desk she begins to switch on the ceiling lights. It's track lighting that targets specific areas. As she switches them on, each area of the room is projected onto and through the glass windows to the outside. It is as if the woman is throwing the office out the window, piece by piece.

Perhaps she really wants to throw herself into the air, like in H.C. Andersen's fable, in order to reach a man who is pacing up and down in the rectangle of a window in the skyscraper opposite. It's a very tall, dark building. But at night, it is lit up by a white light that reveals its spectral emptiness. That restless figure makes the woman inexplicably apprehensive. She knows the name of the firm that occupies that entire floor, but she doesn't know who the man is nor has she ever been in those offices. But whoever he is, it seems as if his presence there is of enormous importance to her, though she doesn't know why. The important thing now is to stop him from leaving, as he might be intending. Keep him there at all costs. She looks in the telephone directory for the name of the firm and dials the number. She waits for thirteen rings, and then she puts down the receiver as if it were a dead weight. Her hand is tired. As she rests it on the arm of her chair, her gaze falls on her husband's telegram. She immediately picks up the receiver and dials another number, three digits only. After a moment, frowning and raising her voice as she does with her secretary, she dictates a telegram. The address is the firm across the street, the text includes the words "immediately" and a phone number: hers.

One hour later, the telegram reaches its destination. She realizes it when she sees the man stop at his window and look out. Obviously he is trying to pick her out. With all the lights switched on behind her, her silhouette must stand out quite clearly. And the man does see her. But instead of running to the phone as she had expected, he opens the window and drops the telegram into the emptiness.

Strangely, the telegram floats into the middle of the street and begins to flutter down into the endless chaos below. A stronger puff makes it spin but only for a moment; the telegram frees itself from the whirlwind and takes shelter in the corner between one building and the next. Here it is sucked back upwards and then down again; it collides with some neon lights and then glides away in harmony with the indistinct background noise. All the laws of physics out there seem to conspire against it. The woman follows it until she can no longer see it, but even afterwards, she continues to listen. She would like to hear the imperceptible rustle as the telegram touches the ground and the garbage truck that immediately carries it away. And with it, all her hopes.

The man has disappeared. The woman returns to her desk. Shortly afterwards, when tiredness catches up with her and she falls asleep with her head resting on her elbow and the light streaming down onto her hair, it almost seems as if she is sleeping in the whirlwind outside the window, in her shattered office. While she is asleep, it begins to rain.

It rains until dawn. Instead of cleaning the air, the storm leaves it dirty, placing a layer of dust over her window. Through this veil, the landscape looks out-of-focus; if you tap your finger on the glass, the landscape shifts. Borges would say that this woman is suffering from unreality. She can't even define what she feels. The emptiness of a few hours before has been filled with a vague but persistent awareness of a thought about that long trial that has been her life. From the indifference of Nature that caused her such suffering as a child, to the indifference of things, even the most common of objects, such as the pen she writes with or the scissors or her house keys or houses themselves. Is there anything more exclusionary than the houses where other people live, themselves the proponents of this absolute indifference?

Some of them will soon arrive at the office. Her secretary, her staff, the doormen. They will smile at her, like strangers. The day before they persuaded her to keep calm so that *they* would be more calm. This conclusion seems to her so blinding that all hatred and rancor towards her husband vanishes, and in its place, like smoke in the damp air, comes a new feeling, a new form for her hatred, a kind of mass hatred that she likes better.

I didn't make this film because at a certain point the character of the woman, who was actually familiar to me, seemed unlikable and even unacceptable. Every time I read this tale, I saw in it different inferences, even political ones. That is, at the visual and narrative level I liked it, but not at the conceptual level.

But if I had made it, it would have been a film about the night and the mingling of people's loneliness. About this relationship between the inside and the outside. As its climax, one would see the woman mechanically grip the scissors and go and stand behind the door. The office starts to come to life with the first sounds of the morning, footsteps and voices. Some of these steps come near, stop on the other side of the door. Someone has come here, more than one person, you can hear them whispering and breathing. In a few moments they will come in.

Gripping the scissors with both hands, the woman raises her hands to strike. It doesn't matter who. Any one of them.

THE CREW[1]

The harbor of a small coastal town. There are not many ships, and what there are pass by at a distance, headed elsewhere, to more important cities. This is a port for small ships unloading goods for sale at the local market, or for larger vessels making emergency stops.

In this port there is a harbor-master's office, staffed by an officer and a few sailors.

In the late afternoon of a normal September day in 1976, the radio in the office announces the arrival of a yacht that a fishing vessel has found out at sea and towed in.

A few people gather at the dock as soon as the two vessels come into view to help with their arrival. As per the standard procedure, someone throws out the mooring lines and they are made fast around the bollards on the dock.

But the yacht arouses people's curiosity. It's a beautiful yacht, a forty-five-foot cabin cruiser called *Irene*, sleek and fast, an ocean-going yacht. Or at least, this is the impression you get if you imagine the ship under normal conditions, for its present state is very far from normal. A hole in one side, its sun canopy torn to shreds, the cabin half-gutted, and the decks whitened by

[1] 1978. Original treatment, 1975-1976.

salt. This ship must have been through a tremendous cyclone.

Three men aboard the yacht help out with the docking. They do so with visible reluctance and seem very tired. They look very much like the yacht on which they were traveling: their clothes ripped and dirty, and their faces ravaged. But what is most surprising is that their clothes aren't the usual sort of sailors' attire. They are strange and rather exotic, and so are the men themselves. One of them is about seventy, and it seems strange that someone that old should be part of a crew like this.

The three of them step off the boat, and their expressions indicate their satisfaction at finally reaching dry land after having spent six days—or so they say—at sea without food or water.

One of the onlookers is a photographer, and the three of them willingly pose for him. In short, they get their brief moment of glory, although it does seem rather ironic that such glory should be bestowed on three people as savage-looking as them.

Anyway, both sailors on the fishing vessel and the three from the yacht are taken to the harbor-master's office. Here the officer asks them to describe what happened. But before they can begin, he asks if they would like anything to eat or drink. The seventy-year-old, who must be their captain, answers for them all and says no. That's a strange reply for someone who spent six days without eating or drinking anything. But the officer doesn't make a point of it and asks them to go on with their story.

They had been hired six days previously for a ten-hour cruise by some guy from _____ (and they mention the name of a big city about a hundred miles along the coast), who was obviously a rich man. They had been offered good pay, in advance, and so they had accepted. But after having gone about twenty miles, the engines had broken down and the boat had been forced by a strong wind out into the open sea.

As if that wasn't enough, they had run into a storm more

violent than any they had seen before that had kept them in fear of their lives for the whole night.

At dawn on the 29th of September, the *Irene* had been about eighty miles offshore. The sea was as smooth as glass. The three of them had been sleeping in the hold when one of them, and here one of the sailors raised his hand to show it had been him, had woken up with a start when he heard a noise coming from on deck. It sounded like someone dragging something away. Then there was a loud noise from the direction of the hatch and then nothing. The sailor had gotten up and climbed the ladder to go up on deck. He raised his arms to push open the hatch to the deck, but it was closed from the outside. Then he had awakened his companions, and with difficulty, they had managed to force it open.

There was a surprise waiting for them outside. On deck, standing in front of the bow, was the yacht's owner with an iron bar in his hand. Threatening them with this, he had managed to drive them back and then had closed the hatch again, this time more securely.

At the time, the three sailors hadn't understood what was going on. They had gone back to trying to get the hatch off its hinges, and after an hour they had succeeded. But a second surprise was waiting for them on deck, bigger than the first one: the boat's owner was no longer there. Disappeared. Most likely, fallen into the sea. Or maybe not, maybe he hadn't *fallen* into the sea; after the incident with the iron bar, it was more likely that he'd suddenly gone crazy and had jumped overboard.

The officer asks them to repeat the name of the boat-owner and asks them what kind of man he was. His name was Daniel Powers, a tall guy, strong with dark hair and a beard, just graying at the temples. Very bright eyes.

A statement is prepared for the three men to sign, and then there are some other formalities. The men from the fishing vessel are demanding compensation for time lost in coming to the boat's rescue, as is the custom. But who is going to pay it? The owner has disappeared; the fishermen turn to the other three, but the idea that they could pay anything is just laughable. The officer solves the problem by saying that they should submit a formal request; he will see that it gets forwarded to the appropriate officials, etc.

The meeting breaks up, and the three men from the *Irene,* together with the fishermen, leave the office.

Outside, it's night, and the group moves off in different directions. The sailors from the *Irene* head towards the town, and the fishermen towards their boat. After a few minutes, the fishing boat slips its moorings, but the *Irene* still rests at anchor there in the darkness.

In the office, the harbor-master and a few sailors are left. The officer is amazed that no request for information has come from the coast guard at _____ in the last few days. Usually when a boat disappears, they send out notices to all the ports. In any case, now they will have to trace the relatives of this Powers guy, and standard procedure dictates this is a job for the coast guard in the deceased's home port.

So the officer gets on the telephone and calls the coast guard at _____. There's an officer on duty there too. An hour later, this officer drives up a street in a residential area of the town. He stops his car at the crossroads of two streets in order to read their names. They are quiet streets, filled with greenery. Little villas and detached houses with gardens. A wealthy, up-scale neighborhood.

The house he is looking for is one of the most beautiful. It's hidden by a lawn and some large trees. It is twilight. An old but carefully dressed woman answers the door. As soon as she sees the officer, she turns pale and begins to tremble. She looks the man in the eye, waiting for him to speak, certain that whatever he has to say will be very painful.

At the news of the disappearance, she bursts into tears, but between her sobs you can make out that she had almost given up hope by now anyway. Mr. Powers was a man of very steady routines, and he had said when he left that he would be back the same day, so it was obvious that something had happened.

The officer asks if there are any family members who need to be informed. The woman answers that Mr. Powers lived alone with her; she had been his governess. She bursts into tears again, and in the deep silence of that house, in the half-light among the antique furniture, her quiet, sincere sobbing seems appropriate.

On the dock where the *Irene* is anchored there is just one street lamp. The light reflects off the glass of a porthole in the bow of the boat. In the night breeze, the light changes, shifting the reflection so that it almost seems as if the glass itself is moving. Or someone behind it is. A face with two bright eyes and a dark beard. The impression lasts for a few moments, and then the face disappears. But after a few seconds, it reappears through a crack in the hatch that is raised just enough for someone to peek out. Then the hatch is thrown open and a man jumps out. Looking around him, he steps off the boat, and after having checked that the dock is deserted, he walks off.

His build is exactly as the seventy-year-old crewman had described the owner of the *Irene*.

He walks along the dock, his hands in his pockets. He has the swaying gait of a man who is used to feeling a heaving deck beneath his feet. At the end of the dock there is a parked car, empty. Its windshield wipers are going and the man stops to look. They must have been left on some hours ago because the battery is dying. The little blades get stuck as if they had no more strength left, then make an effort and continue swishing merrily. The man looks at the car with a strange smile on his face. It's as if he is having a conversation with the wipers, and he even bends down so that when the little blades slow down again, he can help them start up with the touch of a finger. Until they fully stop, and the man says to them, "Good-night."

News of the *Irene*'s adventures has appeared in the newspapers, both the local paper and the one in the big city. There's not much importance attached to it, but there are details given and some commentary. For example, the article says that the most probable thing is that Powers, his mental balance disturbed, threw himself into the sea. The article had reached the editors with a photograph of the survivors, but they hadn't published that.

In the editing department of the newspaper, an assistant editor is looking at the photo. He's curious about these three strange sailors who could have stepped out of the pages of a novel rather than the current affairs section of a newspaper, and he mentions this to a colleague. The first thing that is pointed out to him is that those three hardly look as if they've been six days without anything to eat. Besides, it's hardly likely that anyone would go on a cruise without emergency rations of food and water or without flares to signal their position if the need arose. And then another editor objects that the article says "his mental balance was disturbed." How do they know? Who knows what made him keep three men prisoner in the cabin of his yacht? And then, how come he hired a seventy-year-old man to serve on his crew? From a sailing point of view, there's no reason why anyone would hire someone like that. And how come they didn't send out an SOS?

The discussion becomes heated. Someone else comes up with a totally different thought. How can it be that someone who owns a yacht like that, a man who obviously loves the sea, would choose to commit suicide by drowning? A man like that knows full well that when that final wave washes over you and you are staring death in the face, you will hate the sea, and that's not how a man who loved the sea would choose to go out.

The first editor then asks someone else to look in the archives and see if they've got a photo or other news items about this Powers guy. The other editor goes away and then comes back. Nothing; nobody's ever heard of him. It's strange since they have files on almost everyone. This guy seems to be a first-class recluse. A total blank. "Shall I ask around?" the other editor asks. "No, forget it," says the first one, throwing the photo into the bin.

News of Daniel Powers will never get to the desk of a newspaper editor. Daniel Powers does not make headlines. He is an honest man, tough in business, and formal in his relationships, as in his dress. He has built a calm, bourgeois middle-age life on the foundation of an unworried youth. It almost seems that he's sorry to be so wealthy. He has no family, though he believes in it as a concept. His hobby is the sea, and his boat is a stage on which he acts out his manhood.

Daniel Powers is in his office. His office is in an older style building but is situated right next to a skyscraper that must ruin the view. But Powers can't see the skyscraper from his office; he can see the sea. And the walls of his office are plastered with photographs of boats, motor boats and sailing boats, or of Powers himself in various poses, with the trophies of fishing expeditions or standing at the helm of a yacht. There are women in the pictures too but none are standing near him. Except for one photo, in which Powers looks more or less as he does now. It must be a recent photo.

Powers is in the import-export business. When we see him interact with his employees, they are very respectful towards him. He possesses an innate authority which he exercises with discretion, even if there is no need for him to do so. His business is highly successful in both good times and bad, and he has enough friends to occupy the time he is not at work. In short, he is satisfied—or believes he is satisfied with what he's got. But such moral self-confidence rarely earns men a great reputation: Powers is liked by those who know him well, but nothing more. That's why he is not famous.

It is common knowledge that people only worry about the meaning of life when there is something in one's life that is not going well. But it's not always like that. Such thinking may occur to a person when everything is going marvelously, and he suddenly notices that he needs the stimulus of a little adversity. That is the case with Powers.

One fine morning, he wakes up and feels as if the world around him is completely devoid of interest. He throws open the window and sees the villas and detached houses next to his own so quiet, life going on inside them with such regularity it's frightening. An unruffled, stagnant, lifeless world.

Naturally, the first thing he would like to do is go to sea. But as luck would have it, just the day before he has given his crew of three some time off. This little set-back gives him new incentive. He runs to the harbor but doesn't go to the maritime employment agency as usual. The agency has all the usual people on its books, the best of the profession. Instead, Powers starts wandering around the back alleys of the docks where he meets all sorts of people, from those who are desperate for a day's employment doing anything to con-men and other human parasites. Powers spots three men who look like anything but the seafaring type. But in any case, he doesn't really need highly skilled sailors. He can pilot the boat himself; he knows the sea like he knows the streets of his own town. He just needs someone to help him out with the manual labor. And what attracts him to these guys is, shall we say, their slightly dubious appearances. What he needs right now is a day off from doing things by the book, from respectability.

An hour later, they are all heading out over a clear sea and foamy waves. The morning passes quickly. It's a new kind of morning for Powers. The conversation of this crew, their gestures, behavior, and expressions are worlds away from what he is used to. For example, he could not have imagined that friends— and these three are undoubtedly friends—could have such a relationship. They are mercilessly cruel in trying to wound each other. The seventy-year-old guy treats the others as if they are his personal slaves. He exercises total control over them. The youngest man is undoubtedly the strongest of them, physically. He's like a bull. He's quite prepared for hard work, provided that it's completely useless. As soon as you tell him to do something useful, he becomes recalcitrant. The third man is the whipping boy for the other two. But you get the feeling that he would die if he wasn't allowed to serve their every whim.

All three of them spend their time doing things that are not only useless from a sailor's point of view but also absolutely pointless. It's an unknown world and, in its way, fascinating, even if it is a rather gloomy fascination. Powers only regrets that he has come to know it so late in life.

But Daniel Powers has underestimated the strength of cowardice and stupidity, and he finds himself confronted by both during a storm which blows up towards evening. Black clouds appear low over the horizon, and in little more than half an hour, they cover the whole sky, which seems to become darker with each new gust of wind. The sea begins to get rougher, and soon there is a force eight, force nine, force ten gale. It's absolute hell.

Powers shouts orders that no one pays any attention to or that get lost in the driving wind and rain. With its engines out of action, the boat is dead in the water, completely at the mercy of the waves. There's not a lot they can do about it except throw out sea anchors to hold the vessel upright among the waves and keep its position. But it's an enormous task for one man. It doesn't even occur to the others to help him. The three men of the crew are not only incapable of being sailors under these circumstances, they are incapable of being men. All they do is to shout back obscenities at Powers. They are not scared in the normal sense of the word. Their blood pressures don't rise. But they are mad as hell that the storm won't cease. This is what amazes the owner of the yacht most. Until now, he has seen people react to a storm in two ways: courageously or fearfully. He himself doesn't know what fear is, but he's had many people aboard his yacht and has seen it in various guises. But he's never seen anyone react like his current crew. Despite the chaos of the storm, he can't help noticing it.

With its engines dead, the yacht's movements are completely out of control. And it is this more than anything that seems to anger the three men. They are so furious that at one point, against all reason, they even try to assault the man who is trying to save them. In doing so, they demonstrate their stupidity and cowardice.

One of the three—the youngest and strongest—approaches

him and tries to hit him. But Powers is also strong and, with a kick, he sends the other guy flying, just as a wave sweeps over the deck and drags the man out of reach.

By now, the tension between the three crewmen on the one hand, and the yacht's owner on the other, is exhausting. The struggle that the latter has to keep up is no longer against the sea but against the three crewmen who seem to have focused on him as responsible for getting them into this terrible situation. And as if that wasn't enough, the boat is forced against some floating wreckage, tearing a hole in its side, though luckily it is not very big and is above the water line. But by dawn, the *Irene* looks like a wreck, floating on a dead, glassy sea.

It is during this moment of sinister calm that Powers feels the absurdity of the adventure he's gotten himself into and realizes the danger he's in.

The first thing he does is go towards the bow and lock the hatch to hold the three men prisoner inside. Then he goes to the helm to see if the rudder is still working. It is. He looks over the engines; there's something wrong with the electrical wiring. There's no way of fixing it with the tools he has on board. But the radio is in decent shape. He absolutely must get it in working order to send out an SOS. He's still looking it over when he hears a scraping sound from under the hatch. He realizes immediately that the three men are trying to get out. So he grabs an iron bar and makes for the hatch. He arrives just as the three of them are about to come through the opening. He raises the bar, ready to strike if necessary, and stands there looking them straight in the eye. The sailors take a step forward, but the expression on Powers' face warns them to retreat. The yacht's owner closes the hatch again, this time more securely, and goes back to the radio.

He takes an hour to fix it. When he's finished, he looks up from the equipment and casts his eye over the sea. Looking at the sea is his way of resting, of catching his breath. And it seems almost that the sea is looking back at him and whispering something to him. But no, the whispering is coming from the bow. He turns around, but it's too late. The three of them have managed to get the door off its hinges, and they are just setting foot on deck.

Now Powers is in a really difficult situation. After a moment's hesitation, he moves furtively around the tiller and hides. He's still got the iron bar in his hand. The sea, the storm, the floods . . . the elements hold no fear for him. But the men do. They wouldn't hesitate for a moment to throw him to the sharks and then tell everyone he disappeared. Then they would have his yacht and use it for a smuggling operation or something before sinking it. In the last four years, two thousand pleasure boats have disappeared in the Pacific.

Meanwhile, the three men have gone into the galley. Surely they must see him? But they don't. They move slowly, exhausted by strain as much as by weariness. And Powers can quite easily coordinate his own movements with theirs. His yacht is big and full of places to hide.

From the galley where Powers can hear them eating—there's a noise of plates and glasses, etc.—the three move on to the lounge and there they stay.

Powers doesn't know what to do. The truth is, there is nothing he *can* do except hide. This is what he does throughout the afternoon, using a hundred different tricks. Every so often, one of the three comes out of the lounge and wanders about on deck. Powers has to slip from one hiding place to another like a hunted beast. At one point he finds himself within reach of the strongest of the three, hardly six feet away from him. If he were able to raise his iron bar and strike the man, it would be quite easy to deal with the other two. But violence is not his strong point and he doesn't feel able to strike a man down from behind. He might kill him. And why should he do that? The man hasn't done anything to him yet.

Night falls. As soon as the sun has set, the three men come out of the lounge and go and take possession of the captain's quarters. Powers can then install himself in the forward cabin, under cover, where the others have no reason to go looking for him. He comes out a few hours later to look for food and water. He takes them from the refrigerator, replacing them with more from the stores. He knows where to find things.

After that, he wanders around on deck until he sits down in the bow, ready to take cover at the first noise from below. He returns to his cabin at dawn and follows the same routine during the following days and nights. Each night, while he waits for the sky to get light again, a wave of melancholy sweeps over him. This yacht, which he used to have all to himself, much more so than his own home in the city, is now enemy territory. He's relegated to the status of a stowaway aboard his own vessel. But he doesn't know how to play that role; he feels that the three men have somehow usurped his place, and they now enjoy rights to it, even if only to stay there temporarily and run the boat as if it were theirs. But what amazes him most is that this same fact simultaneously gives him a new experience, that of feeling a sense of doubt. It's almost a feeling of timidity about his future.

But what about the past? He feels his past wash over him like a flood. He sees images from it with frightening clarity. There is a woman in his past, the same one that we saw next to him in the photograph on the wall in his office. Powers thinks about her often. He's never managed to forget her or her laugh. She had a beautiful, silvery laugh that she would use in the most unexpected of moments. He had even heard it when she was telling him that she can't help it, that's just how she is, she'll sleep with any man who asks her nicely because she just can't say no. Powers could not understand that. Because after all, those men would get up and leave her and she would be alone again, left without anything except yet another disappointment, another bitter experience to add to a long list. So why do it? That was when the woman had burst out laughing, and he had left, slamming the door behind him even though he felt that what he wanted to do was stay there with her, even though she would always be like that. But his morals were too strict to allow him to do so. Even now, he feels he had acted wisely, that married life with that woman would have been hell. But then, if he was aware of that, how come he wanted to live with her so badly?

Every morning, the sun comes up as Powers sits there absorbed in these thoughts. It is his signal that he must return to his cabin and go back to sleep.

Sometimes he is awakened by noises the three men make up on deck. He can hear them talking, laughing, and even running. One afternoon, his curiosity aroused, he lifts the hatch and sees them dragging cushions onto the sundeck where they then go to sleep in the sun. They don't appear in the least bit concerned. It's as if the world beyond the yacht has no relevance to them . . . except to provide them with fish. But even this task is left up to the one among them who acts as personal servant to the group. No one is the least bit interested in Powers. They haven't even bothered to look for him.

Every so often, he notices the yacht move suddenly, brusquely changing direction. This is a sign that someone is inexpertly using the tiller to try and find one of the on-shore currents. But it seems that these things, which would have taken precedence over everything else for him, are of only secondary importance to the three men. Is it possible they don't even care if they don't get back? For Christ's sake, it's a matter of life and death. He feels as if there are three madmen, three zombies, moving around on the deck above him.

One night he gets it into his head to go and see what they are doing. If he were to find all three of them sleeping in the stern cabin, he might even try to lock them in there, as he had done when they were in the forward cabin. He cautiously approaches to check out this possibility, but to his surprise, he realizes that one of them is sleeping on the floor in the narrow corridor. God alone knows why, for he could quite easily have had a bunk. But this means that for the moment he can't put his plan into action.

The only thing he can do is to try and make himself useful in some way. Unfortunately, he only has a few brief hours before dawn to do it. He could stay on deck even later because the three of them get up very late, but it's better not to risk it. As soon as the sky is light, he takes his place at the helm and steers the boat into the warm currents near the surface that an expert mariner can recognize at a glance. This direct contact with Nature encourages him after the depression that overcomes him spending all day locked in the little cabin in the bow. It reinvigorates him, like food and water. Powers feels as if he's a part of Nature too. Beneath him, the fish engage in their struggle against each other, as he too must fight against his own kind above. The laws of Nature are the same for all.

Having found the current, Powers locks the tiller in place and goes to sleep. One day he hears the three of them fighting with that usual ferocity that is over as quickly as it begins. And they are fighting about the tiller. One of them blames another for having locked it, and naturally, the other denies it. And so the three of them literally come to blows.

Another day, Powers wakes up very early. He has a feeling that something is happening. The yacht is silent. There are the usual noises like the swish of the wind and the lapping of the waves against the sides of the boat. And yet there is something unusual about it; his instincts are not usually wrong. He gets up and goes to look out the porthole, and there, far away, shrouded in the early morning mist, is the coast.

It's difficult to describe how he feels. He's not just happy for himself, but also for his yacht, which has obediently, docilely cooperated and allowed itself to be carried along by a favorable current. With such happiness in his heart, it is difficult to stay locked inside the cabin. He would like to go out and warn the three men, but then he thinks that it's probably better to let things take their course. Probably, they'll also wake up with the same kind of feeling.

But the hours pass and nothing happens. At midday, the three of them finally appear. They certainly see the coast, which is now clear and sharp. But from the tone of their voices you would hardly think they are thrilled. What kind of people are they?

There's a bit of noise later on when a fishing vessel arrives.

It has seen them and is prepared to give them a tow to land. Powers follows the whole thing, peeking out through the porthole, and he continues to look out even after the yacht is heading towards dry land.

They get there around sunset. A vague and feeble light shows a harbor that he doesn't recognize, a dingy and rather isolated dock. Suddenly, as he looks at this landscape, he realizes something. It's a thought that undoes all his new-found happiness and fills him only with bitterness. He has given too much importance to the things in his life. Instead of smiling contemptuously at Fortune, a tactic that would have enabled him to enjoy its blessings much more, he has taken it too damned seriously.

Meanwhile, a group of people has collected on the dockside. There are only a few of them, but they are curious about this beautiful yacht that has been so badly battered about, and they are curious too about those three motley sailors on board. There's even a photographer who takes a few pictures.

Powers observes the scene from his porthole. He's alone now, watching his three companions happily enjoying their moment of triumph, surely the only one they will ever enjoy in their lives, and now he can finally smile at them with contempt. We can see him quite clearly; the light from the street lamp falls directly onto the glass of the porthole and illuminates his face.

A few moments later, the same face appears coming out of the forward hatch. Powers steps off the boat and sets off along the dock after looking around to reassure himself there is no one to see him. At the end of the dock there is a parked car, empty. Its windshield wipers are going, and Powers leans over the hood to look.

But he's not looking at the wipers. He sees his own image reflected in the glass, and that is what catches his attention. His clothes are as dirty and torn as those of the three sailors; his beard is unkempt and his hair is uncombed. In short, he looks completely different. And Powers seems to regard this difference with a certain amount of pleasure.

As if on a screen, Powers sees himself in the car window, going back to the office to be welcomed with sincere happiness by his staff and associates, who gather round him and congratulate him on having escaped such a danger.

None of the newspapers carry the news of his reappearance. In the city, no one has even noticed it, except for his employees and his former governess. Nobody talks about it. His return has gone unremarked, and they bring him the mail that has piled up in his absence, and he begins to flip through it automatically, feeling himself slowly sinking. The banality of his life takes hold of him again.

But Powers is still standing there, hunched over the hood of the car, watching his reflection in the windshield. But the scene that is now projected onto it is different. Powers goes back to his office in the clothes he is wearing now, all ragged and torn. He smiles happily as he shakes hands with people who are obviously confused and mistrustful of this man who has changed so much, in that degraded state. He laughs and keeps on laughing as his laughter suddenly becomes the laughter of the woman he remembers so well. It's a brittle laughter that seems to take over the whole windshield as Powers stands there looking at it.

Finally, the man straightens up. In the meantime, the wiper blades have stopped, and he says to them (or is it to himself?): "Good-night." As he walks off, he thrusts his hands into his pockets, walking into the darkness with the swaying gait of a man who is used to the sea.

"SOMETHING FOR THE EYE"

by Giorgio Tinazzi

Antonioni has a firm conviction that, "Films are not films until they are on celluloid. A script presupposes a film, it has no autonomy, it is just so many lifeless pages." This quotation confirms the general belief that it is always problematic, if not downright improper, to speculate about film on the basis of the written word, especially when that speculation comes from the man who directed *The Eclipse*. But if it is questionable to critique a written work that is destined to become another form of expression, that critique risks becoming pure falsehood when it is the *quality* of the image and its ambiguous relationship with reality that is the principal focus of the author: "Description can never be generic or wrong precisely because it is about images which very often do not have any concrete referents." Words are "written down on a provisional basis" and serve to describe or create events which by their genesis and their very nature are almost beyond language. For Antonioni, this difficulty has grown as his expressive itinerary has moved on, his aim being to explore the image as the undefinable (for in this lies "its power and its mystery.")

Besides this problematic issue, the study of the projects published in this present volume is complicated by the fact that they are working hypotheses that are chronologically distant from one another (and in between there are crucial years, turning points); in addition, they include different types of material (ranging from sketches to a full screenplay). Moreover, there is the risk of projecting onto them the characteristics of a cinematic style our author has steadily developed over a long period of time which encompasses different periods and phases. Finally, in the case of those projects that predate his career as a director, the difficulties are even greater.

But even with these constraints, it is possible to make some general remarks and even hazard the outline of an analysis. And the first thing it seems necessary to do is to contextualize these projects, no matter how summarily, and to highlight wherever possible the links to Antonioni's other writings from the same time, and even, with the necessary care, to make links to his films.

Green Land, from 1940, is explicitly defined as a "project for the cinema"; therefore it can be considered the first treatment ever written by Antonioni. It is interesting for many reasons; he takes his cue from a previous piece by Guido Piovene and therefore engages in the task of "transposition" or "visualization"; in the original text, there was "something for the eye" and he tries to develop that visual imagery, in particular using color "not to be flamboyant or as mere decoration but as an integral part of the story." Piovene's article, the stimulus for Antonioni's treatment, did not present a complex plot, but there was an initial concept that was sufficiently dense: "I am being faithful to an old conviction: namely, that to make good cinema you need virtually nothing but an image [like that provided by Piovene's "Notes for a Novel"] from which other more precise images can germinate in a way that can only be realized on film." Here we already find Antonioni's firm belief that one image begets others. Moreover, in the story there is a tight link between characters and their environment, and a change in the latter[1] brings about growth, the exterior world has an impact on the interior

---

[1] That "inexorable descent of the glaciers" has obviously made its mark in his memory, for we read in a note to *Quel bowling sul Tevere* (Turin: Einaudi, 1983): "Glaciers in Antarctica are moving at the rate of three millimeters per year towards us. Calculate how long it would take to reach us. Try and visualize in a film what would happen when they do."

life, and cinema demonstrates its capacity to explore subtle transitions. In order to investigate these themes, Antonioni feels the need to include a female character, and in many ways she becomes the *filter* through which he views the changes. We have here a foretaste of some of the most important motifs that characterize his later filmmaking.

There are some supporting notes from those years that Antonioni the film critic (and editorial writer) can offer us about this project, and perhaps they may suggest to us a few observations. In the premise to *Green Land,* he refers to Piovene's piece as a stimulus. In that he is faithful to what he had been writing about as a critic when he had many times expressed the fear that a literary text might prove a burden on a film: "My lady Literature, who inspires us, must submit to my lord Cinema, who achieves." And then Antonioni insists on the fact that the film's "hypothetical realization should be imagined . . . in technicolor." We can see that even in the original story it is the colors that mark the changing climate; certainly the aspiring director emphasizes this aspect of the piece, for example in the white blanket of snow that progressively takes over the fields, the crops, and the farms. Besides, Antonioni had insisted on the importance of color in his critical writings for the *Corriere Padano*: "Color is the most urgent problem we must deal with, for it is destined to restore the artistic dignity of this blessed medium we call cinema." And in a weighty essay from 1942 ("Suggerimenti di Hegel"), his arguments are more complex and more articulate and—among other things—he draws the conclusion that "black and white cinema is to technicolor cinema what the sketch is to the finished painting." He concludes that technical considerations are a compulsory stop on the way to a film's final realization, but we should not be obsessive about this because if artists had always been intimidated by technical problems then no masterpiece would ever have seen the light of day. As a director, Antonioni will make this statement an article of faith.

Green Land is also significant from a thematic point of view: in some ways it takes up old issues and in others it explores new ones. There is a close relationship between character and environment, indeed "the story of these people . . . is the story of their environment." In 1939, Antonioni had published an article in the journal *Cinema* ("A Few Hints for a Film about the Po River") accompanied by some photographs he himself had taken. In this article, it was the land and the people who lived on it that seemed to him really worthy of attention; their "authenticity" would have protected the author of such a film against the dangers of empty formalism: "It should be enough to say," the article concluded, that in "a film that takes the Po as its protagonist . . . it is not folklore that will arouse people's interest (for folklore is just a bunch of external, decorative elements) but rather the human spirit (that is to say, a collection of moral and psychological elements)." The relationship between people and their environment is at the heart of Antonioni's short film, *Gento del Po* (*People of the Po Valley*), shot in 1943. The places in it are a given, they are the *home* of those people, but they are also a visual stimulus, a play of spaces, lines and light, of shades of black and white; they are indeed "something for the eye." And it is certainly not out of place to stress that the *location* in which the characters exist will be one of the salient features of all of his subsequent filmmaking; the director will subsequently claim that "it is always from a character or a place or location where I want to shoot that the subjects of my films are born."

"You just have to go to the Po estuary or to the valleys of the Comacchio to understand the link between these people, their environment and the climate," he asserts in an article written in 1947, "Una città di pianura" ("A Town in the Plains"), the same year that he finished editing *Gento del Po*. This attachment to the land is the same as that described in *Green Land*, so that the dominant dramatic element that appears at the end of the film (the flooding river) recalls his project from 1940 in which "there lies the eternal myth of man engaged in a struggle with the elements."

It was around the 1940s that Antonioni wrote several "prose exercises" in which we can identify a few interesting characteristics. On the one hand, he demonstrates a fine ability to describe atmosphere, to render the climate of a place (*Strade di*

Ferrara [*Ferrara Street*] from 1938), and to capture the fleeting characteristics or outlines of female figures (*Ritratto* [*Portrait*], from the same year). On the other hand, there is the intention to create deliberate and perhaps artificial juxtapositions (the characters who are untouched by time in 1939's *Uomini di notte* [*Men of the Night*]). We can even find evidence of his fascination with the theme of the "journey" and the "adventure" in his review of the book *Il selvaggio* by Brocchieri (1938). However, there is a decadent vein, almost a crepuscular or even pastoral tendency that can also be seen a little bit in *Green Land*: where "life flows happily along," with the girl in the middle of the field of grain, "with a scarf on her head and her lips parted in a radiant smile as she bent to glean the wheat." This vein, which is the product of the atmosphere of the time, will soon disappear; but it will leave a residue that will become a "strong" belief of another kind and will express a need "to go back to one's origins, to try and find oneself again at the most pure, most genuine source": this is the "jungle as a purification of oneself" from *Tecnicamente dolce* (*Technically Sweet*).

A space of ten years separates *Green Land* from *Stairs*. In between is the war and its consequent atmosphere of crisis fostered by Italian Cinema. An era is passing and Antonioni records it. His investigating eye tends to stress the quotidian, extending and almost radicalizing the philosophy behind *Gento del Po*. Those notes for *Stairs* demonstrate the intention to capture, in outline, difference in sameness; and this sameness is a spatial phenomenon. Is it just a coincidence that several key moments in his subsequent filmmaking (I'm thinking of *Story of a Love Affair* or *Identification of a Woman*, as well as others) have steps as their backdrops? At least, the ones that we read in the sketches in this volume are significant: the girl in Number 7 recalls several previous articles, and the dizzying height of the factory chimney in Number 14 cannot help but remind us of *The Cry*. And the last steps remind us of an unmade documentary that Antonioni has talked about,[2] in which there is an "excessive" gaze that lays bare and instills fear and almost seems to be a foretaste of these last steps here. In his notes in this volume there is a hint, at this point quite vague, of a different mode of narration, of linking passages in a different order than was present *in nuce* in *Gento del Po*: the quest for a "free" editing process that alternates subjective and objective shots, that proceeds more by association than by logical sequence.

To get into the joints of a tale and separate each event is already a privileged motif. We find it in *Last Night, Shots Rang Out*. The structure is the structure of a criminal investigation, or—if you like—that of the "thriller," as we find in *Story of a Love Affair* and in *Blow Up,* but also in *The Passenger* and *Identification of a Woman,* as well as—incidentally—in an episode from *Beyond the Clouds* (besides the screenplay for *Sotto il vestito niente* [*Nothing Underneath*]). The intention is to seek out a fact and capture its eccentric ripples, its internal repercussions (such as Giulia's state of mind). Beyond that there is the attention to the world of young people (as a sort of perspective through which to look at events); this can be found in *Those Fun-Loving Girls of 1924* and then in *The Vanquished* (and one might almost make a case, in a different way, for *Zabriskie Point*). One might further remark, with justification: How much does the character of the father matter in that treatment? Is it out of place to find parallels with the minor, but not insignificant role, of the father figures in *The Adventure, Identification of a Woman, The Cry* (Aldo and his daughter/Virginia and her father), and *One of Our Children*?

The final suicide in *Last Night, Shots Rang Out* reminds us of an event that is often present in Antonioni's dramas, from *Attempted Suicide* to *The Girlfriends* to *The Cry* (and *Those Fun-Loving Girls of 1924*). This self-destructive act is the traumatic answer to the difficulties of, or inability to, adapt to change. In all, or nearly all, of Antonioni's works, these difficulties are charted in the paths of individual lives as they cross social or historical events; it is here that the lack of synchronicity between the rhythm of the subject and the rhythm of events becomes painful. The director will progressively tend to tighten the relations

---

[2] C. di Carlo, *Racconti, immagini, emozioni*: 214 of this volume.

among the characters, thus creating a more cogent context.

"The film I was most disappointed not to make was *Those Fun-Loving Girls of 1924*, set in the revolutionary period of Fascism." The project's intention seems to be describing the interweaving of private stories against a background ("the spirit of the times") which only becomes explicit at the end of the film and is revealed in events that *break* the "atmosphere" that has existed up to that point. The aim is to talk about Fascism—the first years of Fascism—"almost without mentioning it by name," as Renzi says, as an atmosphere that no one is aware of until it comes into conflict with their lives. The rites of provincial life and some of the feminine characteristics ("everything is seen through the eyes of the girls") lose their vitality at the end in a traumatic situation. The "fun" ("fun-loving girls") comes to an end, and people's consciences can no longer ignore events, for they invade the private sphere and provoke a crisis.

There is another change in *One of Our Children*. It is the *aftermath* of a historic turning point that gives greater depth to certain events. These characters have a past that imposes a burden on them, and their present circumstances offer no support. The middle-classes, or at least the middle-classes at the time, are the social group that is least able to adapt to the uncertainties of a new world. They are the middle-classes that in "Una città di pianura" Antonioni describes as those "who cannot be reconciled to change."

Each transition leaves deep scars. Even more so when it is a dramatic one, as in *Makaroni*: and let us not forget that Tonino Guerra's personal experience lies behind this treatment. Antonioni and Guerra chart this transition through individual histories in the convulsion of history and the interweaving of personal journeys. What is left out is agonizing ("the war was a kind of second flood"), and the investigation turns—once again—on the *aftermath*. The treatment picks up on the recovery and the sense of adventure in that "freedom in its raw state," in the desperate clutching at new signs of vitality ("Women who have suffered as much as her, and more than her, think that all they have to do is put on a bit of make-up and some lipstick and they'll be able to

blot out the atrocities of the past."). But there is also the redis-
covery of the frailty of feelings, the fear of taking them up again
("We've been through two wars: one general and one personal.
We've all changed."), and the impossibility of "going back to
the old ways, to old feelings" ("I'm afraid of going back to being
a normal person, with a peaceful, tidy life after all this horror
and then all this freedom."). At the end, Roberto entrusts all his
insecurities to his wandering eye. And along his complex and
confused journey, one can discern some important aspects of
Antonioni's style: I am referring for example to how the new
order (the end of fear) bursts out to the tune of an American
song that echoes around the concentration camp; or the group
of prisoners who, from the top of a hill, look down on the deserted town "full of white sheets hanging out the windows"; or
to the love scene on the sand dunes ("everything around them
was calm . . ."). These are individual scenes from a picture that
has a lot of action in it, a background mood that is perhaps the
interpretive key to the whole story.

Moving on to *The Color of Jealousy*, one cannot help taking
into account the fifteen years that elapsed before it was composed, for in the meantime there were other films completed,
turning points crossed, and a demonstrated tendency towards a
type of filmmaking that was a *mise en scène* of Antonioni's vision ("a sincere and instinctive need to reduce everything to images") and which had as its focus all the implications involved
with the gaze, that privileged way of understanding the world.
Antonioni's type of cinema has become defined in particular as
the complex production of imagery, as an analysis of behavior
patterns which suggests internal tensions. At one moment, the
protagonist of this project, Matteo, feels almost tired of "thinking, remembering and imagining." His "sickness" recalls feelings that have already been discussed, that jealousy which is at
bottom the fear of being replaceable. The basic structure of the
story is that of the journey, a movement through space and time;
space produces a change of images,[3] a process of composition
and then disassembly ("an outburst of roaring car engines, flashes
of headlights, squalls of rain and distorted faces seen through

car windows"), the outlines and profiles of landscapes, fragments of things. Time loses its linearity among the returning folds of the past and imaginative tension, in a continuum that has no resolution and no obvious "signposts" (this will be the main stylistic device of *Tecnicamente dolce*). Once again, color is entrusted with rendering these changes. The images reflect, translate, and transform themselves: the raindrop which takes on the form of Yvonne's face ("Yvonne's coloring") or of an eye ("Yvonne's eye"); the green reflection in the window of the service station "that becomes a meadow."[4] Precisely because they are driven by events, these images are the symptoms of a loss of objectivity, and the prevalence of chromatic tonalities, as in the prose of *Quel bowling sul Tevere* (*That Bowling Alley on the Tiber*), fulfills the function, Martinelli comments, "not of enriching or empowering objects, things, and landscapes, but of dissolving their substance." The various modes of perception give reality this mutability. Antonioni even uses this notion to propose some procedures that for him are unusual, like the varying repetitions of the sequence. Moreover, it is easy to find formal indications that have been scattered about like *leitmotivs*; think, for example of the urban landscape that is rendered in a few, essential outlines (a beginning that closely recalls that of *Tecnicamente dolce*); the measured gestures; the protagonist's looking and being looked at (a face watching: how can one not think of the collection of drawings *Sometimes One Stares at a Point?*); and the change of color in the repeated sequence on the telephone that cannot help but recall *Red Desert*.

The telephone is a not insignificant detail. Words are a part of the difficulty of communicating. But the voice is also a stylistic element; it can be a substitute for the image. The penultimate scene of the screenplay *Sotto il vestito niente* rests on this sug-

---

[3] "The headlights . . . catch a cloud that's pure white and dirt black; then they slip down to illuminate a cliff and slide over that to illuminate some trees, a house, and a warning sign, then they fall suddenly on a wall and then directly on Matteo's car."

[4] In *Two Telegrams* we read: "Instead of cleaning the air, the storm leaves it dirty, placing a layer of dust over her window. Through this veil, the landscape looks out-of-focus; if you tap your finger on the glass, the landscape shifts."

gestion. The description of the final events is rendered in a daring sequence that is entirely based on the soundtrack: Commissioner Bonanno listens to the final shoot-out over the telephone, in America.

However, it seems to me that the chief invention of *The Color of Jealousy* rests on images and the revelatory episode of the project. It is a reprise of the recurrent theme of death, the "fact" that ensures all messages are decipherable and there is an objective reality. Matteo "has re-entered the normal world where cars are just cars and the beams of the headlights are just beams of light, merging into the light of the dawn." The final sentence of *Tecnicamente dolce* is, "Then everything becomes dark," and it means that the protagonist has died. Light and darkness, they are the signs beyond which we cannot go, for they are the beginning and the end of vision.

Five years later, Antonioni wrote *Two Telegrams*, and he explicitly states he would have liked to have made this into a film (he would write a screenplay of it in 1985 with Rudy Wurlitzer). The orderly, ritualized life in which the female protagonist is situated is observed via her gestures and behavior, exaggerated and prolonged, against an urban landscape that is "full of hard angles." The eye that records this behavior also describes its alteration, its progressive loss of contact with reality; the final temptation (real or imagined?) is the gesture of breakdown, the traumatic "cut" that separates her from reality.

Something analogous lies behind *The Crew*, a reworking of the story *Quattro uomini in mare* (*Four Men at Sea*), which was subsequently scripted by Mark Peploe and came very close to being made (the actors were supposed to be Burt Lancaster, Robert Duvall, and Joe Pesci). The principal change from the story is that the narrative mode is modified to be told in the third person, and there is a significant digression to explore the protagonist's past life. Once again, the intention is "to search for a fact" (a news item, a photograph), and this fact is full of resonances: a disappearance. Naturally, *The Adventure* springs to mind, but also *The Passenger*. When deciphered, that event again underlines the invasion of *difference*, of chance, and how that produces change. The element which gives rise to this is the violent eruption of Nature ("The storm this yacht has come through must have been tremendous."); other uses of this dramatic device are evident both far (*Green Land* and *Gento del Po*) and near (*Tecnicamente dolce*). But violence also comes from the characters, for Antonioni has indeed talked of violence and madness. And such a profound alteration has consequences: a refusal to abide by the rules, or at least an impulse towards difference that the protagonist "seems to regard . . . with a certain amount of pleasure." An escape? As before, Antonioni feels the *weight* that the final scene could have. In fact, there are three versions of it. One was published in the *Corriere della Sera* (4 Nov. 1976) and the final scene is the only difference with the text published in *Quel bowling sul Tevere* (which is therefore a second version). Then there is the ending published here, which follows the first one only in part. Three variants—always focusing on gestures, lighting, poses, shifts in images, reflections—of the same idea: the unspoken, the withholding of sense. As with other Antonioni endings, it reminds us that not all behavior patterns mean the same thing, and that the images that reflect them are ambiguous.

STORIES, IMAGES, AND EMOTIONS

by Carlo di Carlo

In order to trace and understand Michelangelo Antonioni's *parallel career* as exemplified by his unrealized projects, it is necessary to go back to his own words and find there the reasons behind his choices and refusals. Thus we'll discover through an examination of these writings—in the thoughts, reflections and ideas set out here—how he conceives of writing for and making cinema.

Let us start with a general remark that I found among his typewritten papers; it has no source and has probably never been previously published:

Every subject is a good one, provided that it is sufficiently human as to seem realistic, and given that in art, what is real isn't always realistic. Provided also that it can "grab" the viewer without requiring of him any intellectual participation because, in fact, cinema can count on the public's calm, self-aware attention much less than live theater can. For the supine public loves to have its gaze delighted by images without having to exercise its brain too much.

For the mass audience, therefore, films can be divided into two categories: those that "win over" the viewer and those that don't, and the former are always the good films.

Every writer has projects in his drawer that he could not or chose not to publish.

For a director, however, we know that it is a different matter, for his wishes count for little. In fact, others make the decisions for him. It is the producer who decides if, when, and how a project will become a film.

And in this sense too, Michelangelo Antonioni's experience is singular and unique.

("This is a long and painful story of hours wasted in waiting rooms, or telling stories, or uselessly writing pages and pages. It would be courageous to say that perhaps the experience has been useful, for it is an experience that my generation must always add to another, the war: and that makes a frightening total.")[1]

The first time Antonioni found himself behind the camera was in the early 1940s when a friend in Ferrara gave him a "Bell and Howell," and he went and introduced himself to the director of the local asylum in order to film a documentary:

He was a very tall man, and, with the passage of time, his face had come to look like that of his patients. In order to demonstrate to me how his patients suffered, he made babbling noises. I agreed with him that I would use real schizophrenics. They were very gentle, very sweet-natured. I took them to the room where I wanted to shoot and explained to them what I wanted to do. They listened to me attentively and humbly. When it came to the moment to shoot and we switched on the cameras, all hell broke loose: they couldn't stand the lights and rolled about, hitting themselves and screaming. Faced with that sort of spectacle, I was unable to give any sort of direction, and I gave up the project. It was that unforgettable scene that led us, without knowing it, to begin discussing neorealism.[2]

I don't know why I began to be concerned with feelings in

---

[1] M. Antonioni, *Sei Film* (Turin: Einaudi, 1964), xii.
[2] C. Biarese and A. Tassone, *I Film di Michelangelo Antonioni* (Rome: Gremese, 1985), 29.

film, rather than other, more pressing issues, such as the war, Fascism, social problems, and the way we lived in those days. It wasn't that I was indifferent to those topics; I was involved in them, and I lived them out, even if it was in a quite solitary way. It must have been from an emotional experience of mine that ended in a rather inexplicable way. I didn't need to ask anyone except myself to explain this ending. And the reason became attached to other reasons, and together they became one enormous issue, a really big spectacle with man as its pro- tagonist. Man against his environment and man against man.

My presumption lies in this: that I embarked on the trail of neorealism on my own. It was 1943. Visconti was shooting Ossessione *on the banks of the Po River, and a few miles down- stream, I was shooting my first documentary.*[3]

Antonioni managed to shoot his first documentary, *Gento del Po* (*People of the Po Valley*), at the age of thirty-one, in 1943, but when editing began in 1947, he found that most of his material had been lost because of the war. It was as if he had never shot it, and this was when his parallel career began.

It's a pity—he says—*because the material that was lost was shocking. That bit of land became a muddy swamp. Inside the straw huts they put their babies on tables so they wouldn't drown and hung their sheets across the ceiling to stop the wa- ter coming in from the roof. Cinema at that time carefully avoided all these issues. The Fascist government forbade them. I don't want to seem presumptuous, but it fell to me to deal with them for the first time.*

Shooting documentaries was very useful for me. Before, I didn't know whether I was capable of making films; with the documentaries I realized I could do it no worse than many others.[4]

[3] Antonioni, *Sei Film*, xvi.
[4] Biarese, *I Film*, 32-33.

My attention was captured by these images for other reasons; they suggested different things to me. As I began to understand the world through the image, I began to understand the image itself, its power and mystery.[5]

I am a self-made man. I think my teachers were my eyes.[6]

Antonioni's gaze was born out of this observation, indicating his belief that things received a particular kind of attention from him and made different suggestions to him.

At the height of the neorealist period, of the "pawning of reality," as Zavattini theorizes, Antonioni proposed being attentive to personality, analyzing the symptoms of an on-going evolution and how his protagonists' feelings, psychologies, and even moralities are changing.

Story of a Love Affair (1950, taken from an early screenplay titled "The House by the Sea" that Antonioni had written in 1942 before going to France to work with Carné) was his feature filmmaking debut, but his first screenplay must really be considered as *The White Sheik* (written in 1949). Carlo Ponti liked the screenplay very much and decided to buy it and entrust it to Fellini, giving Antonioni the option of making another film.

In my screenplay there wasn't a very precise plot, just a series of interlinked events. It was quite a free narration, a little like Federico's films today. But at the time, Fellini and Pinelli reproved me precisely because of the fragmentary nature of the story.[7]

Last Night, Shots Rang Out, also from 1949, was a strange and worrying thriller that Antonioni was very fond of, a film treatment of subtle and rarefied atmosphere. At its heart were

[5] Antonioni, *Sei Film*, xvi.
[6] Biarese, *I Film*, 34.
[7] Ibid., 35.

two witnesses to a crime, and a social circle frequented by homo-
sexuals: this was the main reason for the negative response it
received from the board of censors at the time that forced him
to abandon the project.

But the project that had interested Antonioni much more for
the previous several years and that he only abandoned with great
regret was *Those Fun-Loving Girls of 1924*. It was co-written
with Renzo Renzi, who at the time was trying to establish a
production company with Enzo Biagi, based in Bologna:

> *When Antonioni had shot his* Story of a Love Affair—*writes
> Renzi*—*we met to discuss another screenplay. It was* Those
> Fun-Loving Girls of 1924, *which he meant to do as an alterna-
> tive to another screenplay,* Last Night, Shots Rang Out . . . *We
> were enthusiastic about the subject. Set around the time of the
> assasination of Matteotti, the film would have been about Fas-
> cism without ever mentioning it directly. The protagonists were
> caught up in a spiral of increasing violence without knowing
> why. It was a question of those famous reflexes that Antonioni
> wrote about several times. There was a climate of violence.*
>
> *Naturally, the almost total absence of any direct reference
> to politics allowed us to pass the film off as if it was simply a
> period piece: a totally "private" drama, flavored with the dresses
> and songs of a precise historical period.*
>
> *In order to explain his idea, Antonioni took us around Bolo-
> gna, showing us alleys and especially dark, covered porticoes
> with their colonnades, ideal for ambushing someone. They had
> a threatening atmosphere, broken every now and then by glimpses
> of enchanting gardens hidden inside baroque palaces. . .*[8]
>
> *The story for* Fun-Loving Girls—*remembered Antonioni*—
> *was connected to an atmosphere I had lived through as a child;
> certain events were almost autobiographical. It was about Fas-
> cism as seen through the eyes of a group of friends, mostly
> girls, in Ferrara. The presence of Fascism was felt through the*

---

[8] R. Renzi, *Album Antonioni. Una biografia impossibile*, in *L'Opera di Michelangelo
Antonioni*, vol. 3 (Rome: Cinecittà International, 1991), 40.

filter of their youth and their apolitical outlook. To them, Fascism was a fun kind of masquerade. Moravia was right to give one of his books the title The Masquerade. *That's what Fascism was to us children: those "centurions" with their big black capes, the flags, etc. were all like a curious type of play that made us laugh; at the same time, it inspired our respect because we were not able to understand what was behind the mask or foresee the tragic developments it would later lead to. I was very attracted to the idea of showing these early images of happy, carefree Fascism, at least in appearance.*[9]

Renzi continues: *Our attempts to produce this film are quite well-documented in my letters to Antonioni . . . between January and May, 1951. They also mention a project titled* Pane e Fantasia, *written by Piero Tellini, about the Rome cinema circuit. That idea would be the driving force behind Antonioni's future film* The Lady Without Camellias, *while Tellini's project, with the addition of the word* "amore" *would become the first film in the tradition of "pink neorealism,"*[10] *launching Gina Lollobrigida as a star after she had turned down a role in* The Lady Without Camellias, *because, she said, the story of the protagonist was too close to her own . . .*[11]

It is strange that at this time Antonioni also received a proposal from a lawyer (representing the Italian Department of Justice) to make two shorts: one on life in a women's prison, and the other on Rome's Juvenile Hall. From this invitation, one can easily guess why the documentaries were never made. A letter the lawyer sent to Antonioni emphasized: "With due regard to the needs of the filmmaker, the shorts must not give greater weight to the need for spectacle over the need for seriousness and truth that are appropriate to the subject. Furthermore, the Department reserves the right to name an individual

---

[9] Biarese, *I Film*, 35.
[10] *Pane, amore, e fantasia* (*Bread, Love, and Fantasy*) by Comencini, 1953. [Translator]
[11] Renzi, *Album Antonioni*, 41.

of its choosing as technical consultant, after the film is passed by the censors and before it is released to the public, in order to guarantee a successful outcome for the project."[12]

Between 1951 and 1956, Antonioni continued to propose new projects and screenplays in vain. Nothing remains of these anymore, except in his own memory. Amongst others, they include: *Un pacchetto di Morris*, a detective story that won a magazine contest; *Con il tuo perfido cuore*; *Ida e i porci*, written with Rodolfo Sonego and Ennio De Concini, the story of a little girl who becomes a prostitute; and a project for a film with Totò[13] called *Totò and the corpse*.

Antonioni received offers to direct several films that were then withdrawn: *Peccato che sia una canaglia* (*Too Bad She's a Crook*), which Blasetti completed, and *La diga sul Pacifico*, written by Duras, which Clément eventually filmed.

Before shooting *The Girlfriends*, he wrote the screenplay for *The Cry* and admitted eight years later that the idea came to him by staring at a wall.

After *The Cry*, Antonioni met Tonino Guerra, and influenced by his stories about the German concentration camps, he collaborated with him to write the treatment for *Makaroni*.

Almost all of the survivors of World War II have written about "the day after"—the arrival of the Americans and the retreat of the Germans—as the best day of their lives. It was this moment of disorder, chaos, adventure, and freedom that interested Antonioni in *Makaroni*.

Although underrated for years, his films from *Story of a Love Affair* to *The Cry* established his particular gaze and his style; with the passing of time, the arrival of Antonioni on the European cultural scene would be regarded as a historical event. He writes:

In the post-war period, there was a great need for truth,

---

[12] Letter from Zara Algardi, Esq., 12 March 1951.

[13] Totò was a popular Neapolitan comedic actor who appeared in scores of films and was featured by Pasolini in *Hawks and Sparrows*. [Editor]

and it almost seemed possible to photograph it on street corners. Today, neorealism has been superseded in this respect: people tend more and more to create their own reality. This criterion is even applied to feature films in the documentary style and to newspapers dedicated to current affairs, for the majority of these have a pre-established idea of what they want to represent. It's not cinema in the service of reality but reality in the service of cinema.

There is the same tendency in original films. My impression is that the essential goal is to give these films almost an allegorical flavor. That is, each character behaves in an ideal way that is unreasonably in alignment with the way other people behave, so that together they provide meaning to the story itself, but also beyond it in the freedom and intensity of its solutions.[14]

He has a very broad conception of cinema.

It should not be forgotten that for many years Antonioni was confronted with a solid wall of people who would not tolerate his particular style, which was apparently cold and detached but also vital to a deeper understanding of reality. He prefers not to be judgmental precisely because he chooses more subtle, meaningful atmospheres.

According to Antonioni, reality is not a mechanical, conventional, or artificial given, as it is in the stories the film industry churns out on a daily basis.

"Today, cinema," he says, "must be grounded more in truth than logic, and it is the ambience that produces the clash, and the choice."

The Cry was indicative of this development. It was Alexandre Astruc in France who was the first to express the meaning of Antonioni's search when he predicted the new dawn for cinema that was hailed by the showing of Antonioni's *The*

---

[14] Antonioni, *Sei Film*, xiii.

Adventure at the Cannes Festival (even though it was initially greeted by a chorus of boos). *The Adventure* was in fact a work full of expressive maturity in which Antonioni definitively established his style and indicated a new language that penetrated to the heart of an image in an original and highly intense manner.

The 1960s were marked by his most important works which finally got him known and appreciated by a wider public; but they were also a time of profound reflection for him.

His films from the beginning of the decade, *The Adventure*, *The Eclipse*, and *The Night*, are the centerpieces of his film-making career, and at the same time they mark a watershed between the "before" and "after" periods.

The times were changing radically, and so was narrativity, language, art, and cinema, but once again, Antonioni was able to see the first symptoms of these changes.

This habit of keeping one eye open for what is going on inside oneself and the other for what is going on outside is a habit that all directors share, I think. At a certain point, the two perspectives come together, and like two images that overlap, they are brought into focus. It is from this harmony of the eye and the brain, the eye and the instinct, the eye and the conscience, that the impulse to speak and to show is born.

As far as I am concerned, the external, concrete element is always the origin of it. Not a concept or a thesis. There is also a bit of confusion at the beginning, and probably film is born precisely out of this confusion. The difficulty rests in bringing order to it all. I am convinced that success here doesn't only depend on ability but also on training in the use of the imagination . . .

However fascinating an idea seems to me, I can never immediately accept it. I just leave it there, I don't think about it, and I wait. Maybe months or even years go by. It has to be able to float by itself in the sea of things one accumulates throughout life: if it does, then it is a good idea.

One activity that never tires me is watching. I like nearly all the scenarios that I see: landscapes, characters, situations. On the one hand, this is dangerous, but on the other, it is an advantage because it allows a complete fusion between life and work, reality (or unreality), and the cinema.

A director does nothing but seek himself in his own films. So these are not the record of completed thoughts but of a process of thinking.[15]

In 1964, the publishing house Einaudi asked him to republish in a single volume the screenplays of his latest films that had already appeared in the series *From Screenplay to Film* by Renzo Renzi. Antonioni rewrote them carefully, taking out all the technical references and trying to improve their literary form, since for him "these texts should be read as stories, even though they stand in the same relation to film as the *canovaccio* does to the *commedia dell'arte.*"

The chance to re-read and re-adapt his screenplays led him to write a preface. This was a rare opportunity for him to talk about himself and his way of writing for the cinema:

All that screenplays can do is find words for events which defy them.

Writing screenplays is a really exhausting occupation, precisely because it involves describing images with words that are only provisional, that in the end are no good, and that is highly unnatural. Description cannot be anything but generic or even false because it is often about images that have no concrete referents.

As I re-read my screenplays, what I feel most is the memory of the moments that led me to write them. Scouting out certain locations, talking with people, the time I spent living in the place where I would later set an important story, the gradual discovery of the film's most fundamental images, its colors and cadences: these are perhaps the most important moments.

---

[15] Ibid., ix, x, xiii.

The screenplay is an intermediary phase, necessary but transitory. For me, if a film is to come out well, as I shoot it, it must be linked back to those moments before the screenplay; I need to rediscover that original impulse, that conviction . . .

During the writing of the screenplay, the discussions with collaborators, the often cold and competent research into a setting or a solution that comes from experience, all these certainly help to articulate the story in the best possible way. But the risk is that they crush the original impulse. That is why, during the writing of the screenplay there is always a moment of crisis when one loses sight of the story one is trying to tell. Then there is nothing to do but break off and try to go back to thinking about the film as one imagined it during location scouting.

Another feeling that I have as I read these scripts is rather curious: a sort of amazement mixed with irritation. Because now that the films are printed texts, too many things no longer match up. And the ones that do are set out in a kind of pseudo-literary way that, as I say, is irritating. Those who say that screenplays have literary merit are wrong. One could object that mine don't, though others do. Maybe. But in that case they are actually novels and have an autonomous existence of their own.[16]

At this point we discover two interesting projects:

For years, some verses by MacNeice have been on my mind: Think of a number, double it, triple it, raise it to the power of four and then erase it.

I am sure that they could be the beginnings of or at least the symbol of a humorous film. They already exemplify a certain style . . .

I also thought in a moment of exasperation of scripting the first chapters of Bertrand Russel's Introduction to the Philosophy of Mathematics. *It's a very serious book, but in my opinion*

---

[16] Ibid., xvii-xviii.

it is also rich in comic potential. For example: "The number three is not identifiable with the triplet composed of Messrs. Brown, Jones, and Robinson. The number three is something that all triplets have in common." In this case, the triplet of Messrs. Brown, Jones, and Robinson is already invested with something of the ridiculous. Alternatively: "The wife-husband relationship can be said to be the inverse of the husband-wife relationship." You can already see these two inverse couples and their friends and the events that they would get mixed up in. Or again: "The number two is a metaphysical entity, and we can never be certain whether it really exists or whether we have correctly identified it."

This is a frightening statement, from the point of view of the number two. That is, of a number two who is protagonist of some event.[17]

The rejection of drama, the abolition of time, the inversion of *plot*, the analysis of behavior patterns and the elimination of description, the landscape as a place that also expresses impermanence, the unmeasurability of time, the reduction of the number of characters, the brief indications of the story—every detail is reduced to its essentials. Antonioni continues his quest for the internal rhythm of stories, and in all his films, from *Red Desert* to *Identification of a Woman*, he investigates that instability of our times that he defines as "the unknown morality," by which man navigates among fears and uncertainties and records the modifications, conditioning, and reflections in his psychology and in his feelings.

Blow Up—which signaled the transition in Antonioni's filmmaking to the third phase of his artistic career—was the film that, after twenty-six years of film-related activity and nine completed films, determined his international success and finally earned him acclaim as one of the masters of cinema.

Carlo Ponti and MGM gave him a contract (the first for

---

[17] Ibid., xiii.

him) to make three films, and so it seemed that for a while, Antonioni would not have any problem finding money to fund his movies. But *Zabriskie Point*, as we know, had a very unfair reception in the United States and that prevented the film from having the success it deserved.

It is true, despite what people have always believed, that the film had the approval of newspapers, weekly and monthly magazines with wide readerships, and specialized and intellectual publications, especially among young radicals who felt that they were the protagonists of the film. But it is also true that the great liberal press judged the film politically, widely holding that it was an insult to the system.

America was unable to accept Antonioni's perspective, as Moravia wrote: his perspective on a world "where the ends, that is to say, man, become the means, and the means, that is to say, profit, become the end." Antonioni was embittered by this chauvinistic and puritanical attitude from an America that didn't want to look at itself in the mirror and rejected his filmmaking, once again ahead of its time. And Antonioni's employability once again was severely limited.

So when he came back from China in 1972, Carlo Ponti told him that he had no intention of producing the film *Tecnicamente dolce* (*Technically Sweet*), even though he had guaranteed he would when it had been presented to him in 1966 along with *Blow Up*.

Antonioni confided to a critic: "Let us not deceive ourselves that we are special when we are in fact just a chemical process, a biological accident, a genetic deviation. It will be a pitiless film and I like that idea."[18]

This is how he himself tells the story of this "cursed" film:

I have been struggling with this screenplay since 1966. It was a film that I really wanted to make, even though I knew that the undertaking would be very arduous. Why arduous?

---

[18] G Grazzini, "Antonioni nella spirale," *Corriere della sera*, 12 December 1971.

Because it called for a trip to the jungle and staying there for at least two months. I have seen a lot of jungles and virgin forests, I have been around the world looking for the most frightening one, and I have found it: the Amazon. Now I can tell you that the relationship between the horror of a virgin forest and its photogenic qualities are in inverse proportion. The more the forest is frightening, the less photogenic it is. The undergrowth of vegetation is so dense that there are no plains, the foliage merges into everything else, everything is bound up together in a continuous amalgam. The place is dominated by shadows.

The problem in this place of exasperating monotony is how to use the camera. Even placed a few feet away from the actor, there would be branches and leaves, vines and roots, and so on between them, so that the character would not even be visible. If you moved the camera closer to the actor, those branches, leaves, vines, and roots still in the picture would be out of focus, detracting from the quality of the image.

Then there is the light. Because the vegetation is so dense, the sun rarely filters through, making the use of extra lighting necessary. But it is difficult to imagine artificial lighting in the jungle without realizing that it would create shadows and so falsify reality.

My intention was to make a kind of crude summary from this scrap of a film about the struggle between two human organisms and other organisms, vegetable and animal. But also about a more frightening struggle, between the plants themselves as they reach for the light. Or the animals as they fight for food. It was my intention to deal with the subject of cannibalism. Cannibalism has a simultaneous magical and practical value because it persists (if it still persists) in places where there is not enough protein. It is a very complex subject, and therefore a single sequence could hardly scratch the surface of it. I was overcome by doubts and I cut it.

If you add these directorial problems to the production problems we had, above all the logistics of the operation, you will understand how my doubts were legitimate.

In the summer of 1966, I had overcome them all. In the battle between the film and myself, I considered that I was the winner. But I had not bargained for the implacable, merciless, and cynical judge who controls all the strings of any enterprise in the film world: the producer. When Carlo Ponti told me, suddenly and inexplicably, that he no longer intended to produce the film, that he had changed his mind, then the world that I had laboriously constructed in my mind, fantastic but true, beautiful but mysterious, suddenly collapsed. The ruins are still there, somewhere inside me.[19]

When Italo Calvino's book of short stories *T Plus Zero* was published in 1967, Antonioni also turned his attention to the "nocturnal guide." After the failure of *Tecnicamente dolce*, Antonioni threw himself into a project that roused his passion, so much so that one may definitely count it as one of the projects he would have liked to have made. The title of the film would have been *The Spiral* (subsequently, *The Color of Jealousy*).

"It is the story of a man who quarrels with his partner, hangs up the phone on her, and then, instead of calling her back, decides to go and see her, even though she lives in another city. The film was the story of his trip at three different levels: the real trip, the memory of the trip, and his imagined trip. And as the situation and his state of mind changed, so did the colors of the film."[20]

Antonioni wanted to shoot the film electronically, but the technology wasn't sufficiently mature.

The trajectory of the protagonist is what interests me about this film, a man at the end of a violent, sentimental obsession, in contact with events that in his eyes are part of an alarming social and political drama. He rebels against this and matures from a romantic and individualistic position to a more rational, conscious position. He is a man who is prevented from

[19] M. Antonioni, Preface to *Tecnicamente dolce*, ed. A Tassone (Turin: Einaudi, 1976).
[20] I. Bignardi, "Gli amati film che non girai," *La Repubblica*, 30 May 1981.

seeing and thinking clearly about reality. Freud is quite right when he says that each of us is just a shadow of what we might be. Our potential is limited by an infinite number of environmental factors, our daily lives, the mystification we are surrounded by, and so what is "normal" is simply the product of repression, negation, and division . . .

The protagonist of The Spiral, *like all of us, wrestles with the given situation that has been imposed on him and that estranges him more and more from himself. Thus, his alienating dash to the next city becomes faster and faster. It may be a film that deals with the transition from today, when we are surrounded by neuroses, to tomorrow, when alienation has become the norm. Perhaps psychoanalysis will not help to resolve the problems of tomorrow. We are entering the decade of biology and it is probably from this perspective that we should study our problems.*

My great hope is to contribute to people's understanding that while certain words are equivocal today—especially "art" and "politics"—what is unequivocal is our need to measure honestly the drama through which we live.[21]

The failure to realize *The Color of Jealousy* forced Antonioni to accept a counter-proposal from Ponti, who had acquired the screenplay of *The Passenger* from the young British screenwriter, Mark Peploe.

Antonioni, enthusiastic about the project, wrote the script together with Peploe, and began a productive and lasting relationship with him.

The Passenger (1974) was a success, but it was then six years before Antonioni was able to return to the set. His parallel career continued with his rejection of two proposals that were alien to him: Hemingway's *Farewell to Arms* and Morselli's *Il comunista.*

Meanwhile, talking and traveling around with Tonino

---

[21] Grazzini, "Antonioni nella spirale."

Guerra in the middle of the 1960s, a project called *The Kite* began to take shape from one of Guerra's fables that Calvino had liked, and which had been considered and then discarded for *Red Desert*. It is the story of a kite that flies higher and higher and higher and never stops, blown by a mysterious wind, until it ends up thousands of miles from earth.

It is a splendid tale, on the border of science fiction, full of poetry and imagination. At the time, these qualities seemed to have found their natural setting in the extraordinary locales of the Soviet Union, where the separation between the archaic world and the technological world, so necessary to the story, was more obvious. But because of the excessive cost and innumerable technical difficulties, the project could not be realized.

Antonioni continued to write and began his collaboration with the *Corriere della Sera*, where he published a series of stories that were born from his notes for unmade films or from embryonic narratives he had left unfinished in which images and emotions are expressed with great intensity.[22] Among these is *Questo corpo di fango*, from which the screenplay to *Suffer or Die* was born; to write this piece, Antonioni read classic works of mysticism, in particular St. Teresa of Avila, from whom the title was borrowed, and he spent several weeks inside cloistered convents, "breathing the same air that gives life to those women who have renounced life."

On Christmas Eve, a man meets a girl about twenty years old, asks her where she is going, and follows her to mass at the church. She sits down, and during the entire service she watches "this body made of mud" (that's St. Teresa's expression), this figure "bent and immobile in the attitude of prayer."

He escorts her back to her house and at the door he asks to see her the next day. "Tomorrow I am going to enter the convent," she replies.

"What a marvelous beginning for a film," Antonioni has

---

[22] The ones that he judges most important were later collected in *Quel bowling sul Tevere* (Turin: Einaudi, 1983) and two years later appeared in France and Germany.

always said, "but for me, the film ends there." (It is not by chance that this tale, which he has always seen as complete in itself, is among the four tales that make up his last film, *Beyond the Clouds*).

Shooting seemed imminent, but the American financing that was indispensable for the film's international success fell through.

Suffering enforced inactivity, Antonioni accepted the directorship of a remake of Cocteau's play, *The Two-Headed Eagle*, called *The Oberwald Mystery*, where the use of color cameras allowed him to experiment with the use of an electronic medium, the use of color and the transference of the image from tape to film, which had never been tried before.

In 1982, the Franciscan order asked him to make a film about St. Francis, though he objected that he wasn't a believer. They persevered, telling him that they were interested in a film about the man, not the saint. Antonioni accepted because, contrary to the traditional image that people have of the saint, he found in Francis a man of strong and violent temperament.

He wrote the screenplay with Tonino Guerra and Roberto Roversi and confided that "the film—if I manage to make it—will be crude and harsh because in terrible times like the twelfth and thirteenth centuries, full of war and poverty, it was a sign of great courage to preach poverty as Francis did while knights were riding into battle in gold suits of armor."

But even this project met with constant delays and indecisiveness in production, especially from RAI, who a little later commissioned Liliana Cavani to make a second *Saint Francis* with Mickey Rourke.

Although he didn't really believe in it, Antonioni allowed himself to become involved with another project and wrote a screenplay taken from a bestseller by a journalist, Marco Praga, *Sotto il vestito niente* (*Nothing Underneath*). The thriller, set in the world of high fashion, centered around a crime committed by a model who was no stranger to drugs. But when the director suggested working with the top Milanese designers—the heroes of Italian fashion—and shooting in real locations in order to give the story greater realism, barriers were suddenly thrown up and he was rejected as a dangerous intruder.

It was in this climate and with great effort that he managed to prepare and bring to completion *Identification of a Woman*, and he took up again another project (that he had already been thinking about since *Saint Francis*) that he really wanted to make: *The Crew*, another tale inspired by a news item that had been published in the *Corriere della Sera*.

Three men, the article said, exhausted by hunger and thirst, arrived in an Australian port after having been adrift without food or water for six days in a motor yacht called the *Irene*, owned by a wealthy businessman, James Towers. They claimed that engine failure had caused the boat to be driven out to sea by a storm and they had spent the whole night in fear of their lives. When they woke up, the yacht's owner, armed with an iron bar, had threatened them and locked them in the hold. The three of them managed to get the door off its hinges, and when they got back on deck they found that Towers had disappeared.

Antonioni didn't believe any of the explanations the press had provided, nor any of the numerous interpretations of Towers' supposed madness, and even less so the theory that he had suddenly thrown himself into the sea.

A man like that—he writes—knows that there is a moment before one drowns when the world takes on the color of the wave that is about to wash over you and suffocate you. And he knows that at that moment you will hate the sea. No, that is not the feeling that a man like that would choose to experience before he dies.

Meanwhile, the mystery remains. And perhaps it is right that it should. Any explanation would be less interesting than the mystery itself. And yet the story continued to germinate within me for years. In his day, that is, in my own day, I had a lot of respect for Conrad. When I read the adventure of the Irene, *it had that air of Conrad's works about the open sea, those men who had been brutalized and saddened by life, but still had a clean concept of living, and I was very tempted by it.*

Indeed, at one point I decided to set my hand to it like an idea for a film. It was almost a homage to Conrad.

I was in Singapore at the time, waiting for someone. Waiting is a permanent state for a director. I wrote to the Sydney Morning Herald *asking if by any chance they had any further news of the adventure and the characters from it, or if they could find out anything for me. The paper replied: "Unfortunately we cannot accommodate your request for the simple reason that we are not equipped to carry out this sort of investigation."*[23]

It was this mystery that tormented and fascinated him. Together with Mark Peploe, he wrote several versions of it and created a treatment that would certainly have been an extraordinary film, and in a way, a fitting conclusion to his oeuvre, a strong and beautiful story in terms of writing and its emotions.

The project was a production challenge, given its high cost, the complex production plan, the risks its premise implied, especially the personal ones that Antonioni, faithful to his visceral, innate sense of competition, intended to subject himself to. For example, he thought about shooting a real storm, not in a studio, when there would be a force six gale, for this, he believed, was the key to the whole story.

All the producers to whom he showed the story liked it, especially the Americans, but for seven years it had a checkered history of contradictory "yes" and "no" responses, delays, illusions, and an increasing sense of desperation.

Antonioni used this time to dedicate himself to a story that was published in the *Corriere della Sera*: *Two Telegrams*. The first time he read it, he thought it would be impossible to make a film out of it because he did not find the female character convincing.

Between 1981 and 1985, he accepted another personal chal-

---

[23] Antonioni, *Quel bowling*, 66-67.

lenge, writing a screenplay with an American, Rudy Wurlitzer.
But at the very moment he was about to sign the contract to
make the film, he was overcome by illness.

Although it is true that in fifty years of filmmaking,
Antonioni made only sixteen films, it is also true that an ap-
proximate tally of his work shows: twelve other films he wrote
he would have liked to have made but couldn't; another six
written with other people that he could have realized; a further
fifteen original treatments for films that were never developed
further; and at least forty topics suggested for documentaries.

And it is also true that, in beginning to bring some order to
Antonioni's archive along with Enrica Antonioni, I have found
hundreds of "lost pages" (notes, thoughts, and ideas for films)
which, because of the density of his writing and the acuteness
of his observations, constitute another treasury that remains
to be widely discovered and will give further opportunity to
take up this subject again, in an even more detailed way.